The New
Black Politics

The New Black Politics

The Search for Political Power
second edition

Edited by

Michael B. Preston
Lenneal J. Henderson, Jr.
Paul L. Puryear

Longman
New York & London

Senior Editor: David J. Estrin
Production Editor: Helen B. Ambrosio
Text Design: Steven August Krastin
Cover Design: Steven August Krastin
Production Supervisor: Eduardo Castillo
Compositor: Pine Tree Composition, Inc.
Printer and Binder: Malloy Lithographing, Inc.

For Mary, Sherry, Sonja, Andrienne,
Rymicha, Anthony, and Ashly.

The New Black Politics: The Search for Political Power, second edition

Copyright © 1982, 1987 by Longman Inc.

Longman Inc.
95 Church Street
White Plains, N.Y. 10601

Associated companies:
Longman Group Ltd., London
Longman Cheshire Pty., Melbourne
Longman Paul Pty., Auckland
Copp Clark Pitman, Toronto
Pitman Publishing Inc., New York

Library of Congress Cataloging-in-Publication Data

The new black politics

   Bibliography: p.
   1. Afro-Americans—Politics and government.
I. Preston, Michael B. II. Henderson, Lenneal J.
III. Puryear, Paul Lionel, 1930–
E185.615.N38 1987   323.1′196073   86-21427
ISBN 0-582-28554-2
ISBN 0-582-28553-4 (pbk.)

87 88 89 90 9 8 7 6 5 4 3 2 1

Contents

Introduction

The new black politics is in general a story about the "souls of black folks." It is a history not only of political progress but of social progress as well. Yet in its broad general outlines, it is the story of a black minority struggling for equality in a white-majority society. And in this context it is also the story of a democratic society that flaunts its theories of equality, fairness, and equal justice for all—which it seldom equals in practice. American society is proud to attack the violation of human rights abroad while denying them at home. It is in this society that the new black politics must operate and in which the struggle for equality for black people must be waged if minority rights are to be protected and expanded until they are the same as those granted white Americans.

Anybody reading the last statement must surely be aware of the struggle that lies ahead. Yet only a very short-sighted person would argue that blacks have not made substantial progress in the last 20 years. And only a person devoid of foresight would agree that what has been achieved meets the standards of equality enjoyed by white Americans. Thus the black struggle for equality in America will and must continue until the theory of democracy is equal to its practice. The struggle, then, will force America to adhere to its ideals and make it the country it aspires to be, but has yet to become.

More specifically, this book describes the political progress that blacks have made in the 1970s and 1980s. It also describes the growth in the number of black elected officials (BEOs) at all levels of government and analyzes their victories as well as their defeats. In addition, the authors consider the impact of the black vote in the state and nation, not only recording its importance but also explaining its limitations.

The number of black state-elected officials has increased but they are far outnumbered by BEOs at the local level. Of special importance to us has been the growth in the election of black mayors in America. We focus specifically on big city black mayors because these mayors have importance far beyond their city boundaries. For example, Harold Washington, with a sizeable and highly mobilized black electorate, has potential influence not only in city and county politics, but in state, congressional, and presidential politics as well. To a large degree, black mayors, like black congressmen, are not restricted by the geographical location of their constituencies. When Harold Washington speaks of the draconian nature of Reagan's budget cuts on the poor, he is speaking not only for Chicago, but also Philadelphia, Atlanta, Washington D.C., New Orleans, Detroit, and Los Angeles as well. Black mayors, like black congressmen, speak as local and as national representatives of black people in America.

There are several themes that run throughout this book. First, as increasing numbers of blacks register and vote as a cohesive block, they increase their chances of having an impact on local, state, and national elections. In the first section of the book for example, Henderson shows that when presidential elections are close, blacks can become key actors in the outcomes. Lucius Barker's article describes Jesse Jackson's candidacy for the 1984 Democratic nomination by evaluating its impact on American politics and on the participation of black voters. Coleman and McLemore show that black voters in Mississippi, even in majority black counties, voted for a white Republican over a black Democratic candidate for Congress. Their article discusses in detail why black voters made the choices they did. Barker and Barker's article on the courts shows that legal victories are not permanent but last only as long as blacks have a friendly court and national administration.

For those interested in detailed statistics on the overall growth of BEOs, William's article is must reading. She raises some key issues surrounding the growth of BEOs, with one of them being: What difference does it really make?

The section on black mayors highlights the electoral progress that blacks have made in urban politics and shows the limitations of the ballot as well. While the election of black mayors has expanded the political power of blacks in the cities, it has not necesssarily helped those that need it the most: poor, unemployed and underemployed; the underclass has not only remained with us but has grown. Almost all of the authors, Preston, Nelson, Rich, Ransom, Perry, and Stokes touch on this question.

There is a second important theme which runs through the articles on black mayors and that is the "Politics of Personality." One point should be made clear; black mayors are *not* "machine politicians." They govern by virtue of their "personality" not by "political organization." Theirs is the "politics of personality." Most have won election because of their personal popularity and have shunned "the machine" as organizations of the past even when reelected.

There are several good reasons why this is so. First, most black mayors had not had the *support* or *control of* the party apparatus. And even if they could get control, most lack the *resources* necessary to sustain it. Second, most are elected as "independents" (even though almost all are Democrats) and must depend on blacks as well as whites. The whites who support them are normally middle-class and would not be likely to support a machine politician. Third, the establishment and perpetuation of a machine take both money and time, which are scarce commodities where black mayors are concerned. In addition, "political machines" can also lead to factions and corruption, both of which a black mayor does not need. His list of problems is likely to be long, and factions and corruption cut into his major resource: time. Fourth, there is also the possibility that black mayors are more "reformist" than "machinist." That is, they know that when the machine developed, a patron-client relationship existed. Government and voters depended on each other: jobs for votes. Today, welfare is given in most cities by county or state government; patronage jobs are limited by Shakman I and II*; as federal money is no longer available to fuel the patronage armies of the past. In short, black mayors may be reformers because they have little choice.

In conclusion, winning office does not necessarily mean that one will be able to govern; or if one can govern, it does not mean one can solve all the problems of the black community. No mayor can do that—and black mayors are no exception. Thus their election is only one means to the ultimate end—the complete equality of black Americans. We hope the articles in this book give the reader a glimpse of a small part of the overall struggle of black people who won't stop demanding because they can't afford to lose.

Acknowledgments

Several persons were of great help in preparing this book. At the University of Illinois-Urbana, Shirley Burnett of the Institute of Government and Public Affairs and Eileen Gingrich of the Department of Political Science typed the bulk of the manuscript. Thanks also to Anna Merritt, who assisted with the editing, and to Robert Rich, Director of the Institute of Government and Public Affairs, who generously provided me space and secretarial as-

*Shakman I forbids the hiring of municipal employees for strictly political reasons and Shakman II prohibits firing of municipal employees for strictly political reasons.

sistance. Thanks also to David J. Estrin, my editor at Longman and to the production editor, Helen B. Ambrosio, for their patience and assistance in moving the manuscript from development to publication.

Michael B. Preston,
Professor, University of Southern California

PART ONE

National and State Politics

ONE

Black Politics and American Presidential Elections*

Lenneal J. Henderson, Jr.

Both symbolically and substantively, American presidential elections are essential opportunities for black voters to exert national political influence. Black political activity, particularly since the civil rights and black power movements, is manifested most intensely in neighborhood, rural, municipal, and metropolitan politics. Sharp increases in the election of black state legislators and black Lieutenant Governors in Colorado, California, and Virginia within the last 10 years signal an emerging state-centered black politics. Presidential elections, however, provide blacks with a series of opportunities to:

1. influence party politics at the state level in presidential primaries
2. become party delegates and broker with fellow delegates in supporting presidential candidates for the party nomination most supportive of black policy preferences
3. express, pursue, and construct planks in the party platform prior to and during party national conventions in a presidential election year
4. influence national policy issues connected to the presidential campaigns of candidates they support or oppose
5. become party officials, including candidates or prospective candidates for the presidential or vice-presidential nomination
6. play major negotiating and brokering roles in both the campaign strategies of presidential candidates in the general election and in the formulation and projection of issues associated with those campaigns
7. influence U.S. senate and congressional elections associated with presidential elections

*The author wishes to express appreciation to Ronald Brown, Michael Preston, and Ronald Walters in the preparation of this chapter.

8. participate in the formulation and expression of political philosophy and ideology both within and outside mainstream party politics[1]

Taken together, these opportunities represent a range of political options blacks may pursue during a presidential election. What they actually pursue may be considered *a distribution of political choice.* For example, the highlight of the 1984 presidential election for blacks was not the landslide victory of President Ronald Reagan over former Vice-President Walter Mondale, but the ascendancy of Jesse L. Jackson as a serious contender for the Democratic party presidential nomination. Although Channing Phillips and Shirley Chisholm had been among the first blacks to receive some support for their presidential aspirations, Jesse Jackson was the first to seriously challenge other prominent aspirants for the Democratic party nomination.

The Jackson candidacy represented the exercise of an option in the politics of presidential elections never before seriously pursued by blacks. Moreover, the exercise of that option brought new meaning to the exercise of most other political options by blacks. In 1976, black voters were integral to Jimmy Carter's primary as well as general-election victories. In the general election, blacks gave Carter 90 percent of their vote. Assertions and hypotheses about "the pivotal role" of the black voter were frequently heard.[2] Conversely, Ronald Reagan could have triumphed in both the Republican primaries and the general election of 1980 without the black vote. In 1984, the ever-increasing black vote showed widespread dissatisfaction of blacks with the policies of President Reagan. This dissatisfaction, along with the well-publicized elections of black mayors in Philadelphia and Chicago, encouraged Jesse Jackson to become a candidate for the Democratic nomination for President. Jackson surprised and startled many who gave his candidacy little chance. He demonstrated that the black vote could be combined with other political ingredients to pose a serious presidential challenge in the Democratic primary.

In spite of Ronald Reagan's landslide victory in 1984, the Jackson candidacy demonstrates the significance of black presidential voting to the *political self-image* and *confidence* of blacks. The symbolic and substantive association of black voters with the Democratic party encourages blacks when Democrats win and discourages blacks when Democrats lose. But the Jackson candidacy projected new possibilities for black political action during a presidential election year that potentially transcend even the Democratic and Republican party polemics. These possibilities include increased brokering by prominent black presidential aspirants within political parties and the opportunity for a serious third party candidacy, lead by a charismatic black leader, to *influence public policy. Jesse Jackson demonstrated this point during his bid for the presidency* through his help in securing the release of Lieutenant Robert Goodman from Syria and through his policy proposals for Central America, Cuba, and South Africa.

Thus, the varying fates of black voters in the 1976, 1980, and 1984 presidential elections illustrate the agony and the ecstasy of black voting in presidential elections in both *the black political context* and in America as a whole. Black presidential voting therefore assumes both an *internal and external significance;* internal to the politics of the black national polity; external to the economic, social, and political relationship of blacks to American politics in general.

Black voting in presidential elections is tied to many variables: international and national events, economic conditions, mass media influences, political organization, and past patterns of American political behavior in elections. Collectively these variables comprise *the external factors* related to the black vote in presidential elections. Economic conditions, political values, political organization, voter awareness and behavior, and political leadership are *internal* variables among blacks that influence black presidential preferences. Together these internal and external variables constitute *the political environment* in which the black presidential vote takes place.

This chapter examines selected aspects of black voting behavior in American presidential elections. What has been the pattern of black voting in presidential elections? Are there significant differences in black and national voting patterns in these elections? What influence do these differences have? Have recent legislative and judicial policies facilitated black voter participation in presidential elections? How relevant are shifts and changes in national and regional voting trends to black voting behavior in presidential elections? What contributions to black voting in presidential elections has increased black voter mobilization and organization made? What is the conceptual and theoretical significance of the black vote in presidential elections? Finally, what are the strategic implications of black voter participation in presidential elections for prospective presidential candidates and black political development? These questions underscore the importance of black participation and voting for the highest elective office in American politics and government.

The black presidential vote assumes a fourfold significance. First, many political leaders and analysts consider it *a barometer of political participation and influence,* particularly in national politics. Second, as a largely cohesive bloc vote, *it may be pivotal in close presidential elections.* Third, it represents *a symbolic and substantive expression of black values and preferences* through interest-group articulation and mobilization. And fourth, it is *an instrument of political brokering and bargaining by black leaders* seeking to advance black economic, political, and policy goals through the presidency.[3]

Black Presidential Voting and Concepts of Political Participation

Historically, the key issue in the participation of blacks in presidential elections was the acquisition and maintenance of the right to vote. The concept of political participation thus revolved around the vote. The black vote must be examined in conjunction with other concepts of political participation, however. Analysts of electoral trends in presidential elections employ a variety of political participation concepts to explain voting behavior. Milbrath identifies and arranges in hierarchical order 14 types of participatory acts ranging from mere exposure of oneself to political stimuli at the bottom to holding public and party office at the top.[4] Others conceptualize political participation as varied efforts to influence public policy outcomes. Verba and Nie seem sensitive to culture variances in modes of participation.[5] However, their analyses exclude subcultural variances in political participation within a single political system such as the United States. Milton Morris is more aware of these intrasystem subcultural differences. He categorizes black political participation into "electoral and nonelectoral modes."[6] Electoral modes include voting, party participation, and the holding of elective office. Nonelectoral modes include interest-group activity and leadership. Thus the historical evolution of black participation in presidential elections must influence electoral and nonelectoral participatory concepts to embrace those years in which blacks were totally denied the right to vote.[7]

For example, Larry Nelson points out that blacks participated in the presidential election of 1864 even without the widespread use of the vote:

> Although generally denied the vote, black leaders hoped to promote their cause by presenting their views to the electorate. During the winter and spring of 1864, they took advantage of the opportunities presented by abolitionist meetings, informal gatherings, speaking tours, and the press to voice their opinions and anxieties publicly. They seldom spoke without commenting on the fate of slavery.[8]

The activities Nelson describes are examples of nonelectoral political behavior aimed at the candidates in the 1864 presidential election. These activities presaged black voting during the Reconstruction period. Black political conventions, newspapers, race advancement organizations, and other types of political participation were also used in conjunction with the black vote during and after the Reconstruction period to widen the spectrum of black political participation.

Once blacks secured the right to vote through the Fifteenth Amendment, electoral as well as nonelectoral modes of participation in presidential elections became important. These modes included party registration and participation, participation as delegates to party conventions, party office-holding, and election or appointment to public office. Each of these kinds of participation became particularly critical during presidential election campaigns.

For instance, black party affiliation has switched from predominantly Republican from 1866 to 1934 to predominantly Democratic from 1934 to the present. This switch in party affiliation is particularly manifest in presidential elections. Levy and Kramer argue:

> Until 1934 the black vote in the U.S. was decidedly Republican. Those blacks who voted did so for the G.O.P. with the same singlemindedness as Southern whites went for the Democrats, and for precisely the same reason—the Civil War. The G.O.P. was the party of Lincoln and with the exception of his successor, Andrew Johnson, who vetoed a bill providing for black suffrage in the District of Columbia (Congress overrode the veto), the Republicans, perhaps by design, perhaps not, aided the black advance with popular executive orders and selective federal appointments during the succeeding 20 years.[9]

Paradoxically, the budding black influence in presidential campaigns was all but destroyed by a Republican presidential candidate. Rutherford B. Hayes promised to return control of the politics of race to the southern states in the presidential campaign of 1876 if the South promised him their vote. Both Hayes and the white South were victorious.

Until the pernicious compromise, the number of black delegates to Republican national conventions increased. Nowlin points out that there were only four black delegates at the Republican convention in 1868, the year black participation began in Republican convention politics.[10] By 1872, as Reconstruction politics permeated the southern states and registered more black voters for the Republican party, the total number of black delegates to the Republican national convention reached 27. From 1868 to 1896, the politics of these black delegates differed little from their white counterparts. Nowlin suggests that they gave "unstinted support to candidates whose records they believed to favor the welfare of their race and other oppressed people's and in turn for their support, focused the attention of the convention upon the problem of securing civil rights and protection for their groups."[11]

But, following the compromise of 1876, the black-white Republican coalition in the southern states began to disintegrate. White Democratic party leaders viciously attacked the coalition with words, ostracism, and violence. White Republicans began an exodus from the regular party organization and established what came to be known as "lily-white Republican clubs." Following a riot between black and white Republicans at the state Republican convention in Texas in 1888, the white flight from the Republican party increased. Blacks remaining in the regular party organization became known as the Black and Tan Republicans. Hanes Walton and C. Vernon Gray indicate that:

> The lily-white movement gained support and was officially recognized in several states by President Benjamin Harrison in 1889 as the only Republican organization . . . although the era of disfranchisement stripped away most black support of Black and Tan Republicans, both groups became important in the struggle for presidential nomination.[12]

The number of black delegates to Republican national conventions continued to decline between 1880 and 1912 (see Figure 1.1).

By 1934 the economic devastation of the Great Depression, black urbanization, and President Franklin Roosevelt's New Deal combined to turn the majority of the black vote to the Democratic party. This dramatic transition to the Democratic party underscored the increasing importance of the black presidential vote. When the 1942 off-year elections suggested that some black voters were returning to the GOP, some white and black Republican leaders predicted the Republicans would substantially reclaim many black votes in the 1944 presidential election. Two prominent black organizations, the Chicago Citizen's Committee of 1,000 and the National Negro Council, joined with the Republicans in opposing Roosevelt for a fourth term. But the 1944 general election only demonstrated the strength and resiliency of black support for Roosevelt. Blacks provided a key margin of victory for Roosevelt in Pennsylvania, Maryland, Michigan, Missouri, New York, Illinois, and New Jersey. These seven states contributed 168 electoral votes to Roosevelt's victory.[13]

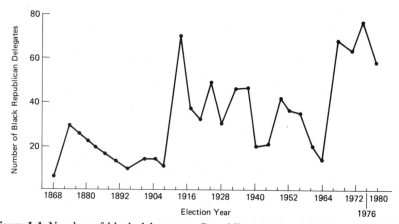

Figure 1.1 Number of black delegates to Republican National Conventions, 1868–1972. (Adapted from Hanes Walton, Jr., *Black Republicans: The Politics of the Black and Tans* [Metuchen, N.J.: Scarecrow Press, 1975], 179.)

Nevertheless, southern states and southern black voters were not pivotal in presidential elections prior to 1944. Seven months prior to the 1944 presidential election, the U.S. Supreme Court, in the case of *Smith* v. *Allwright*[14] declared the white primary unconstitutional, stimulating black voter registration. But not until the massive civil rights and voter registration efforts of the 1950s would the southern black vote become a factor in presidential elections. The focus was primarily on the black voter in large cities in the Midwest and North. Voting registration figures generated by the U.S. Commission on Civil Rights indicate that late in the 1950s, black voter registration in the South began to rise significantly (see Table 1.1).

In 1948, black support for President Harry Truman contributed to his victories in the key states of Ohio, Illinois, and California, accounting for 68 percent of his 115 electoral vote margin. Truman's Executive Orders 9980 and 9981, establishing a Fair Employment Board within the Civil Service Commission and outlawing segregation in the nation's armed forces, proved enormously popular with black voters.[15] There can be no doubt that black voters participated in the presidential contest with a keen rational self-interest and some political acumen.

Nevertheless, in the 1952 and 1956 presidential elections, some blacks defected to the Republican party candidate, Dwight Eisenhower. Also, a number of blacks perceived Democratic party candidate Adlai Stevenson's pursuit of an illusory black-southern Democratic coalition as a political setback. According to a Gallup poll in January 1957, black voting for Re-

Table 1.1   Black Voting Registration in Southern States, 1959 and 1964

	Percentage of Voting Age Blacks Registered		Estimated Number of Blacks Registered
State	*1959*	*1964*	*1964*
Alabama	13.7	21.6	104,000
Arkansas	37.7	43.5	80,000
Florida	39.0	51.1	240,616
Georgia	25.8	39.1	240,000
Louisiana	30.9	31.6	162,866
Mississippi	6.2	6.7	28,500
North Carolina	38.2	45.0	248,000
South Carolina	14.8	34.2	127,000
Tennessee	na	67.2	211,000
Texas	38.8	57.7	375,000
Virginia	23.0	27.7	121,000
Total	—	38.6	1,937,982

Sources: For 1959: *1959 Report*, Civil Rights Commission, 559–86; and *1961 Report*, U.S. Civil Rights Commission, 251–311. For 1964: *Second Annual Report*, Voter Education Project of the Southern Regional Council, Inc., April 1, 1964.

publican candidates rose 18 percentage points from 1952, when only 20 percent of the black vote went to Eisenhower. The poll also indicated that "of all the major groups of the nation's population, the one that shifted most to the Eisenhower-Nixon ticket last November was the Negro voter."[16] The southern black vote seemed particularly important to this trend. An NAACP survey of election returns from predominantly black areas of 63 cities throughout the nation pointed out that the Republicans gained 19.9 percentage points in black communities in 1956. But black voters in 23 southern cities increased their vote for Eisenhower by 36.8 percentage points while blacks in 40 nonsouthern cities increased their support for Eisenhower by only 9.9 percentage points. This dip in black support for Democratic presidential candidates is illustrated in Figure 1.2.

What is also important about the slowly emerging influence of the black southern vote is its underlying nonelectoral participatory base. The Montgomery bus boycott of 1955, the desegregation crisis at Little Rock in 1957, the North Carolina Agricultural and Technical sit-ins of 1960, and other civil rights actions began to infiltrate themselves into the major issues that characterized the 1960 presidential election. Black voters in the North and South began to use events in the South as a method of evaluating prospective Democratic and Republican presidential candidates. Thus, although most civil rights actions in the South were aimed at influencing racial norms and mores, laws, and customs, they also influenced politicians and political systems. As will be discussed later in this chapter, black southern votes would be critical to presidential hopefuls in 1960, 1968, and 1976.

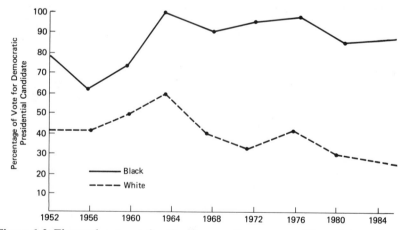

Figure 1.2 Electoral support for the Democratic party candidates in presidential elections, 1952–1984. (Based on Gallup poll survey data in the *Gallup Opinion Index,* 1974, 1977; data from the Joint Center for Political Studies and the *New York Times,* November, 1980, 1984.)

Testing the Pivotal Black Vote Thesis

The focus on voting as the key political resource in the acquisition and maintenance of black civil rights was dramatically illustrated in the 1960 presidential election. John F. Kennedy symbolized a youthful political genesis more sensitive to black goals and aspirations. Black votes substantially contributed to his 110,000-vote margin over Republican Richard M. Nixon. This pivotal role of the black vote in the 1960 presidential election elated civil rights leaders and notified political strategists that black votes were no longer of minor significance.

The 1964 and 1968 presidential elections seemed to argue *against* the pivotal black vote thesis. Although more than 90 percent of the black vote went to Democrat Lyndon Johnson, how critical were these votes to Johnson's victory margin of 434 electoral votes and 61.6 percent of the popular vote? In Louisiana, Mississippi, Alabama, Georgia, and South Carolina, electoral votes went to Republican Barry Goldwater in spite of civil rights activity and the emerging black southern vote. Although it is possible that the visibility of black politics in these states triggered the Goldwater vote, it is clear that the national and southern black vote were minor factors submerged in the Johnson landslide in 1964.[17]

The 1968 presidential election was a more distinctive and complex test for the pivotal black vote thesis. Both the 1964 Civil Rights Act and the 1965 Voting Rights Act were expected to combine with continued black voter registration to increase the strategic significance of the black vote in both the presidential primaries and the general election. Ghetto unrest, the emerging black power movement,[18] the Poor People's Campaign, and other civil rights actions maintained race as a controversial national issue. Moreover, several prominent hopefuls in the Democratic primary intensified interest in the campaign. Edmund Muskie, Hubert Humphrey, and Robert Kennedy all seemed viable presidential nominees at the Democratic convention. All seemed sensitive to civil rights and black needs.

Key circumstances, however, deprived black voters of the opportunity to become electoral arbiters in the 1968 presidential election. First, George Wallace's defection from the Democratic party and his show of political strength as the nominee of the American Independent party seriously weakened the regular Democratic party coalition, which included blacks. Wallace's candidacy was an antidote to emerging black voter strength. He symbolized reaction to increasing black political power. His 46 electoral votes and 9 million popular votes were captured in Arkansas, Louisiana, Mississippi, Alabama, and Georgia—states targeted by civil rights advocates.

Also, the assassination of Robert F. Kennedy during the Democratic primary eliminated the most popular black presidential choice and pitted civil rights against the Vietnam war as the principal issues in the general election.

Black voters supported Robert Kennedy more than any other Democratic or Republican presidential hopeful (see Table 1.2). His association with his brother John F. Kennedy, with civil rights advocacy, and with the liberal wing of the Democratic party made him attractive to many black leaders. His opposition to the Vietnam war distinguished him from Vice-President Hubert Humphrey. Had he become the Democratic party nominee, the Vietnam war would have been less a stigma than it became for Humphrey. Given the saliency of the war and the divisiveness of the Wallace campaign, blacks and civil rights could hardly have elected a President in 1968.

The 1972 presidential election was the antithesis of the 1964 election for the black vote. In spite of the visible role of black party leaders in George McGovern's nomination and the fact that almost 90 percent of the black vote went to McGovern, black voters could not reverse his landslide loss by 503 electoral votes and Nixon's capture of 60.7 percent of the popular vote. Black voters were as submerged in McGovern's loss in 1972 as they were in Johnson's victory in 1964.[19]

The role of the black vote in the 1976 presidential election revived and reinforced the pivotal black vote thesis. According to the Joint Center for Political Studies, the black vote proved to be the margin of Jimmy Carter's narrow 1976 victory in 13 states: Alabama, Florida, Louisiana, Maryland, Mississippi, Missouri, New York, North Carolina, Ohio, Pennsylvania, South Carolina, Texas, and Wisconsin (see Table 1.3).[20] The Joint Center monitored election results from 1,165 predominantly black sample areas in 23 states. Their analysis is based upon careful manipulation of data from these sample areas.

Three elements seemed critical in the 1976 black presidential vote. The full impact of the 1965 Voting Rights Act, renewed in 1970 and 1975, seemed to be felt (See Table 1.4 and Figure 1.3). What is most critical to underscore is the substantial increase in black voter registration in Georgia, President Carter's home state. Black support for Carter in Georgia and Carter's

Table 1.2   Black Perceptions of Presidential Hopefuls, 1968[a]

Wallace (AIP)	Humphrey (D)	Nixon (R)	McCarthy (D)	Reagan (R)
12.1	85.0	55.1	56.5	40.6

Johnson (D)	Romney (R)	R. Kennedy (D)	Muskie (D)
81.5	49.0	90.0	69.3

Source: Survey Research Center, University of Michigan.
[a]Each respondent rated every candidate on a scale of 0 to 100 with 0 indicating great dislike and 100 indicating a very positive evaluation. The scores in the table are mean ratings for each candidate.

Table 1.3 1976 Presidential Election; Black Voter Turnout in States Where Black Votes Were Carter's Victory Margin

State	Black Voter Turnout[a] (%)	Estimated Total Black Vote	Percentage for Carter	Estimated Number of Black Votes for Carter	Winning Margin	Electoral Votes
Alabama	68.1	211,246	86.4	182,517	148,631	9
Arkansas	60.8	74,412	84.3	62,729	229,196	6
Florida	67.3	275,866	94.9	261,797	186,087	17
Georgia	60.3	272,074	96.3	262,007	482,507	12
Kentucky	54.5	49,181	80.0	39,345	85,239	9
Louisiana	67.2	282,708	93.6	264,615	77,308	10
Maryland	55.5	163,709	91.5	149,794	86,638	10
Mississippi	52.9	140,526	87.4	122,819	11,537	7
Missouri	72.6	137,504	91.4	125,678	67,510	12
New York	69.0	681,581	89.5	610,015	275,970	41
North Carolina	55.6	220,670	92.8	204,782	184,508	13
Ohio	75.2	304,091	80.0	243,273	7,586	25
Pennsylvania	70.3	294,551	87.2	256,849	128,456	27
South Carolina	64.8	184,632	90.4	166,907	101,492	8
Tennessee	65.5	150,723	92.2	138,967	188,863	10
Texas	48.2	267,770	96.8	259,202	155,246	26
Wisconsin	84.5	43,741	93.4	40,854	34,017	11

Source: Adapted from *The Black Vote: Election '76* (Washington, D.C.: Joint Center for Political Studies, 1977).
[a]*Percentage of black registrants who voted.*

Table 1.4   Voter Registration in the South Before
and After the Voting Rights Act of 1965

| | Percentage of Voting-Age Population Registered | | |
	1964	*1972*	*1975*
Black	43.3	56.6	54.8
White	73.2	67.8	78.3

Sources: Southern Regional Council Data in the 1968 *Congressional Quarterly Almanac,*
pp. 772, 1055; and in "Revolution in Civil Rights," *Congressional Quarterly,* 70, "The Voting
Rights Act: Ten Years After," *Report of the U.S. Commission on Civil Rights;* (Washington,
D.C.: Government Printing Office, 1975), 43; and Voter Education Project, Atlanta.

"Georgiacentric" black politics can be largely attributed to this substantial
increase in black voter registration in Georgia, as well as the visible and
sophisticated black political infrastructure in the state.

In contrast to the 1960, 1964, 1968, and 1972 elections, black southern
voters were indispensable to a winning presidential candidate in 1976.
Cromwell points out that "with heavy support from black voters, Carter
carried every southern state of the old confederacy except Virginia where
President Ford won with a 23,906 vote margin. Without this massive black
support, many political observers have noted, Carter would have lost his
native South. A majority of whites voted for President Ford."[21]

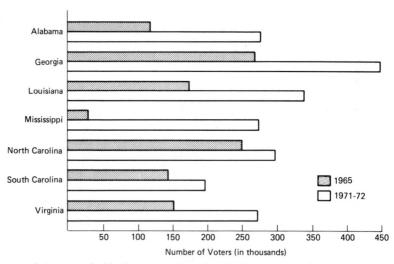

Figure 1.3 Increase in black voter registration in the seven southern states covered
by the 1965 Voting Rights Act. ("The Voting Rights Act: Ten Years After." *Report
of the U.S. Commission on Civil Rights* [Washington, D.C.: Government Printing
Office, 1975] p. 53).

What is somewhat paradoxical about the pivotal role black voters played in Carter's election is that they did so without as much influence in the Democratic party convention as they enjoyed in 1972 and with less overt support for Carter than either McGovern enjoyed in 1972 or Humphrey had in 1968. Once Carter captured the Democratic nomination, black politicians found themselves selling an unknown to black voters. This was particularly difficult because Carter often seemed ambiguous and elusive on major election issues, particularly those of concern to blacks.[22] This may suggest that party participation is less positively correlated with election outcomes than is commonly believed. Campaign issues, the characteristics of presidential contestants, televised debates between presidential candidates, and other variables may be more causal in presidential elections than are party participation variables.[23]

Thus, *external political events* and *internal black political organization* combined to make the 1976 black presidential vote pivotal. The lingering shadow of Watergate certainly favored Jimmy Carter. Ford's association with Richard Nixon reinforced Carter's anti-Washington-establishment image. Black voter mobilization, particularly through Operation Big Vote, stressed not only the necessity of a high black voter turnout but also the need to vote for more ethical and accountable elected officials.

The cumulative impact of internal black political organization began to be felt during the 1976 campaign. The Civil Rights Acts of 1960 and 1964, the Voting Rights Act of 1965, party reforms—particularly those preceding the 1972 Democratic National Convention—and coalitions of black political organizations bolstered the surge of black voters. Moreover, the sharp increase in the number, distribution, and visibility of black elected officials stationed elective leadership in many black communities during the 1976 presidential election. This increase in black elected officials, from little more than 600 in 1962 to 4,503 in 1978, symbolized both the need for and the result of more conscientious black voting behavior.

Despite this temporary rise in the influence of black presidential voting, blacks had yet to realize their full political potential in presidential elections. Of the 15.6 million blacks eligible to vote in 1976, only 9.2 million registered to vote and only 5.7 million (64.1 percent) actually voted. Thus just over one-third of the eligible black voting population actually voted in 1976. Although black voting has increased sharply over past trends, many black adults remain to be registered, and many have yet to vote.[24]

Thus, although the black vote has been numerically pivotal in the 1960 and 1976 presidential elections, whether it will continue to be pivotal is related to the following factors: (1) whether it is the margin of victory in a precinct, county, city, or state needed by a candidate to capture the popular and electoral vote; (2) whether the election is close enough to require a decisive bloc vote; (3) whether blacks contributed to the issues that were decisive in the election; (4) whether black primary votes in individual states and the aggregate primary vote secured the nomination for a candidate; and (5) whether blacks coalesced with other interest groups to contribute to the margin of victory for a candidate.

Ronald Reagan's election severely tests the pivotal black vote thesis. Reagan's victory margin was the second largest (behind that of Richard Nixon in 1972) attained by any Republican presidential candidate in the 20th century. Reagan acquired 43,267,462 popular votes, 489 electoral votes, and 51 percent of the popular vote, despite the 7 percent of the popular vote captured by Independent party candidate John Anderson.[25] Carter obtained 34,968,548 popular votes, only 49 electoral votes, and 41 percent of the popular vote. Approximately 16,967,000 blacks were eligible to vote in the 1980 presidential election, or 10.8 percent of the total voting-age population in America. According to the Joint Center for Political Studies, 61.3 percent of the eligible black votes actually voted, *2 percent more than turned out in the 1976 race.* Only 7 million, or 40 percent of the total black voting-age population, actually voted. The key element in the Joint Center's analysis is the relationship of Reagan's strongest regional support to the strongest regional black voting turnout (see Table 1.5). Reagan's strongest electoral and ideological support came from the West and the South. Turnout by black registered voters, however, was highest in the Northeast (67 percent) and lowest in the South (60 percent). And although black voter turnout was relatively high in the West (64.1 percent), a much smaller percentage of black voters exists in the West than in the South or Northeast.[26]

What is particularly interesting is the comparison between black and Hispanic support for Carter. More than 80 percent of the black vote went to President Carter. But according to the *New York Times,* only 54 percent of the Hispanic vote went to Carter. More than 36 percent of the Hispanic vote went to Reagan. What this suggests is the weakening of the black-Hispanic coalition support for Democratic presidential candidates coupled

Table 1.5   Turnout Rate of Registered Black Voters by Region,[a] 1980 Presidential Election

Region	Number of Precincts	Percent of all Sample Precincts	Total Registered	Votes Cast	Turnout (%)
Northeast	116	21.2	64,857	43,782	67.5
North Central	108	19.7	63,414	39,014	61.5
South	284	51.8	362,884	217,813	60.0
West	40	7.3	21,455	13,763	64.1
Total	548	100.0	512,610	314,371	61.3

Source: Joint Center for Political Studies 1980 election study of sample precincts.
[a]*All data weighted by region.*

with relatively weak black support for Reagan in strong Reagan regions. It is also evident that the southwestern and western configuration of the Hispanic population appeared to be influenced by strong Reagan support in those regions.

In brief, a number of preconditions for pivotal status eluded the black vote in 1980. There were few precincts, counties, cities, or states in which the black vote could have been the margin of victory for Reagan or Carter. National election results were not nearly close enough to make any racial or ethnic bloc vote decisive. Blacks were an unspoken but significant issue in national support for Reagan. Since only 2.7 percent of the Republican party delegates were black, black support in the Republican primaries was insignificant. And black coalitions with Hispanics, labor unions, Jews, and others were considerably weaker than in previous presidential elections.

The 1984 presidential election provided still another variant on the pivotal black vote thesis. Jesse L. Jackson's emergence as a contender for the Democratic party nomination suggested that *blacks are as pivotal to the nomination of the Democratic presidential and vice-presidential team as they are to influencing presidential general election outcomes.* Jackson won more than 400 delegates in the primaries and figured prominently in the selection of Walter Mondale's vice-presidential running mate, Geraldine Ferraro. However, some analysts argue that the Democratic party ignored the Jackson surge and that Jackson's influence peaked at the convention. If this is so, evidence for a pivotal black vote becomes even more difficult to identify.

Components of a Conceptual Framework for Assessing Black Politics and American Presidential Elections

Black Political Values and Interest-Group Aggregation

Whether pivotal or not, "the black vote" exhibits distinctiveness, cohesiveness, and predictability. A general commonality of group values and preferences explain these characteristics. Civil rights, equal educational and employment opportunities, improved social services, and greater political access are among consistent black interest-group values and preferences. Blacks regard presidential elections as opportunities to advance their group interests and goals. As Kirkpatrick argues:

> Elections are, after all, the process through which popular participation and political accountability are secured, the nexus of a system of interlocking institutions through which political leaders are recruited, governments criticized, alternatives presented and examined, and decisions finally made by masses of people about who should rule and to what broad ends?[27]

But two points should be made. First, blacks are historically a submissive group seeking to reduce their dependency on other, more dominant groups through politics. As Mack Jones argues, "the concepts of dominant and submissive groups distill the essence of the black political experience and give us an analytical tool which will allow us to isolate, categorize and interpret the important variables in the black political experience."[28] Participation in presidential elections is a key part of the black political experience through which dominant-submissive group struggle occurs. Second, black voters are less a single, monolithic national interest group than a consistent coalition of local and specialized interest groups that display remarkable voting cohesiveness. Nationally, "the black vote" is the collective expression of values emanating from the black vote in specific cities, states, regions, parties, unions, and other interest groups and institutions. This was well illustrated by the Jackson candidacy for the Democratic Party nomination. Heavy black support for Jackson occurred in some states like Illinois and South Carolina. Conversely, Jackson support was weaker among blacks whose support for Carter was transferred to Mondale. Black political values and aims are expressed through civic, community, union, church, educational, fraternal, and other organizations, as well as through exclusively black political organizations. Black interest-group behavior in presidential elections must therefore be considered at every level and through every institution in which it is manifest.[29]

Black political caucuses are particularly important in presidential elections. Aggregated within or independent of larger organizations, black political caucuses mobilized their members and constituents around strategies that pursue specific political objectives. These caucuses challenge legal or social constraints on their members and constituents. They broker and bargain with larger political entities for concessions, and may form coalitions with other groups and caucuses to pursue mutual interests.

Political analysts have seldom appreciated the role of black political caucuses and organizations in advancing civil rights aims. They attribute increased black voter registration and political action to the removal of legal or institutional barriers. For example, Herbert Asher writes:

> Since 1952, a number of developments have occurred that have increased the potential electorate dramatically. One important set of events is the breakdown of the legal barriers, particularly in the South, that had prevented blacks and other minorities from voting. The 24th amendment to the Constitution abolished the poll tax, while congressional passage in 1965 of the Voting Rights Act enabled federal examiners to register citizens in counties (mostly southern) where literacy tests were used and fewer than 50 percent of the people were registered.[30]

Asher fails to discuss how these legal developments were translated by black organizations into effective political advocacy, particularly during presidential campaigns.

Two kinds of black political caucuses are critical in presidential elections: voter registration/education organizations and intraparty caucuses. Historically and recently, the NAACP, Southern Christian Leadership Conference, Student Non-Violent Coordinating Committee, Voter Education Project, National Urban League, Congress of Racial Equality, Joint Center for Political Studies, and many other organizations have diligently educated and registered black voters. They have translated opportunities provided by voting rights and civil rights law into concrete voter mobilization.

For example, massive voter registration campaigns conducted by Operation Big Vote, the Voter Education Project, labor unions, the Democratic National Committee, and a plethora of local organizations contributed to the substantial black voter turnout that proved so crucial to Jimmy Carter's victory. Big Vote represented a coalition of more than 50 civil rights, labor, business, and community organizations that targeted 36 cities for intensive voter registration activity during the 1976 presidential election year. These efforts to register black voters provide blacks with the instruments to exercise group power to achieve group goals. These campaigns also bolster the political infrastructure of the black national and local communities while mobilizing black voters.

Although essentially external to party decision making, this mobilization of black votes facilitates black intraparty participation. For example, the reforms initiated by the Democratic party in the 1972 convention resulted from the work of a special party task force headed by Senator George McGovern. McGovern revealed that various devices had been used to discourage minorities and other groups from participating in party decision making, particularly at the state level. McGovern's findings were the result of testimony provided by the same civil rights organizations involved in black voter registration and education. The task force findings resulted in structural changes within the party that provided blacks and other groups with greater access to party decision making.

As a result, blacks, women, Hispanics, and youth formed caucuses at the 1972 and 1976 Democratic conventions. Pressman points out:

> The Black and Women's caucuses showed marked organizational development during this period. In 1972 they existed largely as forums to hear speeches by their own members and by presidential candidates. But by 1976 these two caucuses had established stable leadership structure and sophisticated communications networks. They held large meetings for caucus members, whose votes ultimately sanction caucus actions. But their leaders also engaged in a series of concrete, specific negotiations with the presidential nominee.[31]

Perhaps one of the highlights of black participation in the Democratic party was the 1972 Democratic National Convention in which black state delegations and caucuses successfully challenged entrenched party regulars; held critical positions during the convention such as Credentials Committee Chairman, party Vice-Chairman, and Convention Co-Chairman; and spurred a liberal thrust that helped George McGovern capture the Democratic presidential nomination. Key black leaders became conduits for black demands channeled to party leaders and linkages between black delegates and Democratic party leadership.

Black caucus action was particularly crucial to McGovern in California. Gray and Walton write:

> The occasion for the display of black delegate influence was the California challenge. If McGovern won the California challenge, his nomination was assured; if he lost, his nomination would be more difficult to achieve. In a crucial vote on the California challenge, black delegates overwhelmingly voted with the McGovern forces for the seating of the duly elected slate of delegates. Of the 452 black delegates, more than 350 voted to seat the full McGovern delegation.[32]

California Assemblyman Willie Brown, leader of the California delegation, played a key leadership role in the challenge. His brokering and strategy were particularly important to McGovern's nomination.

Although less influential in the 1976 Democratic National Convention, the black caucus enjoyed vestigial authority. Because Carter's early start for the nomination and his surprising control of convention processes left little room for brokering and bargaining among and between groups supporting different candidates, black and other caucuses had less to trade than they did in 1972. This suggests that black caucuses are likely to attain more influence in heavily contested primaries and conventions than those in which a single candidate is dominant.

Conversely, the black caucus at the 1976 Republican National Convention was important because Ford and Reagan ran neck and neck through most of the primaries. Although there were only 76 black delegates to the convention, they held several meetings and receptions with Ford and Reagan during the convention week. The National Black Republican Council, a group closely affiliated with the Republican National Committee, continuously discussed platform planks, candidates, and convention procedures with the members and with prospective nominees. Black Republican delegates and alternates were concerned about the appointment of blacks to top-level administrative posts, soaring unemployment among black youth, the platform's antibusing plank, and other issues. But because several leading black Republican delegates were fearful that too aggressive a strategy would endanger President Ford's nomination, they were neither vociferous nor diligent in pursuing their demands.

At the 1980 Republican convention, the number of black delegates declined significantly, from 76 in 1976 to 56 in 1980. Conversely, an unprecedented number of black delegates attended the Democratic party convention. Of the 3,331 delegates and 2,053 alternates, 481 and 297 respectively were black. Sixty-eight percent of the black delegates supported President Carter, and 32 percent supported challenger Senator Edward Kennedy.[33]

In addition to brokering and lobbying as caucuses within the Democratic or Republican parties, blacks have occasionally pursued more independent action during presidential campaigns. At the 1964 Democratic National Convention, the Mississippi Freedom Democratic Party (MFDP) mobilized a 68-member delegation to unseat the regular white Democratic party delegation from Mississippi. Although they failed in 1964, they continued political activity in Mississippi. In 1968, former MFDP leaders returned as the Mississippi Loyalist Party (MLP) to again challenge the regular state Democratic delegation. The MLP was seated with Aaron Henry as a delegate.

Also in 1968, the District of Columbia nominated Channing Phillips as a black favorite son for the Presidency. He received 67.5 votes. Black Georgia state legislator Julian Bond was nominated for the vice presidency, but declined. Also in 1972, without the endorsement of the Congressional Black Caucus or the National Black Political Convention, Congresswoman Shirley Chisholm announced her candidacy for the Democratic party nomination for President. Chisholm entered the 1972 Democratic National Convention with only 26 delegate votes. However, the Congressional Black Caucus failed to agree on the endorsement of a presidential candidate in 1972 and 1976.

What is important to underscore about black political caucuses in presidential elections is the two-dimensional nature of their function. They simultaneously mobilize their membership and constituents to consolidate themselves internally while seeking to affect productive exchange relations with other groups and institutions external to themselves. The emergence of the National Conference of Black Elected Officials, the National Caucus of Black State Legislators, the National Caucus of Local Elected Officials, the National Conference of Black Mayors, and other black caucuses will seek greater influence in upcoming presidential elections both as voter mobilization institutions and as effective sources of black demands and policy preferences. More than 85 percent of the 4,912 black elected officials in 1981 served local government. Caucuses representing black local elected officials as well as black congresspersons are particularly important stimulants to black voter mobilization.

The extent to which present or future black political caucuses influence presidential outcomes depends upon a host of variables beyond the control of the caucuses, however. The socioeconomic status of the black voter, state and local election systems and law,[34] the level of black civil and community participation, the characteristics of particular presidential aspirants, including black presidential aspirants like Jesse Jackson, international events, and the national mood and condition during a presidential year are variables that black political caucuses must address. These variables are causally related to black voter participation in presidential elections (see Figure 1.4). Some, like the socioeconomic status of black voters and state and local election systems, are independent variables. Others, like the level of black civic and community activity and the characteristics of presidential aspirants, are intervening variables.[35] Whether independent or intervening, these variables comprise the strategic environment in which black political caucuses strive.

International and National Conditions and Events

In addition to black interest-group aggregation, international and national conditions and events are critical in presidential elections. Although black interest-group aggregation is an example of an *internal black political variable,* international and national conditions and events are *key external variables* related to the black presidential vote. Public satisfaction or dissatisfaction with the way in which incumbent presidents handle international and national conditions influence voter propensity to support or oppose incumbents. Combined with the charisma, conviction, and image of the challenging presidential aspirant, the public mood can swing from incumbent to challenger or from challenger to incumbent.

For example, McGovern's unsuccessful effort to generate voter support by exploiting Nixon's method of "winding down" the Vietnam war contributed to his electoral demise. Ford's failure to dissociate himself from

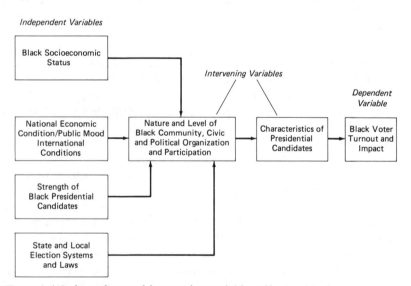

Figure 1.4 Independent and intervening variables affecting black voter turnout.

the Nixon administration and respond adequately to the energy crisis helped Jimmy Carter in the 1976 general election. Carter's inability to stimulate the economy and win freedom for Americans held hostage by the Iranian government contributed substantially to Reagan's electoral margin.

Somewhat ironically, in 1984 Jackson's adept handling of the release of Lieutenant Goodman and his peace efforts in Central America demonstrated his capability in international affairs and won significant support for him among Democrats.

Continued Mobilization of Black Voters

In addition to black interest-group aggregation, continued direct mobilization of black voters will be necessary to maintain and expand the level of black influence in presidential elections. The continued efficacy of Operation Big Vote, a nonpartisan coalition of some 80 local, regional, and national organizations will be essential. As Hillman indicates, "through voter registration and get-out-the-vote campaigns, Operation Big Vote coalitions in 50 target cities not only raised the level of participation in those cities, but helped to raise political consciousness and participation in other areas as well.[36]

Specifically, black voter mobilization must consider the following:

1. Targeting key precincts, cities, counties, and states where presidential sweepstakes in the primaries may be close
2. Increasing the *number and distribution* of black elected officials, particularly in Congress and statewide offices. This will contribute visible black leadership able to influence party decisions and electoral strategies in a presidential election year.
3. Increasing the proportion of eligible black voters
4. Strengthening black voter coalitions with other key interest groups
5. Continued internal review of values, policy preferences, and political strategies between and among political caucuses and organizations within the black community.

Blacks, Presidential Elections, and Public Policy

Black political caucuses articulate black public policy concerns during presidential campaigns. The success of these caucuses in persuading presidential candidates and party leaders to incorporate black public policy concerns into party platforms determines whether blacks can hold an elected president accountable for implementing them once in office. The saliency, clarity, and consistency of black public policy positions coupled with the role of the black vote during the primary and general presidential elections can increase or decrease the ability of black political leaders to bargain with

successful presidential candidates for political or public policy concessions.[37] For example, in 1960 black leaders were vocal and clear about their
civil rights demands during the presidential election, particularly within the
Democratic party. The saliency of the civil rights issue and the key role of
black votes in the general election put black leaders in a favorable position
to bargain with John F. Kennedy for civil rights and antipoverty legislation.

In contrast, in the 1972, 1976, and 1980 presidential elections, the linkage
between black public policy demands and the role of the black vote was
less firm. In 1972 blacks articulated a strong and clear set of public policy
issues for George McGovern; but the black vote failed to elect McGovern.
In 1976 blacks were less unified and clear about their public policy expectations of Jimmy Carter; but the black vote was decisive in Carter's election. As a result, both in 1972 and in 1976, the ability of blacks to successfully bargain with the president-elect was more limited than in 1960.
Once Carter was nominated in 1976, many black politicians who in 1968
and 1972 were almost ideological purists on such issues as affirmative action, aid to the cities, black participation in Democratic party decision making, and other concerns now exchanged a belated and bewildered commitment to Jimmy Carter in the hope that he would be responsive to black
concerns.[38]

In 1984, black public policy demands were largely embodied in the candidacy and, following Mondale's nomination, the advocacy of Jesse Jackson. However, this focused advocacy did not appear to influence the outcome of the general election. Reagan would have won the election whether
Jackson and Mondale were closely allied or unified within the Democratic
party or not.

It is important to note that public policy issues are not the sole concerns
of black leaders in presidential campaigns. Frequently, the price of black
voter support is the appointment of blacks to key leadership and administrative positions in the party or the new administration. The assumption
is that a black presidential appointee will be sensitive enough to blacks to
pursue their public policy concern while in office. But the failure of black
leaders to clearly identify those blacks best able to implement specific black
policy concern leaves the president-elect with the discretion to appoint a
black who may or may not inspire the confidence of the national black
community. For example, when President Carter appointed Housing Secretary Patricia Roberts Harris, many black leaders complained that she was
not the ideal choice for the post. *After,* rather than *before,* the appointment, black leaders identified other, "more acceptable," choices for the
post of Secretary of Housing and Urban Development.

Nevertheless, the public policy issues identified as critical by black leaders during presidential campaigns reflect both national and black economic,
social, and political conditions. These policy issues must therefore be con-

sidered in relation to larger national public policies and policy issues to determine whether they are politically feasible. Often, black leaders will demand that a presidential aspirant declare himself on a policy issue that is politically unfeasible. They may do so as a political ploy rather than a genuine attempt to evaluate the suitability of the presidential prospect. In either case, larger policy issues must be considered by black leaders in presidential elections not only to know who the significant others of the various presidential prospects are but also because those larger issues may have overt or covert implications for the black community. For example, the fiscal and monetary policies of presidential aspirants are seldom explicitly racial but have underlying implications for the economic opportunities of nonwhite communities.

Summary

Ultimately, blacks participate in presidential elections to affect public policy outputs and outcomes. Their social, economic, and political development and quality of life depend heavily on government action and intervention. The policies that influence the nature and extent of that government action and intervention are therefore of principal concern to black voters. Given the importance of multidimensional participation in presidential elections, factors that encourage or restrain black voters, black party officials, black elected officials, and other black leaders must be isolated in order to identify strategies for maximizing black participation in the selection of the president. Historically, blacks have struggled from virtually negligible participation in presidential elections to an occasionally pivotal role. As black voters increased, black delegates to the Democratic and Republican conventions increased. As black delegates increased, more conscious and collective black group strategies resulted. Black group strategies not only occasionally affected the nomination of presidential candidates but also resulted in the periodic development of black presidential and vice-presidential aspirants.

It is important to reiterate that black southern votes are growing in political influence in presidential elections. Unable to overcome racist third-party mobilization or the incursion of conservative Republicans into the South for decades, black southern voters gave Jimmy Carter decisive support in southern states in 1976. Still, Reagan victories in these states in 1980 reminded black voters of the mobilization yet to be done and the limits of even maximum black voter mobilization.

Although the role of the black vote in 1976 illustrates how pivotal black presidential voting can become, the Reagan elections illustrate that the black vote is only pivotal when elections are close, when black votes help presidential candidates win key states, and when blacks forge effective coalitions with other groups whose support is indispensable to the presidential candidate.

Whether pivotal or not, black votes result in and are the result of effective black political caucuses and organizations. These entities exist at the local, state, and regional levels as well as at the national level. Often they emerge in a union, church, or other large organization. But their leadership, advocacy, and strategies during presidential campaigns determine whether black interest-group values are effectively articulated and accommodated by political parties and party leaders.

It is also important that these black political organizations and caucuses articulate clear and consistent public policy goals for presidential aspirants and their parties. If they fail to do so, their ability to bargain with successful presidential candidates, even when the black vote is pivotal in the election, may be significantly reduced. Blacks must therefore articulate their public policy expectations effectively, formulate workable participatory strategies for black voters, design efficacious group strategies within and outside party structures, and bargain effectively with successful presidential candidates if they are to maximize their role in presidential elections.

Notes

1.   See, for example, Michael B. Preston, "The 1984 Presidential Primary Campaign: Who Voted for Jesse Jackson and Why." University of Illinois, Institute of Government, November 1985; Ronald E. Brown, "Group-based Determinants of Campaign Participation in the 1984 Presidential Election." University of Michigan, Institute of Survey Research, 1985; Robert C. Smith and Joseph R. McCormick, "The Challenge of a Black Presidential Candidacy." *New Directions* 11, no. 2 (April 1984): 38–43; and Thomas E. Cavanagh, *Inside Black America: The Message of the Black Vote in the 1984 Elections* (Washington, D.C.: The Joint Center for Political Studies, 1985).

2.   See Lucius Barker and Jesse McCorry, *Blacks in the American Political System* (New York: Winthrop, 1980).

3.   Scholarly literature on blacks and presidential elections is surprisingly scarce. Among the key works are Henry Lee Moon, "The Negro Vote in the Presidential Election of 1956," *Journal of Negro Education* 26, no. 3 (Summer 1957): 219; Hanes Walton, Jr., *Black Republicans: The Politics of the Black and Tans* (Metuchen, N.J.: Scarecrow Press, 1975); Milton Morris, *The Politics of Black America* (New York: Harper and Row, 1975), chaps. 8 and 9; Hanes Walton, Jr., *Black Politics: A Theoretical and Structural Analysis* (Philadelphia: Lippincott, 1972), chap. 5; Eddie Williams and Milton D. Morris, *The Black Vote in a Presidential Election Year* (Washington, D.C.: Joint Center for Political Studies, February 1981); see also Ronald W. Wal-

ters, "Black Presidential Politics in 1980: Bargaining or Begging?" *Black Scholar* 11, no. 4 (March/April 1980): 22-31.

4. Lester Milbrath, *Political Participation* (Skokie, Ill.: Rand McNally, 1965).
5. Sidney Verba and Norman Nie, *Participation in America: Political Democracy and Social Equality* (New York: Harper and Row, 1972).
6. Milton Morris, *Politics of Black America,* 147.
7. Lenneal J. Henderson, "The Historical Evolution of Black Political Participation." Howard University, Department of Political Science, 1978.
8. Larry Nelson, "Black Leaders and the Presidential Election of 1864," *Journal of Negro History* 6, no. 1 (Jan. 1978): 43.
9. Mark R. Levy and Michael S. Kramer, *The Ethnic Factors: How America's Minorities Decide Election* (New York: Simon and Schuster, 1972), 38.
10. William Nowlin, *The Negro in American National Politics* (New York: Russell & Russell, 1970; originally published in 1931).
11. Ibid., 65.
12. Hanes Walton, Jr., and C. Vernon Gray, "Black Politics at the National Republican and Democratic Conventions, 1868-1972," *Phylon* 36, no. 3 (1975): 272.
13. Henry Lee Moon, *Balance of Power: The Negro Vote* (Garden City, N.Y.: Doubleday, 1948).
14. *Smith* v. *Allwright,* 321 U.S. 649 (1943).
15. Ruth Morgan, *The President and Civil Rights* (New York: St. Martin's Press, 1970).
16. Quoted in Moon, "The Negro Vote in the Presidential Election of 1956," 219.
17. *Presidential Elections Since 1789* (Washington, D.C.: Congressional Quarterly Service, 1975).
18. Stokely Carmichael and Charles V. Hamilton, *Black Power: The Politics of Liberation in America* (New York: Vintage Books, 1967).
19. James A. Michener, *The Presidential Lottery* (New York: Random House, 1969).
20. *The Black Vote: Election '76* (Washington, D.C.: Joint Center for Political Studies, 1977); and Oliver Cromwell, "Black Impact on the 1976 Elections," *Focus,* November 1976, 4.
21. Cromwell, "Black Impact on the 1976 Elections," 5.
22. Lenneal J. Henderson, "Black Politics and the Carter Administration: The Politics of Backlash Pragmatism," *Journal of Afro-American Issues* 5, no. 3 (Summer 1977): 245.
23. A good discussion of sex and race differences in political participation may be found in Susan Welch and Philip Secret, "Sex, Race and Political Participation," *Western Political Quarterly* 34, no. 1 (March 1981): 3.
24. *The Black Vote: Election '76,* 31.
25. Anderson, a Republican, captured 5,588,014 votes as an independent candidate. He received only 1.49 percent of the black vote.
26. Williams and Morris, *Black Vote,* 229.
27. Jeane J. Kirkpatrick, "Changing Patterns of Electoral Competition," in *The*

New American Political System, ed. Anthony King (Washington, D.C.: American Enterprise Institute, April 1980), 249.

28. Mack Jones, "A Frame of Reference for Black Politics," in *Black Political Life in the U.S.,* ed. Lenneal J. Henderson (San Francisco: Chandler, 1972), 10.

29. Harold F. Gosnell and Richard G. Smolka, *American Parties and Elections* (Columbus, Ohio: Charles E. Merrill, 1976).

30. Herbert Asher, *Presidential Elections and American Politics: Voters, Candidates, and Campaigns Since 1952* (Homewood, Ill.: Dorsey Press, 1976), 44.

31. Jeffrey L. Pressman, "Groups and Group Caucuses," *Political Science Quarterly* 92, no. 4 (Winter 1977–78): 673; see also Jeffrey L. Pressman, Denis G. Sullivan, and F. Christopher Arterton, "Cleavage, Decisions, and Legitimation: The Democrats' Mid-Term Conference," *Political Science Quarterly* 91, no. 1 (Spring 1976).

32. Walton and Gray, "Black Politics," 270.

33. Williams and Morris, *Black Vote,* 219.

34. Steven J. Rosenstone and Raymond E. Wolfinger, "The Effect of Registration Laws on Voter Turnout," *American Political Science Review* 72, no. 1 (March 1978): 22.

35. Christopher Arterton and Harlan Hahn, *Political Participation* (Washington, D.C.: American Political Science Association, 1975).

36. Garcia Hillman, "Black Voter Participation Rose by 2 Percent in 1980." *Focus* 8, no. 12 (December 1980): 5.

37. On blacks and public policy, see Marguerite Ross Barnett and James A. Hefner, eds., *Public Policy for the Black Community* (New York: Alfred Publishing, 1976); Michael B. Preston, "Blacks and Public Policy," *Policy Studies Journal* 6, no. 2 (Winter 1977): 245; and Lawrence Howard, Lenneal J. Henderson, and Deryl G. Hunt, eds., *Public Administration and Public Policy: A Minority Perspective* (Pittsburgh: Public Policy Press, 1977).

38. Henderson, "Black Politics and the Carter Administration," 246.

TWO

Ronald Reagan, Jesse Jackson, and the 1984 Presidential Election: The Continuing American Dilemma of Race

Lucius J. Barker

One signal from the 1984 presidential campaign and election, and a disturbing one, is that the status of black Americans is at a critical point and remains very much an American dilemma. The dilemma affects not only blacks; it affects all institutions and segments of American politics and society. This can be discerned in several contextual areas, among them: 1) the Reagan administration's lack of commitment to the basic principles and structures of civil rights law; 2) Jesse Jackson's campaign for the Democratic presidential nomination; and 3) differential voting behavior and patterns between blacks and whites in the 1984 presidential election. These contextual areas reflect the stakes involved in the 1984 presidential election, and the outcome of that election suggests that it served to shore up rather than weaken the policies and practices of the Reagan administration. The position taken here is that the election results are likely to exacerbate and perpetuate the American dilemma of race, and that unless we are able to deal directly and effectively with this continuing dilemma, we might be moving once again toward what the 1968 Kerner Commission described as "two societies, one black, one white, separate and unequal."[1]

National Commitment to Civil Rights

The national commitment to civil rights developed slowly and over time. Perhaps the major stimulus to the development of this commitment was the decision of the Supreme Court in *Brown* v. *Board of Education*.[2] This decision, and the subsequent impact of the civil rights movement, spurred the presidents, especially Kennedy and Johnson, and Congress to action. Laws were enacted committing the nation to take concrete steps to achieve the principles enunciated in the 1954 Court decision.[3] These steps were accelerated by the urban unrest of the 1960s. After a national soul-searching symbolized by the Kerner Commission report, the nation reaffirmed its commitment to the full inclusion of blacks and similarly excluded groups into the political-social order. These changes in our law and practice portended massive changes in prevailing patterns of influence, privilege, and benefits, and not unexpectedly, they encountered massive resistance. However, this resistance was overcome or at least quieted by the resolve and commitment of the nation to support the principles imbedded in the court decision. Indeed, as one writer put it, "developments in . . . civil rights . . . over the past forty years reflect the nation's acceptance of 'life, liberty, and the pursuit of happiness' on an equal basis for larger groups of its citizenry; and second, that the federal government should play a major role in vindicating civil rights."[4]

Despite variations in levels of support, up until the Reagan administration these premises and the legal regime and environment spun therefrom had provided the operational framework for both Democratic and Republican administrations, including those of Eisenhower, Kennedy, Johnson, Nixon, Ford, and Carter.[5] Leadership and authority of the president and his chief administrative officials—such as the attorney general—have long been turned to for the implementation and enforcement of civil rights law. In contrast to such presidential leadership and support, the Reagan administration has acted to impede and frustrate the structure and spirit of legal change envisioned by *Brown* and subsequent civil rights legislation.

The record of the Reagan administration has been documented meticulously elsewhere and need only be highlighted here.[6] Consider, for example, the administration's efforts to permit racially segregated private schools to receive tax benefits from the public treasury.[7] Or consider the efforts, ultimately successful, of the administration to narrow the reach of the federal funds cut-off provision of Title VI under the Civil Rights Act of 1964.[8] Or the administration's assault on the Civil Rights Commission, the premiere symbol of civil rights in this country.[9] Or still further, consider the continuing negative posture of the administration toward busing to achieve school desegregation and the Legal Services Program.[10] And, of course, the administration's attempts to scuttle and dilute the Voting Rights Act was a strong signal that it hoped to slow civil rights progress.[11] The administration's posture in regard to this act was especially disturbing since it is through the electoral process that ordinary groups can expect to protect their interests. More recently the administration has again tipped its hand by calling for revisions in the long-standing posture of the federal government toward affirmative action.[12] Its concern here was whether to tone down (or remove altogether) basic federal policies and guidelines used to encourage and promote job opportunities for long disadvantaged minority groups, e.g., blacks and women.

When viewed in its totality there is overwhelming evidence that the actions and attitudes of the Reagan administration have impeded civil rights progress. This administration posture has raised anew controversy and doubts concerning the legal basis upon which our civil rights law has developed. Equally disturbing is how quietly, even approvingly, we seem to be accepting this erosion of our civil rights law. A silver lining to this unhappy situation is that the policies of the Reagan administration may have aroused the concern of black political leaders and led them to do something in the 1984 presidential election to protect their interests.

The Jackson Candidacy

Jesse Jackson's campaign for the Democratic presidential nomination will undoubtedly go down in history as one of the most significant aspects of the 1984 presidential election. Consider the context out of which the Jackson candidacy developed.[13] Problems facing black politics and black political leaders as they looked toward the 1984 presidential election were indeed enormous, and they were growing. Earlier progress in achieving policy goals and objectives seemed to have become stalled, perhaps even in a state of retrogression. Studies conducted in early 1982 document the glaring socioeconomic inequities that persisted between blacks and whites. Moreover, blacks were confronted with presidential actions and attitudes that were unprecedented in terms of their scope and hostility to civil rights interests. And the considerations and benefits flowing to blacks from the Democratic party were in no way equal to the support and loyalty given by blacks to the party.[14] Overall, there was a growing concern among blacks over the current state of affairs. This "politics of frustration" led to suggestions that something had to be done to deal with the mounting problems and stem the growing sense of despair.

Ultimately, it was the attitudes and actions of the Reagan administration itself that increased the frustrations and stirred the search for coping strategies within the black community; and it was the drive and determination of Jesse Jackson that kept the issue of a black presidential candidacy alive and who by his decision was able to bring this strategy to fruition. Not all agreed with his strategy, however.

Criticisms of Jackson's candidacy were strikingly similar to those levelled against Martin Luther King and the civil rights movement.[15] When placed in the context of American politics and history, those criticisms still do not appear well grounded. It should be mentioned, however, that as Jackson's campaign developed, and as he achieved notable successes in presidential primaries, criticism of his candidacy along these lines subsided noticeably. Nonetheless, a brief review of these criticisms demonstrates their thrust and effect.

The "now is not the right time" criticism, for example, is the perennial argument used against those who launch major initiatives. Similarly, history clearly shows that the "can't win" criticism is not likely to deter important political-social movements. Fighting against overwhelming odds was the very hallmark of Martin Luther King and the civil rights movement. Jackson's candidacy was of "movement" character and dimensions. But realistically, under present conditions, neither Jesse Jackson nor any other black American, no matter how qualified, could have won the 1984 Democratic presidential nomination. One could view Jackson's candidacy as an attempt to change such conditions. But obviously this was a momentous undertaking, one that is continuing. Thus, "winning" for Jackson had to be defined in new ways, including black and minority voter registration and turnout, and his contributions to increasing the political education and consciousness of those not previously activated. On the basis of available data,[16] Jackson's campaign met with great success and took the steam out of the "can't win" criticism.

Those who charged that Jackson's candidacy was "merely symbolic" and would do nothing to feed the hungry and provide jobs for the poor somehow misread the important role and influence of symbols in politics.[17] Symbols influence peoples' thinking, guide their behavior, and shape the political environment. Symbols draw attention and get people to vote their interests. They may help reach people who are typically not motivated. Through his charisma and appeal, Jackson provided the sort of symbolism that activated large numbers. This is strongly supported by data showing dramatic increases between 1980 and 1984 black voter registration and turnout in presidential primaries.[18] What must be emphasized is that important political actions, such as running for president, serve and promote symbolic needs while simultaneously serving and promoting more material interests. Certainly Jackson's candidacy was symbolic, but so was Hart's, Mondale's, and Reagan's. It was the very symbolism of Jackson's candidacy that gave it an importance far beyond what any ordinary candidacy could command.

The Jackson candidacy served other functions that would seem to hold long-term benefits. These include an unprecedented "level and kind of political mobilization among Black Americans and minorities not heretofore experienced in American politics."[19] It involved fashioning for the first time a national campaign structure and the identification of "leadership and specialist cadres among persons whose talents had been largely dormant, untapped, underdeveloped and under utilized."[20] The experience gained through such activity can prove useful for other endeavors, including future campaigns.

In addition we should not overlook the political education benefits of Jackson's campaign. Jackson skillfully developed and used campaign opportunities to discuss and analyze not only substantive policy issues, but rules, procedures, and structures that might facilitate or impede the use of the electoral process to achieve goals and objectives. Above all, through his charisma and communication skills, Jackson was able to activate a sizable number of blacks who participated in politics for the "first time."[21]

Jackson's candidacy appealed to all segments of the black community as evidenced by support in presidential primaries.[22] Even in Alabama (50 percent) and Georgia (61 percent) where he was opposed by key black leaders, Jackson still polled a majority of black voters. In the 11 other primary states with sizable black populations, Jackson's totals were in the 70 to 80 percent range.[23]

However, Jackson did not receive much white support, particularly in the South; the lowest level was about 1 percent in both Alabama and Georgia.[24] The highest was about 9 percent in California. This is quite consistent with voting patterns over time, which show vividly that black candidates, no matter how qualified or how they conduct their campaigns, simply are unable to attract strong white support. This holds true as much for mayors Wilson Goode of Philadelphia (20 percent) and Andrew Young of Atlanta (11 percent) as it does for Harold Washington of Chicago (19 percent) or Richard Hatcher of Gary (14 percent).[25] To be sure, Jackson's support among white voters in the presidential primaries, ranging from 1 to 9 percent, is considerably less than the white support black mayoral candidates have attracted. However, the overall context of those elections—the arena, the nature of the office, and the issues—are quite different from that of the presidency. Of course, the levels of support may vary with individual candidates and campaigns. But the evidence is overwhelming that black candidates in the main find it difficult to attract sizable white support. By contrast, blacks have and do support white liberal candidates in large numbers.

Some "Downsides" to Jackson's Candidacy

Obviously there were some "downsides" to Jackson's candidacy. Such downsides exist for any candidate for the presidency, although Jackson was not *any* candidate. First, there was the view—somewhat implied in the "now is not the right time" criticism—that Jackson's candidacy would arouse the anxiety and fears of white voters and hence possibly jeopardize racial progress, sharpen racial divisions, and worst of all, drive whites, particularly those in the South, to vote for Reagan and lead to his reelection. As we discuss later, whites—especially southern whites—did vote overwhelmingly for Reagan, which did lead to his reelection. While we must await more study and analysis, it does not make sense to blame Jackson for this outcome. More fundamentally, it may be properly asked, should Jackson or anyone else be deprived of the right to run for the presidency because of these perceived or actual fears? This becomes a matter of political judgment for the individual involved. In other words, this was a matter for Jackson and his supporters to discuss, not one to be decided by law, tradition, custom, or fears.

Still others throught that Jackson was not "qualified" to run for president, referring to his not having had experience in elective or appointive public office. The criticism was less openly expressed but was certainly held by a number of persons, white as well as black. While this criticism might influence individual voters, the criticism itself is somewhat erroneous since it assumes that there are indeed "special" qualifications, over and above the constitutional ones, that a person must meet to be a good president. Dwight D. Eisenhower, whom some might rate as a "great" president, is a prime example of one who had no prior experience in political office. On balance, however, experience in public office would seem to be a plus although it may be overcome by other experiences in the "public arena."

Perhaps most damaging to Jackson's candidacy was the "Hymie" affair and the subsequent Farrakan involvement. Of course, Jackson's handling of this matter, plus intense and wide media coverage, served to keep the matter alive. In general, the situation appears to have hurt Jackson. Apparently, however, it did not seem to detract from Jackson's appeal and support from black voters.*

This may be a useful point at which to discuss the role of Jackson and blacks generally at the Democratic National Convention.[26] That role was shaped by several factors. First, Mondale's nomination seemed assured and thus his forces were in control of the convention. Second, somewhat more

---

*In a *Washington Post* story (February 13, 1984), Jackson, in an "off-the-record" conversation was reported to have referred to Jews as "Hymies" and to New York as "Hymietown." At first, Jackson denied the story but later apologized and admitted his having made the comments. Farrakan's involvement came when he warned Jews and others not to "harm this brother" (referring to Jackson), and over the course of the next few weeks made remarks considered derogatory to Jews. Thus Farrakan's involvement exacerbated Jackson's problems (see also *New York Times,* February 28, 1984, p. A 20).

than half of the record 700 black delegates supported Jackson; Mondale had the support of most of the remaining black delegates.

The Democratic Convention

Because of the split among black delegates, and very importantly, the strong open support Mondale received from some highly visible black leaders during the nomination campaign, Jackson's leverage in the convention and in the developing campaign organization was obviously reduced. But apparently so was that of Mondale's black supporters. This lack of unity among black leaders, plus the fact that blacks tend to vote overwhelmingly Democratic in presidential elections anyway, allowed Mondale much more discretion than he otherwise would have had in dealing with blacks. Seemingly, Mondale used this discretion to minimize the benefits that might otherwise have been needed to win support of a major constituent group such as blacks. Accordingly, Mondale supported only one of Jackson's four minority planks, and that only after reaching agreement to substitute "verifiable measures" for the word "quotas" in the affirmative action plank. To be sure, Mondale forces soundly defeated Jackson's litmus test plank dealing with enforcement of the Voting Rights Act. However, Mondale did agree to a Fairness Commission whose functions would include a review of delegate selection rules, one of Jackson's major complaints.

In addition, Jackson was accorded the opportunity to address the convention during prime time. Obviously Mondale expected such a speech to benefit his cause as well. To many this was no more than one would have expected if Mondale hoped to achieve unified support from blacks. In any event, it was clear that Jackson attempted to use the speech to satisfy a number of interests.[27] However, Jackson's speech, as well-crafted, eloquent, and moving as it was, did not quiet the concern felt by many of his delegates over the treatment and respect accorded Jackson by the Mondale forces. This concern spilled over into other arenas, as for example, in my own Missouri state caucus where black delegates openly expressed strong disapproval of the treatment accorded Jackson, and emphasized that "things must change" if Democrats expected continued black support in elections, including state and local elections.[28]

For the record, it should be stated that at various points during the convention Jackson told his delegates to "await his signal," since they had not received fair consideration in exchange for the expected support. That signal never came, and so, beneath the cloak of unity, many Jackson delegates left San Francisco in frustration, disappointment, and anger. Only at a subsequent meeting of Mondale and black leaders, after the convention, was some accord reached with respect to the role of blacks in the Mondale campaign. This action permitted Jackson and others to finally offer their support to the Mondale campaign.

The Two Societies and the 1984 Election

That black and white Americans still view much of the world, including their politics, differently is reflected well by the voting behavior of the two groups in the 1984 presidential election.[29] A summary overview of that election indicates that estimates indicate that Mondale received 90 percent of the black vote, up from the 85 percent received by Carter in 1980; at the same time Reagan won 9 percent of the black vote, down from 11 percent in 1980. On the other hand, Mondale receieved only about 33 percent of the white vote, slightly down from the 36 percent Carter received in 1980, while Reagan's share of the white vote rose dramatically from 55 percent in 1980 to 68 percent in 1984. Among Democrats, Mondale won 96 percent of the black vote but only 68 percent of the white vote, while Democratic votes for Reagan increased slightly to 31 percent from the 30 percent he received in 1980. Black support for Democrats was up in the East and Midwest and down for Reagan. In the South black support for both parties remained the same (89 percent for Democrats and 9 percent for Republicans). White support for Reagan increased in all areas with a range from 57 percent of the white vote in the East to a high of 72 percent in the South. Mondale received less than a majority of the white vote in all areas from a low of 28 percent in the South to a high of 42 percent in the East. This represents a decrease in white support for Democrats in two areas—the South and Midwest. Ninety-three percent of Jackson's supporters in the Democratic primary elections voted for Mondale, with only 6 percent for Reagan. Parenthetically, a little more than one-third of Gary Hart's primary election voters supported Reagan, while 65 percent voted for Mondale. Gender made little difference in the overwhelming support given Mondale by black men and women (85 percent and 93 percent), and the strong majority support of Reagan by both white men and women (68 percent and 64 percent).

In general, along just about every dimension, available data show rather sharp divisions between black and white voters. The sharpest division is in the South, where blacks voted by an overwhelming majority (89 percent) for Mondale while whites supported Reagan by a huge majority (72 percent).

This sharp division between whites and blacks is further demonstrated by data collected from exit polls.[30] For example, when asked the question, "Compared to four years ago, would you say your family now is financially better off?" about one-half (48 percent) of all whites said "yes," while only

about one-tenth (11 percent) of the black respondents answered affirma-
tively. On the other hand, nearly one-half of all blacks (45 percent) thought
they were "worse off," while only 15 percent of the whites thought so.
Nearly 40 percent in both groups thought their condition, compared to four
years ago, was the same (whites, 35 percent; blacks, 39 percent). The "two
society" picture becomes even clearer when voters were asked, "If Ronald
Reagan is reelected, do you think the policies of his administration will be
fair to lower income people?" 50 percent of all white voters felt that Reagan
would be "fair," but only 7 percent of blacks thought so. Indeed, an overwhelming majority of blacks, more than four out of five (82 percent)
thought Reagan would be "unfair" to lower income people. What is somewhat surprising, and even more disturbing, is that more than one-third of
all whites (37 percent) agreed with blacks that Reagan's policies would be
"unfair" to "lower income people." Of course, "lower income" is often
used as a euphemism for blacks and minorities.

Conclusions

National Threat to Civil Rights Law

The events and statistics presented here suggest that the national commitment to civil rights law is under severe strain, even to the point of breaking.
Perhaps most serious of all, the very legal basis of that commitment appears
to be under attack by the Reagan administration not only through its civil
rights enforcement policies and legislative activities, but also through the
courts. Moreover, divided attitudes among major constituent groups within
the Democratic party over these issues cloud the picture even more. That
commitment could be further jeopardized should the president have the
opportunity to make additional appointments to the Supreme Court. To be
sure, there may not be as many opportunities as might be suggested by the
fact that several of the justices are over 75, nor may the president have his
way given the composition of the Senate. Nonetheless, the addition of one
or two justices could alter the balance and the extent to which the Supreme
Court might be able to keep alive the national commitment to the rights of
blacks and minorities. It should also be pointed out that President Reagan
has had and will continue to have many opportunities to make appointments to federal district courts and to courts of appeal.[31]* These oppor-

---

*Since this chapter was written, the President has indeed had the opportunity to alter the
composition of the Supreme Court due to Chief Justice Burger's resignation. The President
nominated Associate Justice William Rehnquist to become chief justice and Judge Anthony
Scalia to fill the Rehnquist vacancy as associate justice. Many believe, particularly civil rights
advocates, that Rehnquist and Scalia will not bolster the nation's commitment to civil rights
and in fact might well do harm or damage it.

tunities allow the president to implant his philosophy and ideas in the one branch of government where they may be perpetuated long after he leaves office in 1988.

Bluntly stated, whereas in the past disadvantaged groups could at least look to the federal government for protection of their fundamental rights, the Reagan administration is perpetuating an environment in which this protection can no longer be relied upon or is shaky at best. More serious, the federal government itself is supporting those who wish to pull back from the nation's commitment to civil rights law. Even more serious, through his judicial appointments, the president is attempting to influence the decisional behavior of our federal courts toward this particular position. Unless we forget, it has been the federal courts that have provided the stimulus and leadership for the major political-social changes with respect to improving the lot of blacks and minorities.[32] Obviously, this puts blacks and minorities in an uneasy position. It also places the nation in an uneasy position.

Reagan is the first president who has persistently and broadly challenged the long-standing policy consensus on civil rights. Such a challenge presents the frightening possibility that the widely shared policy consensus of our civil rights law will once again be thrust into the public arena with potentially divisive consequences. And the attitudes of the American public as manifested through public officials elected to office in the 1980s makes the outcome of this debate even more frightening and uncertain.

Jackson's Use of Electoral Process

One of the fundamental but largely unnoticed contributions of Jackson is that by resorting to electoral politics at the highest level, he has clearly opted for the maximum use of the electoral process as the major route by which to achieve political objectives. As such, Jackson's effort broadens the scope and possibilities of election politics already symbolized by the election of black mayors and other officials. That Jackson has focused on the electoral route holds enormous implications and challenges for the future of black politics and American politics generally. Obviously this direction does not rule out the use of litigation and protest, but it does increase the emphasis on electoral politics to achieve policy objectives.

Divisiveness Between Black and White Voters

The Jackson candidacy relates to black politics in more direct ways. There is a very strong congruence among blacks, in contrast to whites, in their attitude on public policy matters. Opinion specialists find that the degree of "liberal attitude consistency for blacks across such a diverse set of issues (school integration, foreign policy, size of government, economic welfare) is greater than for any other group"[33]—more than 60 percent. This has led these specialists to conclude that "no other group in American society is as distinctively liberal as blacks."[34] In short, there is an unusually strong level of cohesion and unity among blacks on policy issues, and this obviously contributed to the strong support Jackson received from blacks.

When this phenomenon is viewed in a larger context, however, it becomes clear that during the same period (1950s–1970s) the white South has become the most conservative group in America. By the 1970s over 60 percent of middle and high status white southerners fell into the conservative category.[35] "The dilemma," as Nie and his colleagues point out, "is clear: if blacks, on the one hand, and the white South, on the other, represent a major proportion of the nation's Democratic supporters, how does any party with such a polarized base maintain (in the long run or in any specific election) the allegiance of both groups."[36] The 1984 elections dramatically show that the party was unable to do this. And how, or whether, this sharp division of attitudes between whites and blacks will be handled by both major parties in 1988 and beyond will obviously do much to shape the future terrain of black politics and American politics generally.

Benefits of Jackson's Campaign

As intimated earlier, it is the symbolic side of Jackson's candidacy that calls for closer examination. The causes represented by Jesse Jackson's candidacy transcended the Democratic nomination and the 1984 presidential elections. By seeking the very highest election office this country has to offer, Jackson dramatically called attention to the very deep concerns and aspirations held by many blacks and others. These very fundamental concerns and aspirations include the right 1) to be treated as fully worthy members of the American community, not as objects of condescension, as "outsiders wanting in"; 2) to share in power not because votes force reluctant power holders to make concessions—although this is true—but because it is the *right* and *fair* thing to do if fair and equal treatment is to be accorded to all; and 3) to be accorded respect and dignity due individuals as equals in our politics and society, since *full* citizenship in a democracy requires nothing less. To be sure, these may be viewed as intangible, symbolic benefits but they determine the basic ground rules and character of the political environment in which the allocation of substantive benefits takes place. They are so important to our very deep fundamental underpinnings of government that they really are nonnegotiable. The extent of their absence of presence can impact directly on whether people feel happy, frustrated, enraged, or dispossessed. And the effects of these feelings on political participation and political behavior are obvious.

Jackson's candidacy directly challenged the rituals and myths (two symbolic forms) that many Americans would like to believe in. It challenged Americans to live up to the ideals symbolized by the often-heard views "that any person (even blacks or women) can be president, or that all persons should be accorded every opportunity to reach their full potential." In addition, the Jackson candidacy challenged more directly certain myths and rituals of the political process such as those that relate to electoral politics. Specifically, Jackson challenged directly the notion that elections confirm the "will of the people," when in fact there remain a number of barriers and arrangements—including voting registration procedures, run-off primaries, at-large elections and other schemes—designed to restrict and minimize the influence and participation of blacks and minorities in the electoral process.[37] He also challenged the rules for selecting delegates to the 1984 Democratic convention.

In another vein, Jackson's candidacy also challenged certain myths and beliefs, very much a part of symbolic politics, that impact negatively on blacks, minorities, and others. These include the myth that blacks do not have high aspirations or ambitions and that they are not articulate about, conversant with, or interested in issues beyond those termed "civil rights" or "minority issues."

When Jackson attacks our election system, or talks about the unfairness or unrepresentativeness of our other institutions and practices, he undoubtedly upsets many good, sincere Americans. And this discomfort is due in part to the strong influence that symbols and symbolic forms have in our culture on the role and importance of these institutions. Undoubtedly, during the 1984 Democratic presidential nomination campaign a good number of Americans would have preferred all candidates, including Jesse Jackson, to play by the "rules of the game" and shut up. However, those who held such views missed altogether one of the significant dimensions of the Jackson candidacy. That dimension was to dramatically remind the nation of its unfulfilled commitment to the principles and goals of our civil rights laws. These causes are a part of, but also transcend, their leaders, party politics, and even presidential politics. And vigorous advocacy of such causes, as Jackson did, is not likely to quiet anxiety and controversy. But it was very congruent with deep cultural and political strains in the black community.[38] This is why it was possible, even in face of adversity, for Jackson to continue to achieve enviable support and success from an overwhelming majority of black Americans.

Redefinition of Political Parties

With respect to strategy options, the view is once again being expressed that continued overwhelming black support for one party has allowed that party to take black support for granted, and the other party to ignore blacks or focus attention on its own supporters. But suggestions or inferences that blacks should split their allegiance and support between the two parties, no matter how appealing as an abstract proposition, will perhaps remain hollow unless accompanied by concrete evidence that major concerns and interests of blacks and minorities are being addressed by those parties. This could well be a matter of "which comes first"—the initiative of the party toward blacks and minorities, or the initiative of these groups in joining the party which in turn would spur party concern, etc. This is a difficult question involving elements of trust, respect, and persuasion.

Realistically, however, evidence from the 1984 election, and resulting agenda priorities, suggests that the concerns of blacks and minorities may be in for rough times. After the election, some leading Democrats began focusing on how best to recapture the white middle class, particularly white voters in the South. And the interests of these groups, as discussed earlier, will undoubtedly prove difficult to reconcile with the interests of blacks and minorities. On the Republican side, attitudes and policies of the Reagan administration have primarily benefited middle and upper classes, i.e., mainly whites. And there is little evidence to suggest that in any redefinition of its future the Republican party will be any more attractive to blacks than it has been in the past. Overall, as the parties redefine themselves for the future, they might do well to seriously entertain the need to reaffirm (through word and deed) the nation's commitment to equal justice and opportunity for all. Otherwise, should racial polarization and divisions be allowed to fester and continue, we could once again face the dire consequences of "two societies, one white, one black, separate and unequal."

Formation of Independent Coalition

As to specific strategy options, we might expect continued strong efforts of blacks and minorities to win office in local, state, and congressional elections. But in view of the close and important relationships between accomplishments in these arenas and the White House, continued efforts might also be directed at influencing presidential politics. In addition to party participation blacks, minorities, and like-minded persons might well consider an independent national organization that could throw its weight to either party under particular conditions. Jesse Jackson's "Rainbow Coalition" provides an example of this possibility. Forging such an organization will not be easy, and could well encounter some of the same problems experienced by Jackson's candidacy, e.g., a division among black leaders. However, such an organization would provide these groups with a unified structure through which to push for their interests undiluted by the broader compromises usually needed in larger coalitions such as the two major parties.

Unification to Protect National Civil Rights Laws

Jackson's candidacy affords us the opportunity to take note of the capacity and limitations of the political process. Indeed, maximum use of electoral politics—given the structure and operation of the American political process—may not *in itself* be sufficient to achieve the objectives sought. This raises the more basic question about how more or less "permanent" minorities achieve their objectives in a majority oriented political system. One way, of course, is to pursue the strategy used by Jesse Jackson: Go out and develop political power that becomes sufficiently important that it *has to be dealt with* in the political process.

The history and persistence of racism in America indicates that, insofar as blacks are concerned, this will be an extremely difficult undertaking. Specifically, what is to be done when a group (blacks), long deprived and oppressed, attempting to improve its status through political mobilization, is met with a massive counter-mobilization of political forces from the major group (whites)? This matter must be given more attention, for it holds serious and long-term implications for American democracy. Ultimately, it is the answer to this question that will determine whether we can overcome tendencies toward "two societies," and once again work toward fulfilling the national commitment to the basic principles and goals embodied in our civil rights law.

Notes

1. *Report of the National Advisory Commission on Civil Disorders* (Washington, D.C.: U.S. Government Printing Office, 1968.) The commission became informally known as the Kerner Commission after its chairman, former Governor Otto Kerner of Illinois.
2. *Brown v. Board of Education,* 347 U.S. 483 (1954).
3. Refers primarily to the Civil Rights Acts of 1964 and 1965.
4. Drew Days, "Turning Back the Clock: The Reagan Administration and Civil Rights," *Harvard CR/CL LR* 19 (1984): 309.
5. Ibid.
6. Ibid.
7. *Bob Jones University v. United States* and *Goldsboro Christian Schools, Inc. v. United States,* 461 U.S. 574 (1983).
8. *Grove City College v. Bell,* 104 S. Ct. 1211 (1984).
9. For background on this controversy, see "Civil Rights Commission Reconstituted," *Congressional Quarterly Almanac* (1983), 292–295.
10. For an overview of the administration strategy in these areas, see Lucius J. Barker and Twiley W. Barker, Jr., *Civil Liberties and the Constitution* (Englewood Cliffs, N.J.: Prentice Hall, 5th ed., 1986), 363, 543–545.

11. For information about this issue, see "Voting Rights Act Extended, Strengthened," *Congressional Quarterly Almanac* (1983), 373–377.

12. For background and summary of this controversy, see "Administration Ignites New Conflict Over Affirmative Action Enforcement," *Congressional Quarterly Weekly Report* (October 29, 1985), pp. 2106–7.

13. See Lucius J. Barker, "Jesse Jackson's Candidacy in Political-Social Perspective: A Contextual Analysis," scheduled for publication in Barker and Walters, *Jesse Jackson's 1984 Presidential Campaign: Continuity and Change in American Politics* (Urbana: University of Illinois Press, 1986).

14. Over time, at least since 1952, the black vote has been overwhelmingly Democratic, and from 1964 to the present the black vote has been about 90 percent for Democrats.

15. For an overview of similarities and differences among civil rights groups, as well as friction points in the civil rights movement, see Lucius J. Barker and Jesse McCorry, *Black Americans and the Political System* (Boston: Little Brown, 1980), 169–190.

16. Some of these data are available at the Joint Center for Political Studies. In addition, this writer participated in Jackson meetings and delegate caucuses and served as a Jackson delegate to the San Francisco Democratic National Convention in 1984.

17. Murray Edelman, *The Symbolic Uses of Politics* (Urbana: University of Illinois Press, 1967).

18. See Thomas Cavanaugh and Lorn Foster, *Jesse Jackson's Campaign: The Primaries and Caucuses, Election '84* (Washington, D.C.: Joint Center for Political Studies), 16–17. Also see table on "Southern Voter Registration, 1980–1984," in *Point of View* (Washington, D.C.: The Congressional Black Caucus Foundation, 1984), 13.

19. Lucius J. Barker, "Black Americans and the Politics of Inclusion," *PS* 16, no. 3 (Summer 1983): 504.

20. Ibid.

21. Cavanaugh and Foster, *Jesse Jackson's Campaign,* 17.

22. Ibid.

23. Ibid.

24. Ibid.

25. See Marguerite Ross Barnett, "The Strategic Debate over a Black Presidential Candidacy," *PS* 16 (Summer 1983): 489–491.

26. Much of the information in this section is based on the personal participant-observation of the writer as a Jackson delegate to the 1984 Democratic National Convention.

27. For text of Jackson's speech, see *Official Proceedings of the 1984 Democratic National Convention* (1984), 293–301.

28. Comments made at caucus of Missouri delegates, July 18, 1984.

29. See election analysis in *The New York Times,* November 8, 1984, p. 11.

30. NBC Election News Exit Polls, 1984.

31. For a summary of Reagan's appointments to federal district and appeals courts, see "Reagan Gaining Control of Federal Judiciary," *Congressional Quarterly Almanac* (1984), 293–95.

32.   Refers to Supreme Court decisions in certain landmark cases, e.g., *Smith* v. *Wainwright,* 321 U.S. 649 (1944); *Brown* v. *Board of Education,* 347 U.S. 483 (1954); *Baker* v. *Carr,* 369 U.S. 186 (1962); and *Gideon* v. *Wainwright,* 372 U.S. 335 (1963).

33.   Norman Nie, Sidney Verba, and John Petrocik, *The Changing American Voter* (Cambridge: Harvard University Press, 1979), 253–4.

34.   Ibid.

35.   Ibid.

36.   Ibid.

37.   For review of these problems, see Barker and Barker, *Civil Liberties and the Constitution,* Chapter 6, "Political Participation," 454–463.

38.   For an informative and interesting analysis in this regard, see Matthew Holden, *The Politics of the Black Nation* (New York: Chandler, 1973), 16–25.

THREE

Continuity and Change: The Power of Traditionalism in Biracial Politics in Mississippi's Second Congressional District

Mary Delorse Coleman
Leslie Burl McLemore

Introduction and Purpose

In the 1984 national congressional elections 13 black challengers ran unsuccessfully in House races.[1] Eleven challengers were Republicans; six of them ran against incumbent blacks.[2] All black incumbents except Democrat Katie Hall of Indiana won re-election. Georgia, South Carolina, Mississippi, and Alabama, the states with the largest percentage of blacks, do not have any black congresspersons.[3]

Peter J. Visclosky defeated Katie Hall of Indiana by 1.9 percentage points.[4] In this 71 percent white district, the battle for a congressional seat was racially divisive. Nonetheless, Hall's primary percentage seems to suggest that at least 7 percent of the votes she received were cast by whites.

A chance to offset the loss was narrowly missed when Democratic candidate Robert Clark of Mississippi was defeated in his second bid to become Mississippi's first black Congressman in this century. In a rematch of their 1982 mid-term contest, against Republican challenger Webb Franklin, Clark was unable to unseat him. As with the Indiana primary, the Mississippi Second Congressional District campaign was racially divisive.[5] In this chapter we examine voter choice and voter turnout in a biracial election in Mississippi's Second Congressional District. We answer two basic questions: what factors influenced voter choice for Robert Clark, the black Democratic candidate, and were there differences in the voting behavior of blacks and whites by county size and percentage of blacks in the population?

As in 1982, the Second Congressional District was the poorest in the nation.[6] Although it elected a Republican to the House in 1982, the new Second Congressional District is consistent in its Democratic voting habits.[7] Only one of the 11 counties picked up in redistricting, Warren County, supported Ronald Reagan in 1980. But, close county totals were registered in the Reagan/Carter bid throughout the state.[8] Thus, as a moderate "Southern Democrat" Carter was able to neutralize what might have been a Republican presidential victory in the district in 1980. In Warren County alone, Webb Franklin's (Republican) vote increases, from 1982 to 1984, exceeded, by two to one, his vote increases elsewhere.[9] The 3,784 vote increase there permitted him to expand his victory margin. Moreover, in majority black Sunflower (51 percent) and Bolivar (54 percent) counties he received 55 and 52 percent of the votes cast, respectively.[10]

Unquestionably, white Democrats voted Republican in 1982 and in 1984. Reagan's coattails, though skimpy elsewhere throughout the nation, assisted whites in jettisoning the Democratic ticket and its black moderate contender. Nevertheless, in 3 of 4 counties in which Jesse Jackson held voter registration drives, black voters increased appreciably over 1982.[11] However, these increases were not enough to offset racial block voting and ticket splitting.[12] Former Governor Winter, a white Democratic Senate contender, outpolled Clark (black) in the Second Congressional District.[13] Furthermore, fewer votes were cast in the Congressional race than in the Senate race containing the Second District. Hence, the actual vote percentage in the Senate and House races was the same.

Although no black challengers nationally won any Congressional seats, at least five of them showed promise as future contenders. The outcome of elections are often influenced by redistricting. At least in the Mississippi case, the Delta district is marginally black and after two unsuccessful attempts to seat a moderate black, different election strategies will be necessary in the future. In both Indiana and Mississippi, most whites in the Democratic party appear unwilling to vote for black candidates—incumbent or challengers.[14]

Robert Clark, the black Democratic challenger, and 16-year veteran of the Mississippi legislature, lost two bids to become Mississippi's first black congressman since 1890. Why was his candidacy unsuccessful? Was black non-voting pervasive? Did white ticket-splitting surface in a district consistently casting ballots for Democratic state, local, and national candidates? These questions beg another question: Was the Democratic challenger the candidate most able to maximize black voting and minimize white ticket splitting in a 48 percent black voting age electoral district?

Historical Overview

Like most major electoral campaigns, Robert Clark's race for Congress was underway informally before the 1982 primary.[15] Voter registration projections had been made and prior black independent candidates' performance had been evaluated. A three-county area of the newly redistricted Second Congressional District fell in the heart of the Delta's plantation economy: an area where wealthy planters and black rural poverty had historically co-existed.[16] Additionally, the size of the district was anticipated as a delimiting factor in Clark's organizational efforts. The locals had been wondering aloud about the salience of race as an issue in the contest. If Clark emerged as their choice should he run as a Democrat or an independent? In case he chose the former, should not a black independent wait in the wings to challenge the Republican?

Typifying the old guard black leadership's response to the independent course was long-time civil rights activist and moderate, Aaron Henry. Representative Henry put the matter thusly: "I think that when you lie down with independents you get up with Republicans. I am not about to participate in an action that would lead toward the election of Webb Franklin."[17] That was strong language, indeed. All of the minor party candidates as well as black independents seeking congressional office since 1982 had lost. There was another sentiment: if the white Democrats are not tested, what barometer will black Democrats use to measure the strength of the black-white Democratic coalition. Unforgotten was the 1980 election, in which a Republican was elected to Congress after a racially divisive three-way election jettisoned black support from the Democratic contender to an independent black candidate. Thus, prior to the 1982 mid-term election, the Democratic party leadership had been mending fences. At long last two-party politics—a transition eased by a black Democratic challenger and Reagan's popularity on the horizon. Black and white Democratic party leadership was understandably anxious to support Robert Clark should he emerge victorious in the primary.

Research Design

Why was his an unsuccessful candidacy? In order to answer this question it is important to examine historical factors associated with black political participation in Southern politics. In the Old South, white hostility to black voter registration and participation generally increased as the size of the black population increased. The late V. O. Key established the relationship between majority black rural delta counties and white resistance in 1949: he found that white hostility toward blacks increases as the black population reaches and/or exceeds majority. In the deep South (Alabama, Georgia, Louisiana, Mississippi, and South Carolina) black majorities resided primarily in the black-belt.[18] The black belt is also characterized by fertile alluvial soil on which cotton was the primary crop, and blacks, as slaves, sharecroppers, and/or tenants worked in the field. It seems, worthwhile, therefore, to examine county size as one factor influencing voter turnout in the delta district. The county size variable, as does the statistical technique, regression analysis, masks a plethora of important substantive concerns. However, it is one way to look at the black vote by county size and turnout. A second historical consideration is the economic dependency of blacks in the delta. A reasonable facsimile of that phenomenon is an examination of the influence of black median income of the county on voter choice. With the advent of the Voting Rights Act there was an increase in the number of black elected officials. That increase has meant, among other things, increased awareness of public policy issues and the ability of blacks to assist in governance. Does not the presence of black elected officials also influence black voter mobilization? Was Clark the choice of voters in counties with extant black elected officials?

Regression analysis is well suited to an examination of internal level data. To assist in an explanation of voter choice in the 1982 Congressional election we examine the influence of three independent variables, county size (whether large, medium, or small), median black income by county, and the number of black elected officials by county.

In subsequent analysis voter turnout data are analyzed as a way to assess black/white differential in voting behavior.

Findings

Table 3.1 presents the results of the multiple regression equations of the votes received by the two major candidates in the 1982 Mississippi Congressional race. In the Clark vote, three independent variables: median black income, black elected officials, and county size produced coefficients of 0.03, 0.11, and 94 respectively. However, as Table 3.2 shows, the corresponding standard error for the black-elected officials variables is so large as to render analysis trivial. When we adjusted the equation to eliminate the black elected officials variable, 3 percent of the variance previously explained was lost. Hence, two independent variables, the black mean income of the counties in the Second Congressional District and the county size (whether the county was determined to be large, medium, or small within

Table 3.1   Regression Coefficient for 1982 Mississippi Congressional Race

	Clark Votes				Franklin Votes		
	B	Standard Error	T Value(s)		B	Standard Error	T Value(s)
Mean Income	0.03	(0.12)	−10.04		0.05	(0.26)	−7.28
County Size	0.11	(0.01)	6.14		0.00052	(0.04)	−5.09
Black-Elected Officials[a]	94	(51)	7.18	−19		(115.2)	7.15

[a]Not significant at the 0.001 level of significance

the context of the counties composing the district) accounted for 74 percent of the variance; of that amount 60 percent is accounted for in the county size variable alone.

We look further to determine how the county size variable relates to the votes received by the two candidates. When we refer to Table 3.1, we see that as county size increases by 1 unit, the number of votes received by Clark increases by 0.11 units. Contrast this with Franklin and we again see that as county size increases by 1 unit, the number of votes received by Franklin increases only minimally. Hence, the larger the county the more likely it is that turnout for Clark is greater; a trend reversed in the 1984 rematch.

As we turn to the second most important independent variable in the equation, it is evident that as the black mean income of a county increases by one unit, voter turnout for Clark increases by 0.03 units. The vote for Clark's opponent, Webb Franklin, however, increased by 0.05 units as black mean income increases. Hence, lower income voters were more likely to vote for Clark than were voters with income above the mean. While the differences are slight, they are statistically significant at the 0.001 level. Furthermore, extant studies continue to demonstrate a positive correlation between high income and Republican identification. This single finding presented here does not strongly suggest that higher income black voters are likely to vote Republican even in biracial contests but this finding is, nonetheless, substantively interesting. In both contests, Franklin received 5 to 9 percent of the black vote. Clark, by contrast, received less than 7 and 4 percent of the white vote in 1982 and 1984 respectively.

High-income citizens, whether black or white, are more likely to have higher turnout rates that their low-income counterparts.[19] Hence, Republican voters tend to be disproportionately drawn from high-turnout groups

Table 3.2 Summary Table: Multiple Regression

Variables	1982 Votes Received by Democrats			1982 Votes Received by Republicans		
	R^2 Change	R^2	Standard Error	R^2 Change	R^2	Standard Error
Mean Income of County	0.22	0.22	0.12	0.0021	0.0021	0.26
County Size	0.53	0.75	0.01	0.00002	0.00219	0.04
Number of Black-Elected Officials	0.04	0.80	0.51	0.0018	0.00402	115.2

like college graduates and high-income persons, exactly the groups from which a disproportionate number of blacks remain excluded.[20]

We recall from Table 3.1 that when the black-elected officials variables were entered into the equation a mere 3 percent more of the variance was explained with the Clark vote as the dependent variable. Nonetheless, as the number of black elected officials in a county increased by one unit, the number of votes received by Clark increased by 94 units. However, the relatively small percentage of black-elected officials in a county obscures what is potentially an important finding: as the number of black-elected officials increased, the number of votes for Clark substantially increases. (However, as previously stated, the standard error is so large that the proposed interpretation would be an increase or a decrease of 43 units.) For the white Republican, however, as black elected officials in a county increase by 1 unit, the number of votes for Franklin *decreases* by 96 units. There is, therefore, an inverse relationship between the number of black-elected officials in a district and the votes received by a white Republican.

Several other observations about the 1984 election are warranted. As Table 3.3 demonstrates, the Democratic challenger was edged out in large Delta counties by incumbent Franklin. In 1982, Clark won four of the seven large counties, in 1984 he won three and lost four, including majority black Washington and Sunflower counties. Only 8 percent of the votes received by incumbent Franklin in 1984 were cast in the new counties; whereas 20 percent of the Clark vote was cast in the new counties. *From 1982 to 1984, Clark lost 9 percent of the vote he received in the same counties in 1982;* Franklin gained 13 percent of his 1984 vote in old counties of the district. These data suggest competitive biracial voting behavior. Increases made by Franklin, in the old counties, also bears evidence to the advantage of incumbency and the leverage Ronald Reagan's coattails gave to his reelection bid. Clark, on the other hand, was unable to maintain his voting base in the old counties. His defeat in Washington and Sunflower counties requires further inquiry. It is in Sunflower county that Franklin outpolled the incumbent U.S. Senator and President of the United States.

The benchmarks used to explain correlates of voting in Congressional elections do not explain the 1982 and 1984 elections in Mississippi's Second Congressional District. Several variables: region,[21] legal restrictions,[22] socioeconomic factors,[23] psychological factors,[24] and political mobilization[25] influence turnout. In general, this literature is consistent with Socioeconomic Status (SES) as a correlate of voting. As SES increases, so does voter turnout. The SES model and the attendant controls do not explain the voting behavior of black Americans, and where the model does serve as a useful explanatory tool, it does not appear to explain black voting behavior in competitive biracial elections. In particular, the Second Congressional Dis-

Table 3.3 Second Congressional District Election Results—1982 and 1984

Big Counties	General Election 1982 Percent Increase	General Election 1984 Percent Increase	Location	Winning Party 1982	Winning Party 1984	BVAP Percent 1980	1982 Percent of County Voting	1984 Registered Voters Casting Ballots (Percent)	1982 Mean Party Increase	1984 Mean Party Increase*
Bolivar	52	77	Delta	D	D	54	51	59	50 Dem.	75 Dem.
Coahoma	34	73	Delta	D	D	58	44	48	51 Dem.	77 Rep.
Madison	60	75	Hill	D	D	50	46	40		
Warren	61	77	Hill	R	R	34	41	58		
Leflore	44	57	Delta	R	R	54	48	54		
Washington	55	74	Delta	D	R	50	39	50		
Sunflower	49	75	Delta	R	R	57	34	54		
Medium Counties										
Holmes	22	52	Hill	D	D	64	58	52	22 Dem.	52
Yazoo	46	62	Hill	R	R	46	57	59	51 Rep.	68
Attala	44	25	Hill	R		35	57	NA		
Leake	64	*	Hill	R		30	52			
Small Counties										
Webster	80*		Hill	R		16	51		44 Dem.	54
Choctaw	48*		Hill	R		24	37		62 Rep.	55
Carroll	52	54	Hill	R	R	47	64	45		
Quitman	62	56	Hill	D	R	49	54	54		
Humphreys	28	51	Delta	D	D	59	53	53		
Montgomery	69*		Delta	R		35	61			
Sharkey	51	66	Delta	D		58	58	56		
Issaquena	46	58	Delta	D		51	39	NA		
Tunica	37	57	Delta		D			53		

*Counties changed in redistricting, Senate Bill 2001.

trict contains a huge heterogeneous geo-political area: a successful black Democrat or independent will need enormous grass-roots support and organization to offset higher Republican voting in a presidential election year. Furthermore, in biracial elections where the race of a candidate is itself an issue, it seems to constrain the ability of black moderates to wage highly race-conscious campaigns. A race-conscious campaign seems crucial unless black *economic resource* mobilization is present. For the most part, Franklin rather than Clark had the economic resources with which to mobilize voter turnout.[26]

Robert Clark was, in 1982, the only choice for crossover white Democratic support. His political philosophy had been one of moderation. In 1968 he became the first black to sit in the Mississippi legislature since 1894. He was gradually accepted by the House leadership and gained chairmanship of the House Education Committee. He won the Democratic primary for Congress in 1982 with strong support.[27] He polled 57 percent of the vote to beat three white Democratic challengers. Of his primary win, Republican Webb Franklin retorted: the Democratic party's backing will not be enough for Clark.[28] Table 3.4 suggests that Franklin's view was vindi-

Table 3.4   Vote Percentage of Democrat in General Election, by BVAP

County	BVAP 1980	Voter Turnout 1982	% of County Vote Exceeding BVAP Received by Democrats
Bolivar	54	52	−2
Coahoma	58	50	−8
Madison	50	53	±3
Warren	34	40	±6
Leflore	54	44	−10
Washington	50	50	−
Sunflower	57	48	−9
Holmes	64	68	±4
Yazoo	46	46	−
Attala	34	43	±9
Leake	30	43	±13
Webster	16	29	±13
Choctaw	24	35	±11
Carroll	40	40	−
Quitman	49	56	±7
Humphrey	59	53	−6
Montgomery	35	39	±4
Sharkey	58	57	−1
Issaquena	51	58	−7
Tunica	67	53	−14

cated on election day in 1984. Two trends appear evident: turnout for the Democrat in the majority black counties was, on an average, nine percentage points below the actual black voting age population percentage. However, as the percent black in voting age population reached 36 percent, voter turnout for the Democrats increased on an average of 10 percent above the black voter age population.

However, these increases occurred in relatively small populated counties. Furthermore, a majority of the small counties in which the 1982 Clark vote percentage exceeded the black voting age population percentage was excluded in the 1984 redistricting. Despite findings to the contrary, it would appear that counties at or near 55 percent black majorities have impacts on biracial voting that favor the white candidate. Stated differently, it is in these populated black counties that both black apathy and/or economic dependency is greatest and where, coincidentally, white hostility toward blacks is greatest and is manifest in white voter mobilization in biracial elections.

Discussion

In general, black access to electoral politics in Mississippi has been mitigated by three factors: (1) the ideological stagnation and/or economic dependence of black leadership; (2) structural barriers; and (3) improper mobilization of the black poor, and concomitantly, failure to decrease the black poor's dependency on white entrepreneurs and/or the federal government.

It has been only in the last two decades that blacks have gained real access to governmental and political processes. As a group, black leaders lack the power to get people and/or institutions to do that which ordinarily would have been done.

The actions blacks and those sympathetic to their cause have used are those traditionally used by other groups. Although the means have been traditional, their effectiveness have been mixed: litigation, as a major mode to black participation, is a slow, albeit efficacious means by which to redress grievances; affecting legislation through demonstration and civil disobedience has been an effective short-term means of influencing what government does; voting has limited utility if the voting constituency is not organized to influence how elected officials behave once in office. All of these tactics are externally driven, they each seek to determine the policy behavior of others toward blacks.

Inside black politics in Mississippi little appears to be going on. Leadership training, through the active recruitment and participation of black youth into old line organizations such as the NAACP appears wanting. Fear and economic intimidation have not been totally eliminated as causes of nonparticipation.[29] Black leadership has not attacked apathy by creating a sense of group consciousness. Class antagonisms have not been recognized and thus, have not been broken down. In general, except for campaign attempts, political education is missing in black communities. Whatever the goals of black leadership in Mississippi, black communities need to be made aware of strategies needed to achieve their goals. Largely, though not totally, financial and organizational resources are very limited.

However, on the positive side, it is no longer true that "accommodating types" have a monopoly on leadership in Mississippi. There are at least three leadership groups in Mississippi: (1) the old timers; (2) the Student Nonviolent Coordinating Committee (SNCC), Mississippi Freedom Democratic Party (MFDP) Jesse Jackson supporters; and (3) a younger generation of professionals. Competing leadership is one by-product of political conflict and change. Despite conflict among these three groups, each leadership tier suffers from an inadequate economic base from which to mobilize black mass publics. Finding the machinery with which to mobilize blacks across income groups is a challenge of the next decade. Can black leadership and followership rise to the occasion? Does either entity have the economic potential to mobilize black politics across all income categories? It is clear that if blacks in Mississippi are to gain political power where they have the numbers, more political education and organization is needed.

Summary

A segment of the black electorate's political personality seems to differ from whites irrespective of SES.* Though blacks are characteristically cynical about the responsiveness of government to black people they (blacks) retain confidence about their own ability to influence what government does. This seeming paradox lies, argues Shingles,[30] in black consciousness. It is not clear what proportion of blacks in the Second Congressional District have high black consciousness. However, if they are to elect a black congressperson in the future it will have to be developed.

Clark, the first black to be elected to the Mississippi legislature this century, was very much aware of the state's past race relations. Thus, for reasons consistent with his political socialization, his campaign strategy did not appeal to race pride as a way to generate mobilization. Such a strategy might have been advanced if his electoral constituency had been at least 65 percent black. Structural arrangements influence campaign strategy but should not determine it. Nonetheless, Clark, who hoped to turn out blacks

---

*Mike Espy defeated Webb Franklin in the 1986 Mississippi Second Congressional District election to become the first black elected to congressional office in Mississippi since Reconstruction.

at 75 to 80 percent of their registered voter strength, ran an issue-based campaign. This campaign strategy did not net the 15 to 20 percent white crossover the Democratic challenger targeted.

In a close election district a black Democratic challenger needed to fight for and win substantial black and white votes. The vicious cycle in which black leadership existed and out of which it developed created dual and sometimes incongruent expectations among blacks and whites—leadership and followership.

The 1982 and 1984 campaigns in Mississippi's Second Congressional District were a reminder that the more things change the more they remain the same. Links of continuity and change coexist in the Mississippi delta as comfortably as rich planters and rural poor. *Robert Clark and Webb Franklin mirrored the area's past and present,* and the past won. In the 1982 campaign, Franklin used the television medium to show Clark's color—he resurrected white fears of black rule and won. In 1984, he expanded his base and Clark, *both a victim of tradition and of change,* was defeated. Clark was victimized by change because in the process of gaining white acceptance he did not develop in blacks the perception of his legitimacy as a black leader. His defeats raise questions about the conditions under which the black poor can be mobilized to view voting as policy behavior within the framework of a political culture of black economic and educational dependency and white political supremacy.

Notes

1. Joint Center for Political Studies, telephone interview with Linda Williams, September 27, 1985.
2. Ibid.
3. Andrew Young of Georgia was the last black person to represent a Deep South State.
4. "Women, Minorities Barely Hold Own in 99th," *Congressional Quarterly Weekly Report,* vol. 42, no. 45, 2920.
5. Ibid.
6. U.S. Bureau of the Census, 1984 *Current Population Reports,* Sen. p-60, No. 380.
7. F. Glenn Abney, *Mississippi Election Statistics 1900–1967* (University Mississippi, 1968). For recent trends see also *Mississippi Statistical Register,* 556–557.
8. Ibid., pp. 556.
9. Official Recapitulation Date (1984) Secretary of State's Office, Jackson, Mississippi.
10. Ibid.
11. Coleman, et al., "Voting and Non-Voting in Ten Mississippi Towns," (Atlanta: The Voter Education Project, 1983).

12. On election day exit polls taken by one of the authors showed that at least 92 percent of the whites interviewed had voted for the Republican incumbent, Webb Franklin.

13. Official Recapitulation Data compiled by the authors.

14. See the *Congressional Quarterly,* op. cited for a discussion of the Indiana primary.

15. About 200 people representing 15 of the district's 21 counties gathered in Greenwood in early July to discuss electoral strategy for the 1982 Second Congressional District. In fact, the decision about Clark's candidacy had been made weeks before at a meeting of leaders and public officials in the district. Thus, the July meeting was a formality. Both authors participated in and observed the July meeting.

16. The district has historically had acute regional rivalry, which can be traced back to the divergent economic interests of gentry in the Delta and farmers in the hills. Moreover, as is true for Mississippi in general the income and educational disparities by race are alarmingly high. For example, in Coahoma County, the 1980 census show that the median income for blacks was $6,556, for whites $19,738; median education was 8.1 years for blacks and 12.5 for whites. These income and educational disparities can be generalized throughout the district.

17. Karen Hinton, "For a Lack of Interest Small Turnout Expected," *Jackson Daily News,* August 17, 1982, Section B, p. 1.

18. V. O. Key, Jr., *Southern Politics* (New York: Vintage Books, 1949).

19. Ibid.

20. Charles Bullock, "The Impact of Income and Black Political Participation: Legislative Voting in the South," *Civil Rights Research Review,* vol. IX, no. 3-4, 1981, 7. See also Gary H. Brooks, "Black Political Mobilization and White Legislative Behavior," in *Contemporary Political Attitudes and Behavior* (ed.) Tod A. Baker and Robert P. Sneed, (New York: Praeger, 1982), 221–237.

21. Margaret Conway, "Political Participation in Mid-term Congressional Election: Attitudinal and Social Characteristics During the 1970s" *APQ* 9:221–224.

22. Lester Milbrath, *Political Participation: How and Why Do People Get Involved in Politics* (Chicago: Rand McNally, 1965).

23. Alan T. Abramowitz, "Economic Conditions, Presidential Popularity and Voting Behavior in Mid-term Congressional Elections," *JOP* vol. 47, no. 1, Feb. 1985, 38.

24. Angus Campbell, et al. *The Voter Decides* (Evanston: Harper, Robinson and Company, 1954).

25. Gregory Calderia, Samuel Patterson, and Mankko Gregory, "The Mobilization of Voters in Congressional Elections" *JOP* vol. 47, no. 2, May, 85, 490–509.

26. According to financial statements filed with the Federal Election Commission, Franklin reported at least $501,649 in 1984 while Clark reported at least $367,291 for the same period.

27. James Young, "Strong Vote Help Clark Avoid Runoff," *The Commercial*

Appeal, Jackson, Mississippi Bureau. Clark won 57 percent of the primary vote. His nearest opponent, Pete Johnson, a white Democrat, whom Clark endorsed for the 1986 elections, received 22 percent of the primary vote in 1982. Clark endorsed Johnson despite the candidacy of black Democrat Michael Espy.

28.   Karen Hinton, "Party Loyalty to Be Tested in November," *Jackson Daily News,* p. 1-A.

29.   In a 1983 gubernatorial race in which 500 blacks were interviewed, only 18 percent identified fear and/or economic intimidation as a reason for nonvoting. See Coleman, et al., op. cited, 21.

30.   Richard D. Shingels, "Black Consciousness and Political Participation: The Missing Link" *APSR* vol. 75, 1981, 77.

FOUR

The Courts, Section 5 of the Voting Rights Act, and the Future of Black Politics

Twiley W. Barker, Jr., and Lucius J. Barker

The Voting Rights Act (VRA) of 1965 was hailed as a great victory in America's attempt to end racial discrimination. The chief purpose of the act was to remove the vices and vestiges of practices that prevented blacks (and other minorities) from voting. If there is one sacred feature of the American democracy, it is the right to vote. The sacredness of this right is grounded on what is perhaps an oversimplified belief that through political participation (mainly the right to vote), individuals and groups will be able to safeguard, protect, and promote their interests. Put another way, the intense competition for votes in our electoral system acts as a leverage on actions by government officials that might alienate large numbers of voters. In any event, regardless of theoretical or practical considerations, there is widespread popular support for guaranteeing and safeguarding the right to vote. To be sure, it took a long time for this widespread support to be converted into specific support to protect the voting rights of blacks. It began with the elimination of the most blatant devices (e.g., grandfather clauses, white primaries) that disenfranchised significant numbers of blacks and continued with the actions taken by Congress in the civil rights acts of 1957, 1960, and 1964. These acts, while indicative of a change in congressional mood, were not very effective in increasing the number of black voters. White officials, primarily in the South, continued to find ways to keep blacks off the registration rolls and from voting. Indeed, the major defects of these measures were that they left registration machinery in the hands of hostile state and local officials and that they relied too much on litigation.

The 1964 elections made clear that the right to vote was still not a reality for black Americans in the South. A year later, stirred by massive civil rights demonstrations and pressed by the strong initiative of President Johnson, Congress finally enacted comprehensive voting rights legislation. The major improvement of the Voting Rights Act of 1965 over earlier laws is that it provided federal machinery to secure voting registration. In addition, the 1965 law abolished literacy and understanding tests in states and voting districts where less than 50 percent of the voting-age population had been registered in 1964 or had voted in the 1964 presidential election. To be sure, white southern officials challenged the constitutionality of the Voting Rights Act, but the U.S. Supreme Court upheld its validity in 1966.[1]

The new legislation proved effective. There were significant increases in black registration and black voting.[2] These increases, coupled with well-established demographic factors, raised the possibility that blacks might gain control of local governments in some jurisdictions.[3] Southern reaction to such an eventuality had been indicated by a situation that resulted in the 1960 Supreme Court case *Gomillion* v. *Lightfoot*.[4] Here, the Alabama legislature had attempted in a rather bold (and somewhat crude) manner to prevent a black takeover of a municipal government by redefining the corporate boundaries of Tuskegee and thereby excluding nearly all black voters from the city electorate. The plan did not survive judicial scrutiny, and the Supreme Court found it an obviously racially discriminatory scheme in violation of the Fifteenth Amendment.

The decision in *Gomillion* indicated that "racial gerrymandering" could not be used as a device to blunt the impact of an increasing number of black voters. Nonetheless, those who pushed for the passage of the Voting Rights Act knew that safeguards against the use of such discriminatory devices had to be included in the legislation. It was directed at state or locally imposed changes in voting practices that might thwart or blunt the increase in black voters and prevent black majorities in given jurisdictions. More specifically, the VRA forbids a "covered" jurisdiction[5] to institute voting qualifications, practices, and procedures different from those in effect on November 1, 1964, unless it first obtains from the district court of the District of Columbia a declaratory judgment that the changes do "not have the purpose and will not have the effect of denying or abridging the right to vote on account of race or color."[6] To expedite matters, the provision allows jurisdictions to change the voting and election laws if the U.S. attorney general does not interpose any objections to such changes within 60 days after their submission. The ultimate outcome of such changes are then subject to judicial determination. In terms of its potential impact on black voting, Section 5 therefore looms as one of the most important safeguards against the use of discriminatory voting devices. The effectiveness of that safeguard depends in great measure on the position of the judiciary, and ultimately on the U.S. Supreme Court.

The chief burden of this chapter is to discuss how the Supreme Court has dealt with actions brought under Section 5 of the Voting Rights Act.[7] This discussion, in turn, allows us to comment on the importance of court actions to the achievement of black policy objectives. It also permits us to view the influence of such court activity on the future course of black political participation and political representation.

Section 5: Developing the Law

The initial impact of the Voting Rights Act came during the first decade of the so-called reapportionment revolution.[8] To be sure, the reshaping of electoral districts had long been used as a mechanism for manipulating the voting strength of particular groups, a fact specifically referred to in the *Gomillion* case. A key question about Section 5, therefore, was whether Congress had had such actions in mind when it created the measure.

This was the question before the U.S. Supreme Court in the 1969 case *Allen* v. *State Board of Elections*.[9] In its decision the Court rejected efforts to exclude reapportionment activity from the judicial and or administrative scrutiny required in Section 5. Mississippi had argued that since some reapportionment plans are the result of judicial mandate and must have judicial approval before implementation, Congress could not have intended a judicial conflict in the area by having such plans subjected to judicial scrutiny. The Court did not accept this rather curious and strained argument.

Two years later, in *Perkins* v. *Matthews*, the Court explicated further its *Allen* decision when it held that several changes in the electoral procedures of a Mississippi municipality were subject to Section 5 clearance before they could be implemented.[10] In this case the city of Canton had sought (1) to change the location of polling places, (2) to provide for different municipal boundaries through annexation, and (3) to shift from single-member districts to at-large elections. A federal district judge, relying on *Allen*, temporarily restrained the first election where the modified electoral procedures were scheduled to be implemented, only to have the restraining order dissolved by a three-judge district court upon its examination of the merits. In the Supreme Court's subsequent reversal, Justice Brennan emphasized that a correct reading of *Allen* made prior Section 5 clearance of such changes mandatory. Brennan also said that the three-judge court had examined the substantive aspects of the electoral changes but that such an examination was beyond its authority. Under the Voting Rights Act only the district court for the District of Columbia has jurisdiction to examine the substantive issues concerning changes in voting procedures that occur in "covered" jurisdictions.

In *Georgia* v. *United States*, the Court once again affirmed its *Allen* ruling that state reapportionment actions are subject to Section 5 scrutiny.[11] Georgia had made extensive changes in its state legislative districts, including the creation of several multimember districts to replace single-member districts. Noting that "Section 5 is not concerned with a simple inventory of voting procedures, but rather with a reality of changed practices as they affect Negro voters," Justice Potter Stewart made it clear that because such changes could dilute the votes of blacks, they were within the "standards, practices, or procedures" to which Section 5 is directed. Stewart observed further that, in considering the 1970 extension amendments to the Voting Rights Act, Congress had had an opportunity to make substantive changes regarding Section 5 coverage, but had declined to do so. Hence, the *Allen* ruling remained the proper interpretation of Section 5 with respect to reapportionment.

Despite these favorable procedural decisions, the Burger Court adopted rather narrow standards of review in judging the substantive effect of reapportionment actions under Section 5. This has resulted in the dilution and/or blunting of black voting strength in several jurisdictions. In *Beer* v. *United States*, for example, when the New Orleans City Council reapportioned its wards and continued to combine an at-large election format with a single-member district (ward) plan, the Burger Court did not find the action in conflict with Section 5.[12] But the federal district court for the District of Columbia pointed out the "dilution" consequences of the plan. Looking at the seven-member New Orleans City Council and the black percentage of the population, the lower court noted that the "mathematical potential" of blacks was the control of three of the seven seats. The "predictive reality" under the plan, however, the lower court indicated, was control of only one of the five single-member districts.[13] Indeed, the history of racial bloc voting in New Orleans made it realistic to assume that blacks would be frozen out of the two at-large seats. But the U.S. Supreme Court disagreed. It reasoned that since the at-large seats were established in the city charter a decade before the Voting Rights Act, they did not represent a change in established voting arrangements and procedures. Hence, they were not subject to Section 5 scrutiny. Accordingly, the Court reasoned that the at-large dimension of the election scheme and the consequent dilution of black voting power were "sealed in" the city charter and would have to remain unless or until the charter was amended.

More significantly, the Burger Court majority found the New Orleans plan valid since it did not diminish the electoral position of blacks. Indeed, as seen by the Court, black electoral representation would in fact be enhanced since, prior to the reapportionment, there were *no black council-men*, and under the new plan blacks would constitute a population majority in two of the five districts and a registered voting majority in one of them. Thus, to the Court majority, the reality of the reapportionment plan was that prior to the institution of the plan there were no blacks on the council, and now under the plan there would almost certainly be *one* black (the district having a registered black voting majority). On this basis the Court concluded that black representation would be increased by *100 percent*, and this certainly would not offend Section 5.

Justice Thurgood Marshall sharply criticized the Court majority for what he termed a simplistic application of its "non-retrogression" standard. A plan might be ameliorative and produce some gains for blacks but none-theless be discriminatory in its overall effect. The inescapable fact, said Marshall, is that while blacks constituted 45 percent of the New Orleans population at the time of the 1970 reapportionment, under the plan accepted by the Court they could realistically expect to elect (and did in the next election) only one black person to the seven-member city council. To be sure, as Justice Marshall noted, proportional representation of blacks is not constitutionally required. But he did think that the burden of proof should be shifted to those officials who allegedly caused the dilution of black voting strength, compelling them to show that the revised election structures and processes are equally open to participation by the complaining blacks.

Marshall's view did not prevail, and the *Beer* decision was a definite blow to black political aspirations in New Orleans. When the history of racial bloc voting in the city is coupled with the entrenched at-large plan for the election of two-sevenths of the council, it seemed clear that blacks were effectively frozen out of the at-large seats and could hope to elect black candidates only from the remaining single-member districts. The at-large scheme could be viewed as part of a total plan for the election of the New Orleans City Council and not separate from the changes in election procedures subject to Section 5 scrutiny. Whatever the motives of those who adopted it in 1954, the overall plan *at the time it was instituted* served to "seal in" discrimination against black voters. Under current Court doctrine, the bifurcated election scheme seems to be safe, at least until political realities remove the at-large dimension from its pre-VRA shield that *Beer* erected.[14] Interestingly, however, subsequent developments, including demographic changes, resulted in 1986 elections that saw blacks gain majority control of the New Orleans city council.

In 1976, the Court appeared to push aside the distressing message of *Beer*, and approve legislative action that was required to enhance the voting potential of blacks in a Section 5 preclearance action in *United Jewish Organizations of Williamsburg* v. *Carey*.[15] In that action, however, those challenging the state action were not blacks, but Hasidic Jews. In meeting the Attorney General's objections under Section 5 to several legislative reapportionment actions, New York's lawmakers focused its remedy on the *size of the nonwhite majorities* in certain districts, rather than the total number of districts with nonwhite majorities. The aim was to arrange a nonwhite population large enough in certain districts (given historic voting behavior) to effect the election of nonwhite representation. To accomplish this, population shifts were made in racial terms. One of the results from this exercise in "geometry and geography" was the splitting of a natural community of Hasidic between two districts.

In their constitutional challenge, the Hasidic Jews contended that their voting strength was being diluted for the purpose of enhancing the political position of blacks. Three members of the Court supported Justice Byron White in rejecting this position. They held that New York's use of racial criteria in fashioning its legislative districts was in effect an attempt to comply with Section 5 and obtain the attorney general's approval. As such, the challenged plan was not intentionally racially discriminatory. In fact, the Court held that the New York plan *while enhancing the possibility for nonwhite representation in several districts, did not "minimize or unfairly cancel out white voting strength."* The Court concluded that as long as whites as a group were provided with fair representation in the overall reapportionment plan, increasing nonwhite majorities in some of the districts, did not constitute discrimination against whites.

The crucial lesson of *UJO* v. *Carey* was the Court's approval of the use of a racially based remedy to meet the mandate of Section 5. It may be argued that in doing this the Court opened the door to racial gerrymandering. However, the effect of shifting the percentages of nonwhite voters in several districts was not an invidious manipulation. Rather, the result reflected a possible fairer share of legislative representation to their population in the areas involved. It does not disturb the "nonretrogression" principle. And, as noted in *Beer*, rigid application of that principle can result in a severe dilution of black voting strength.

Chief Justice Burger's dissent in *UJO* poses an interesting dilemma for the future of black voting strength. Questioning the proposition that racial interests can be represented properly only by persons of that race and that this would result in a move away from a "truly homogeneous society," the chief justice sounded a note of caution for the future:

> This retreat from the ideal of the American "melting pot" is curiously out of step with recent political history—and indeed with what the Court has said and done for more than a decade. The notion that Americans vote in firm blocs has been repudiated in the election of minority members as mayors and legislators in numerous American cities and districts overwhelmingly white. . . . [16]

Burger's cautionary note does not seem to represent a realistic view of political behavior in the United States. Certainly it is possible to applaud the election of Mayor Bradley by a predominantly white electorate in Los Angeles. Nevertheless, this single instance does not reflect racial voting behavior in most American jurisdictions. The simple fact is that in the overwhelming majority of governmental units in the United States, black candidates do not get elected to any office unless they can count on a large black vote, usually a majority of the electorate. For this reason, the "proportionate" principle is crucial to such political events as reapportionment.

The Court resurrected the *Beer* non-retrogression rule almost a decade later to validate a Texas municipality's electoral arrangements that Mexican-Americans charged had the effect of blunting their voting power. At issue in *City of Lockhart* v. *United States* were the use of "numbered posts" in an at-large scheme and "staggered terms" that in practice were alleged to frustrate "single-shot" voting practices that would allow minority groups to concentrate their votes in support of a single candidate. In holding that these arrangements did not have the effect of abridging the right to vote that would require their rejection under Section 5, the Supreme Court recognized that, in some circumstances these arrangements when used in the context of racial "bloc voting" may have a discriminatory effect, but they do not relegate Mexican-American voters to a *worst position*. The Court noted that the city of Lockhart had employed "numbered posts" under its old electoral system with the same affect on "single-shot" voting as possible under the newly adopted arrangements. It also concluded that the introduction of staggered terms had not diminished the voting strength of the city's minorities either. As Justice Lewis Powell contended:

> "Minorities are in the same position every year that they used to be in every other year. Although there may have been no improvement in their voting strength, there was not retrogression either."[17]

In dissent, Justice Thurgood Marshall took issue with the majority for its construction of Section 5 that allows jurisdictions under the "non-retrogression" test to perpetuate discriminatory practices. For him, such a construction was contrary to the intent of Congress when it adopted the preclearance requirement in Section 5. Clearly, he contended, the intent was to advance the "goals of the Fifteenth Amendment". He certainly would not accept the majority's action, which he characterized as permitting the adoption of electoral schemes that could be discriminatory in effect so long as they were not "more discriminatory" than the arrangements they replaced. In short, he argued that such construction, "reduces Section 5 to a means of maintaining the status quo." Indeed, such a result would seem to be in conflict with the larger goal of the Voting Rights Act and certainly at odds with the language of Section 2 of the Act added in the 1982 extension.

Some jurisdictions have resorted to territorial annexation as a more direct (if not lasting) strategy of staving off black control of their governments. Illustrative of this strategy was the action taken by the city of Richmond, Virginia, in 1969. Up to that time, there had been a steady flight of whites to suburbia, resulting in an increasing black proportion of the Richmond population. Annexation proceedings had commenced in the early 1960s but had languished in controversy over an extended period of time. In fact, Richmond dropped its effort to annex one parcel as not being in its "best economic interest." But continued negotiations led to the annexation of some 23 square miles in the Chesterfield County area in 1969. Just prior to the annexation, the black proportion of Richmond's population had increased to 52 percent, and given the at-large election procedures for the city council, coupled with the historic practice of racial bloc voting, a black takeover of the city in the not too distant future was a realistic assumption. The new territory added slightly more than 47,000 inhabitants, of whom 45,700 were white or nonblack.[18] Hence the postannexation black proportion of Richmond's population was 43 percent, a substantial 10 percent decrease.

Upon the initial request under Section 5, the attorney general refused to approve the annexation because it portended the dilution of black voting strength. The attorney general did suggest that the "impermissible adverse racial impact" of the annexation on black voting strength might be avoided by the use of single-member districts for ward elections. Thereupon, Richmond devised a single-member district plan with the population apportioned so that four of the districts had substantial black majorities, and four were substantially white. For all practical purposes the Ninth District was white-dominated with a 59 percent white, 41 percent black population. Following the 1971 Supreme Court ruling in *Whitcomb* v. *Chavis*, Richmond officials sought a modification of the single-member district proposal.[19] The effort failed.

While the city was attempting to get approval of the annexation from the attorney general, litigation was commenced alleging that it constituted a violation of the voting rights of blacks as protected by the Fifteenth Amendment.[20] The district court for the eastern district of Virginia accepted the plaintiff's racial-purpose argument and ordered elections under a bifurcated scheme for the original city area and the annexed territory to avoid dilution of black voting strength. But the court of appeals did not accept such an application of the Fifteenth Amendment to the annexation action, and the Supreme Court sustained this position when it denied the plaintiff's petition for *certiorari*.

The district court for the District of Columbia (as provided for in Section

5 of the VRA) entered the controversy when Richmond sought a declaratory judgment to validate the annexation. Upon a special master's findings, the district court held that the annexation had a dilutive effect on black voting contrary to the proscription of Section 5.[21] Citing the Supreme Court decision in a 1971 case on the applicability of Section 5 to annexation actions, the district court noted that the obvious was implicit: if blacks constitute a lessor proportion of the population in the new jurisdiction with the annexed territory than they constituted in the old territory (prior to annexation), and when this fact is coupled with the well-established pattern of racial bloc voting, the voting strength of blacks as a class is diluted.[22] The lower court made it clear that the annexation had a discriminatory purpose and effect and that the city of Richmond had not met the burden of proof that there were "objective, verifiable legitimate economic and administrative reasons" supporting annexation.

The Burger Court rejected the district court's holding.[23] Justice Byron White, who spoke for the Court, discounted any racial motive in the 1969 annexation. On the contrary, Justice William J. Brennan noted in dissent, that the district court had explicitly pointed to such a motivation:

> Richmond's focus in the negotiation was upon the number of new white voters it could obtain by annexation: it expressed no interest in economic or geographic considerations such as tax revenues, vacant land, utilities or schools. The mayor required assurances from Chesterfield County officials that at least 44,000 additional white citizens would be obtained by the city before he would agree upon settlement of the annexation suit. And the mayor and one of the city councilmen conditioned final acceptance of the settlement agreement on the annexation going into effect in sufficient time to make citizens in the annexed area eligible to vote in the city council elections of 1970.[24]

The Court majority was not satisfied with the evidentiary considerations of the district court, particularly the current justifications for annexation, and remanded the case for a further consideration of the justification issue.

The crucial part of the Court's decision in *Richmond* was its holding that Section 5 does not proscribe a city from annexing territory (and adding new voters) and thereby diminishing black voting strength so long as *there is no finding of a discriminatory purpose*. The discussion at any stage of the annexation for any "legitimate" and "justifiable" reasons, such as administrative and economic benefits, seems to be the Court's standard for meeting Section 5 scrutiny in such cases. To the majority, the fact that the proportion of the black population—and hence voting strength—diminishes when compared with the preannexation proportion does not in and of itself make the action defective. Of crucial importance is whether or not the enlarged jurisdiction gives fair and equitable recognition to blacks.

In 1980 in *City of Rome, Georgia* v. *United States*[25] the Court, speaking through Justice Thurgood Marshall, affirmed a federal district court's ruling rejecting several annexation actions because of their vote dilution effect. The territory proposed for annexation would have added almost 2,600 whites and about 50 blacks to the city's population, including 823 white and only 9 black registered voters. Under *City of Richmond* these facts alone do not condemn the annexation. But the Court found that Rome did not meet its burden of proof that the new electoral jurisdiction "fairly reflects the strength of the black community after annexation." This "fairly reflects" standard continued to guide the Court in subsequent annexation preclearance actions brought during the 1980s.

Efforts to stave off possible black political control have produced some other interesting (if not imaginative) electoral arrangements. In late 1977 and 1978, the City of Port Arthur, Texas for example, used both consolidation with two smaller municipalities and annexation of unincorporated territory to expand its geographic area and increase the number of white residents and voters. As a result of these consolidation and annexation actions, the black population decreased by about 5 percent. Initially, two different schemes for the election of the city council were formulated. First, a nine-member body that would be elected at large was proposed. A short time later this was replaced by a 4-4-1 plan that involved a combination of single-member districts and at-large members. A majority-vote requirement for election under each plan was ensured by providing for run-off elections. The district court found both schemes inadequate under Section 5. Not only was a discriminatory purpose undergirding each plan, the lower court contended, but it concluded that, given the history of racial "bloc voting" in Port Arthur, neither plan reflected the minority's potential voting strength in the enlarged city as required by *City of Richmond, City of Rome,* and *City of Petersburg, supra.*

Subsequent to the court rejection, Port Arthur and the Attorney General agreed on another bifurcated plan—the so-called "4-2-3" plan—that combined four single-member districts with two superimposed single-member districts and three at-large seats. All the seats were governed by a majority-vote requirement ensured by run-off elections. Under this arrangement, blacks were assured of extraordinary majorities in three districts. This was almost equivalent to the black population in the enlarged city (35 percent). The District Court for the District of Columbia, however, was not impressed, and concluded that the plan did not neutralize sufficiently "the adverse impact upon minority voting strength" that resulted from the territorial expansion. In its rejection, the court suggested a remedy to correct what it considered the plan's major defect—the elimination of the majority vote for the two non-mayoral at-large seats.

In its affirmance of the district court (*City of Port Arthur, Texas v. United States*),[26] the 6-3 Supreme Court majority took notice of racial proportions of the population in the enlarged municipality and concluded that the plan undervalued the political strength of the black majority. Hence, it considered the lower court's call for eliminating the majority-vote requirement for the at-large seats to be an "understandable adjustment." Reduced to its simplest term, the Court reasoned that the majority-vote requirement (in the context of historical racial "bloc voting") would result in a black candidate facing a white candidate in a "one-on-one" contest in a white majority jurisdiction. Hence, in practice, the rule would effectively foreclose election of blacks to the at-large seats.

In ruling as it did, the Court seemed to be backing away from the "no retrogression" rule followed since *Beer, supra.* It should be noted that a black candidate faced the same obstacle in New Orleans. In dissent, Justice Lewis Powell argued that what the majority had done was to adopt erroneously a new theory of Section 5 under which the district court exercises equity powers whereby it can fashion a remedy that enhances political strength of minorities rather than merely preserving it. But, if anything, the holding was little more than an aberration, for just two months later Justice Powell led seven members of the court in an unmistakable reaffirmation of the "non-retrogression" rule in the Court's *City of Lockhart, Texas* decision, discussed earlier.

Preclearance into the Twenty-First Century

While the Supreme Court actions reviewed here highlight a few of the more blatant attempts to keep black citizens from a major share of political power, the considerable activity is more clearly focused by an enumeration of the scope and nature of the legislative changes that have come within the purview of the Attorney General since 1980 (see Table 4.1).

The reports chronicled a wide variety of electoral structure and voting requirement changes adopted in several "covered" jurisdictions. The major culprits designed to thwart the political advancement of blacks continue to include annexation of new territory with largely white residents, at-large

Table 4.1 Preclearance Activity Under Section 5, 1981–1984

Year	No. of Submissions	No. Voting-Related Changes	No. of Objections Raised
1981	2,001	6,072	21
1982	2,800	13,300	41
1983	3,000	10,000	53
1984	3,400	16,700	Not Available

Source: Annual Reports of the Attorney General

elections with numbered posts and majority-vote requirements, and unfair redistricting of electoral areas.[27] And this is understandable. Federal legislation makes it difficult to pare down the number of voters by restrictive voter registration. Hence, the strategy has been to effect a *dilution* of the numbers to achieve the same end. And in the effort, a deeply embedded commitment to federalism has proved a reliable supportive principle. State laws permit local governmental units to annex new territory. State laws have routinely provided for majority or plurality elections and, for much of this century, state laws have allowed local governments considerable latitude in the adoption of their governmental and electoral arrangements. Hence, this helps to explain the increased enactment of at-large election schemes or numbered posts or majority vote requirements or redistricting plans designed to ensure continued white control despite the changed demographic configuration of the jurisdiction. To be sure, these more "visible" strategies designed to curb black voting power have been highlighted in the political controversy over the last 20 years. However, other restrictive strategies have also been used on occasion. These have included, for example, restrictive availability of polling places and discontinuation of community-group voter registration drives. An extreme example of the former involved the elimination of 12 of 13 polling places in a hospital district in a Texas county. The Attorney General objected in a Section 5 preclearance action because the one remaining polling place was 19 miles from the residential area of the highest concentration of black voters and some 30 miles from the area where most Mexican-Americans lived.[28]

Almost from the moment of passage, VRA supporters expended considered resources to keep the political-power potential for which they had struggled so long from eroding. Certainly, vigorous enforcement by the administration was essential. They were well aware of possible retrenchment actions of the several state and local legislative bodies and timely objections by the Attorney General to such "debilitating" acts were considered an important shield against forces seeking a return to and continuation of pre-VRA white political domination. The several annexation, reapportionment, and at-large elections challenged during the first decade of VRA enforcement underscored the necessity for extending the Act in 1970, 1975, and 1982. Generally the Nixon, Ford, and Reagan administrations came to recognize the essentiality of Section 5 as a shield against state and local voting procedures and requirements that could effectively deny or dilute black voting rights and power. Accordingly, they supported, with varying degrees of intensity, congressional actions in those years to extend the preclearance mechanism of Section 5 for limited periods.

To be sure, during the 1982 extension debate, VRA supporters argued that the considerable evidence developed during the life of the Act supported the view that Section 5's preclearance provision should be *perma-*

nent. The number of totally covered states (nine) and those where partial coverage is mandated (13) underscored continuous difficulties encountered by blacks and minorities in exercising the franchise. House action supported a permanent extension, but the Reagan administration thought that a 10-year extension would be sufficient. In the end, a compromise of the two positions produced at 25-year extension until the year 2007.

While hearings on the extension measure underscored the need for the continued application of the preclearance mechanism in some jurisdictions, the changing socio-political climate in others (produced largely by the steady increase in black voter registration) indicates no further need for pre-clearance coverage. Consequently, the Act's current "bail-out" provision can be used to remove coverage when a jurisdiction convinces a three-judge panel for the District Court of the District of Columbia that it has had a clean voting rights record for the preceding 10-year period. A clean record can be substantiated by showing that: (1) no discriminatory devices or tests for voting have been used; (2) there has not been a judicial finding of a voting rights law violation; (3) federal examiners to assist in voter registration have not been required; (4) timely submissions for Section 5 preclearance were made; (5) election changes where the Attorney General interposed objections were repealed; and (6) implementation of constructive efforts to end intimidation and harrassment of voters and to bring minority groups into the electoral process. This new bail-out procedure became effective in August 1984.

Though important, the 25-year extension of the Voting Rights Act gives little cause for its supporters to relax. There is evidence, for example, that "many jurisdictions continue to defy the Act by making changes and ignoring the requirements of the law."[29] For example, a study done by the Southern Regional Council shows that in just three states (Alabama, Georgia, and South Carolina) there are 536 "illegal voting law changes 'enforced but not submitted for preclearance under Section 5.' " In short, the effectiveness of Section 5 depends on whether such changes are *brought to the attention* of proper authorities (the Attorney General or the D.C. District Court) for preclearance. This means that if state and local officials fail to bring forth such changes, the burden is effectively left to those most concerned, blacks and their supporters.

The discussion of how the Supreme Court has interpreted Section 5 points up several important factors with respect to the future of black politics. First, the enactment of Section 5 and the Voting Rights Act itself suggests the incremental nature of the development of public policies. The Civil Rights Act of 1957, the first such civil rights legislation enacted since Reconstruction, represented an initial congressional response to the civil rights movement designed to safeguard the right to vote. But the effectiveness of the 1957 law, as well as the voting rights provisions of the 1960 and

1964 acts, depended primarily on the use of lawsuits and litigation to protect voting rights. Moreover, such court orders as might be forthcoming depended for their enforcement on state and local officials. Thus the protracted and limited coverage of such legal action, plus dependence on generally hostile white southern officials for enforcement, made it obvious that the voting provisions of such legislation would prove ineffective. The futility of these earlier laws was vividly pointed up by massive civil rights demonstrations that eventually led to the passage of the much stronger Voting Rights Act of 1965. This act allowed federal officials to register black voters and see that such persons could vote and have their votes counted honestly. Overall, then, starting with the very weak 1957 legislation, it took some eight years before an effective congressional policy evolved with respect to black voting rights.

Second, this discussion points up the enormous resources needed to win a major public policy enactment. The 1965 Voting Rights Act, for example, required a broad coalition of racial, religious, ethnic, and labor groups; persistent and massive street demonstrations; bipartisan support from congressional leaders; and vigorous support and arm-twisting from President Lyndon B. Johnson. This means that the enactment of major public policies, especially controversial ones (as civil rights laws tend to be), requires efforts and resources that are very difficult to harness, and even more difficult to maintain.

Moreover, the enactment of policy is only one stage, albeit a very important one, in the overall policy process. Policies, once enacted, must be implemented. And this implementation depends in large measure on how various institutions and individuals interpret and enforce the policy. As this chapter illustrates, both the U.S. attorney general and the federal courts can be important in determining whether or not Section 5 will be effective in deterring racial discrimination in voting. The attorney general, for example, may be called upon to determine initially if a particular change in voting qualifications, practices, or procedures in "covered" states has the effect of "denying or abridging the right to vote on account of race or color." A decision at this state can prove crucial, for it signals that the nation's highest legal officer has reviewed the matter and rendered an opinion. The fact that officials have such authority clearly demonstrates that blacks must be constantly concerned about who holds key administrative positions, such as that of attorney general. Whether an Edward Meese rather than a Ramsey Clark holds the post of attorney general, for example, can be of crucial importance in this regard. Or that a Ronald Reagan rather than a Lyndon Johnson is president can obviously affect the substance and tone of civil law enforcement generally.

The major focus of this chapter has been the role of courts, specifically the U. S. Supreme Court, in the formulation of public policy. The application of a law or public policy (e.g., Section 5) to specific cases allows courts to determine, in large measure, their meaning and effectiveness. Taking our example of black political participation and representation, a Court decision opting for "at-large" or "single member district" elections might well determine the electoral opportunities open to blacks. The nature of electoral politics today and in the future would seem to indicate that *race* will be an important—perhaps the determining—factor in voting behavior in areas having sizable black populations. With few exceptions black officials are elected from constituencies in which blacks comprise a majority or nearly a majority of the population. This applies to national, state, and local elections. Because of losses in big-city populations and reapportionment subsequent to the 1980 census, however, some black officeholders may have a difficult time retaining the kind of constituency from which they were elected. Obviously, in terms of Section 5-type voting policies, who the judges are and what they do remains important to black political participation and representation. This is why blacks and minorities are concerned by the trend and types of appointments being made to the federal judiciary by the Reagan administration.[30]

In any event, studies of the role of courts in the policy process indicate that (1) the position of courts can prove important in the struggle for policy objectives; and (2) court decisions, though important, are not necessarily determinative and are subject to change by courts themselves and by the "pushes and pulls" of the political process.[31] Given the nature of American politics—and the relatively meager representation, resources, and influence that blacks have in the nation's political councils—black citizens may well continue to need strong and persistent judicial support if they and other minorities are to reach threshold enjoyment of the responsibilities and benefits of the American political-social system. But, as history clearly shows, even this support is uncertain and subject to change.

Notes

1. *South Carolina* v. *Katzenbach*, 383 U.S. 301 (1966).
2. With respect to increases in black registration and voting, see Lenneal J. Henderson, Jr., "Black Politics and American Presidential Elections." Chapter 1 in this volume.
3. Most significant was the increasing proportion of urban black voters left behind by whites fleeing to suburbia.
4. *Gomillion* v. *Lightfoot*, 364 U.S. 399 (1960).
5. The following states (or counties therein) were initially covered by the statutory definition: Alabama, Alaska, Arizona, Georgia, Louisiana, Mississippi, North Carolina, South Carolina, and Virginia. Counties in several other states were covered thereafter. In subsequent amendments to the Act,

a large number of jurisdictions were required to conform with special language provisions to reduce the language burden on non-English speaking citizens. The U.S. Commission on Civil Rights reported in 1981 that over 100 counties and cities nationwide were covered by the Minority Language provision of the Act.

6.   42 U.S. Code 1973c. The statute requires the constitution of a three-judge court to make such determination.

7.   A fairly extensive literature exists on this general topic. See generally: "Voting Rights Act of 1965—Municipal Annexation." 10 *Georgia Law Review* 261 (Fall 1975); "Section 5 of the Voting Rights Act of 1965 and Reapportionment," 7 *Indiana Law Review* 579 (1974); "Multi-Member Districts and Minority Rights," 87 *Harvard Law Review* 1851 (June 1974); Robert L. Bell, "The At-Large Election System," *Howard Law Journal* 19:177 (Spring 1976); James W. Ozog, "Judicial Review of Municipal Annexation Under Section 5 of the VRA" 12 *Urban Law Annual* 311 (1976); Paul W. Bonapfel, "Minority Challenges to At-Large Elections—The Dilution Problem," 10 *Georgia Law Review* 353 (Winter 1976); Dennis J. Nall, "Multi-Member Legislative Districts: Requiem for a Constitutional Burial," 29 *University of Florida Law Review* 703 (Summer 1977); H.M. Yoste, Jr., "Section 5: Growth or Demise or Statutory Voting Rights," 48 *Mississippi Law Journal* 818 (September 1977); Richard L. Engstrom, "Racial Vote Dilution: Supreme Court Interpretations of Section 5 of the Voting Rights Act," 4 *Southern University Law Review* 139 (Spring, 1978); L. McDonald, "The 1982 Extension of Section 5 of the Voting Rights Act of 1965: The Continued Need for Preclearance," 51 *Tennessee Law Review* 1 (Fall, 1983); and Note, "The Voting Rights Act Amendments of 1982: Real Gains or Illusions?" 8 *Thurgood Marshall Law Review* 129 (Fall 1982).

8.   *Baker* v. *Carr*, 369 U.S. 1986; *Reynolds* v. *Sims*, 374 U.S. 533; *Avery* v. *Midland County*, 390 U.S. 474 etc.

9.   *Allen* v. *State Board of Education*, 393 U.S. 544.

10.   *Perkins* v. *Matthews*, 400 U.S. 379.

11.   *Georgia* v. *United States*, 411 U. S. 526.

12.   *Beer* v. *United States*, 425 U.S. 130 (1976).

13.   *Beer* v. *United States*, 374 F. Supp. 363 at 393 (1974).

14.   When the multimember district format invidiously discriminates against blacks, the Court has required that that segment of a reapportionment plan be excised and single-member districts be substituted. See *White* v. *Register*, 412 U.S. 755 (1973).

15.   *United Jewish Organizations of Williamsburg* v. *Carey*, 430 U.S. 144 (1977).

16.   *United Jewish Organizations of Williamsburg* v. *Carey*, 430 U.S. 144 at 187.

17.   *City of Lockhart* v. *United States*, 460 U.S. 124 at 133 (1983).

18.   Only 1,557 people in the annexed territory were classified as black.

19.   In *Whitcomb* v. *Chavis*, 403 U.S. 124 (1971), the Court upheld the power of the Indiana legislature to restructure its electoral districts (by establishing multimember districts) against challenges that the primary purpose and result were to dilute black representation.

20. *Holt* v. *City of Richmond*, 334 F. Supp. 228 (1971); 459 F. 2nd 1093 (1972). The U.S. Supreme Court denied *certiorari*.

21. *Richmond* v. *U.S.*, 376 F. Supp. 1344 (1974).

22. *Perkins* v. *Matthews*, 400 U.S. 379 (1971).

23. *Richmond* v. *U.S.*, 422 U.S. 358.

24. Ibid., at 382.

25. *City of Rome, Georgia* v. *United States*, 446 U.S. 156 (1980).

26. *City of Port Arthur, Texas* v. *United States*, 459 U.S. 159 (1982).

27. U.S. Commission on Civil Rights, *The Voting Rights Act: Unfilled Goals* (Washington: 1981) 64–65. Among the changes were reapportionment plans for state houses and senates, congressional districts, and local governmental units; numbered posts and majority vote requirements; restrictions on voter registration drives; and voter reidentification procedures.

28. See Senate Judiciary Committee Hearings on the *Voting Rights Act Extension*, 97th Cong. 2d Sess., 1982, Senate Report No. 97-417, 11.

29. See generally the excellent manual by Barbara Y. Phillips, *How to Use Section 5 of the Voting Rights Act* (Joint Center for Political Studies, 1983), 3d ed., 12–13.

30. For data and commentary on Reagan judicial appointments see "Reagan Gaining Control of Federal Judiciary," *Congressional Almanac* (Congressional Quarterly, Inc., 98th Congress, 2d sess., 1984) 243–245.

31. See generally: Lucius J. Barker, "The Supreme Court from Warren to Burger: Implications for Black Americans and the Political System," (1973) *Washington University Law Quarterly* (Fall 1973), no. 4, 747; Robert Dahl, "Decision-Making in a Democracy: The Supreme Court as a National Policy Maker," 6 *Journal of Public Law* (1975); and Jonathan Casper, "The Supreme Court and National Policy Making," 70 *American Political Science Review* (1976): 50–62.

FIVE

Racial Factors in the 1982 California Gubernatorial Campaign: Why Bradley Lost

Charles P. Henry

Despite a substantial lead in the polls throughout the 1982 California gubernatorial campaign, Los Angeles Mayor Tom Bradley lost his bid to become the first black elected governor in the history of the United States. His loss to Republican George Deukmejian is more surprising in light of Democratic victories throughout the nation. In California, Democrats retained control of the legislature, strengthened their grip on the congressional delegation, and elected every statewide partisan officer below the rank of governor. Moreover, Democrats proclaimed a psychological victory of sorts by seeing five costly bond issues passed and Jerry Brown's supreme court judges retained (which Deukmejian opposed).

A number of factors have been proposed to explain the Bradley loss. These range from negative opinions of Bradley's wife to the large turnout of voters against the proposition to ban handguns. Although it is true that in a close election—Deukemejian won by 93,345 votes out of 7.5 million—any one or a combination of factors could have been fatal, we will contend that race was the major factor in Bradley's defeat. No other factor so readily explains the loss of a well-known, well-financed mainstream Democratic candidate in a Democratic state during an election in which Democrats who shared many of his positions won.

The dramatic rise in the number of black mayors over the last decade and a half (223 in 1982) represents a new stage in the evolution of American politics generally and black politics in particular. However, the increase tends to obscure the fact that black elected officials still represent only about

1 percent of all elected officials. The election of black mayors had almost always depended upon exceptionally high black turnout in cities with majority (or near majority) black populations. In other words, white votes have not supported black candidates, as the recent Chicago mayoral campaign has demonstrated. This white crossover to white Republicans or independents has occurred even though the black candidates have usually been Democrats in heavily Democratic cities.[1]

The fairly extensive literature on black mayors provides at least an indication of the obstacles facing a black gubernatorial candidate. William Nelson and Philip Meranto report that the first black mayors of major American cities received only a small percentage of the white vote even though they ran as Democrats in heavily Democratic cities. For instance, in the 1967 mayoral race in Gary, Indiana, Richard Hatcher received only 14 percent of the white vote. Carl Stokes was victorious in Cleveland in 1967 even though he received only 15 percent of the white vote.[2] Similarly, Newark's first black mayor, Kenneth Gibson, received a mere 15 percent of the white vote even though the white incumbent had been indicted for extortion and income tax evasion.[3] In New Orleans, Ernest Morial won the 1977 mayoral race with 19 percent of the white vote. Four years earlier the black candidate, Coleman Young, won with a mere 9 percent of the white vote in Detroit. Also in 1973, Maynard Jackson polled 23 percent of the white vote to win the mayor's race in Atlanta.[4] Obviously black mayoral candidates have been heavily dependent on the large black populations in these cities. Without extensive voter registration efforts, high black turnout and bloc voting from 88 to 97 percent, the black mayoral candidates in these cities would not have been successful. At the same time, white voter support ranged from 9 to 23 percent.

Tom Bradley's election as mayor of Los Angeles presents us with a different case, although even here race was not an irrelevant issue. In a city with a black population of only 18 percent (in 1970), race was a key factor in Bradley's loss in 1960 and in his 1973 victory. In the former case the incumbent, Sam Yorty, ran an openly racist runoff campaign after finishing second in the primary. He won with 53 percent of the vote. In both elections political scientists Donald Kinder and David Sears found that symbolic racism (sociocultural prejudice) was the major determinant in voting against Bradley among voters who felt threatened by blacks as well as those who did not. In other words, whites voted against the black candidate, regardless of whether or not blacks threatened their jobs, neighborhoods, or schools, because he represented a threat to traditional American values and the racial status quo.[5] The irony is, however, that these moral values—which include individualism, self-reliance, the work ethic, obedience, and discipline—are the very essence of Bradley's personality.

Much of the analysis of Bradley's efforts in Los Angeles have focused on the socioeconomic characteristics of white Bradley supporters. Harlan Hahn and his colleagues have argued that Bradley received greater support from white blue-collar workers than from middle and upper-middle class whites. They suggest that black politics may represent more than symbolic "recognition" of the racial group. It may mark a transition from ethnic to class politics.[6] Hahn's interpretation of working class white support from Bradley has been challenged by Robert Halley, Alan Acock, and Thomas Greene. They contend that middle-to-upper class whites supported Bradley to a greater extent than working class whites.[7]

Regardless of the socioeconomic status of white Bradley supporters, it appears that Bradley has increasingly diffused white opposition and gained increasing support in successive elections.[8] To the extent that this reflected a decline in white opposition was of little concern to Bradley. However, it undoubtedly also reflected a decline in black voter interest in Bradley.[9] The unreliability of survey polls on racial issues is a further cause for concern. In 1969 a *Los Angeles Times* poll predicted that Bradley would win by 53 percent.[10] Early in 1978 former black Congresswoman Yvonne Burke had led Deukmejian comfortably in the race for attorney general. However, two months prior to the election Burke's lead in the *California Polls* shrank from 12 to 4 percent.[11] Deukmejian won, carrying 48 of the 58 counties. In that same year, Mervin Dymally lost his bid for reelection as lieutenant governor while his running mate, Jerry Brown, won. Dymally won 43 percent of the vote and 12 counties. This split in party between the governor and lieutenant governor has occurred only twice in California history—both involved black candidates who lost—Dymally and Bradley.

While a number of reasons have been advanced for why Bradley lost the gubernatorial race, it is this author's contention that race was the major factor. It is interesting to note that the polls showed Bradley as the likely winner. We start, then, by discussing why they chose Bradley and end by explaining why and how Bradley lost in spite of the polls.

The Campaign and the Pollsters

Given the cases of Dymally and Burke, along with the data on black mayors, one must closely examine the conduct of the campaign as well as the polling data from a variety of sources to appreciate fully the role of race in the final results.

Bradley and Deukmejian agreed from the outset to conduct a "gentlemanly campaign." Both argued that race would not be a significant factor in the campaign. Of course, the overt use of race—unlike the Booker T. Washington era—would likely backfire in today's California. However, issues like law-and-order and welfare have been more recent, subtle appeals to white voters. The fact that Deukmejian centered his campaign around the issue of "getting tough on crime" might be taken as a covert appeal to white voters. Yet when one examines the Republican candidates' political career, it is difficult to find any other issue he could credibly run on.[12]

More importantly, Bradley was able to counter these subtly racial issues. His first televised commercials stressed his background in law enforcement and his willingness to be "tough on crime." Indeed, an early poll found Bradley scoring higher as a tough crime fighter than Deukmejian.[13] Furthermore, polls generally indicated that unemployment rather than crime ranked number one among voters as California's most pressing concern.

Bradley also campaigned as a fiscal conservative who did not raise taxes and had frequently balanced budgets with cuts in social services while mayor of Los Angeles. In addition, his pro-business, pro-development views were emphasized in an effort to attract business support and distance himself from incumbent governor Jerry Brown. Thus, the Democratic candidate made it difficult for Deukmejian to attack him as a "bleeding heart, big spending liberal."

Only one major California newspaper article focused on the racial issue. According to that *Los Angeles Times* story a number of political experts felt that race would be a factor in the campaign. Both Deukmejian and his campaign manager, Bill Roberts, insisted that race was a taboo issue and would not enter the campaign.[14] Ironically, less than two weeks later, it was Roberts, a former Reagan campaign manager, who introduced the subject. In an October 7 response to reporters, Roberts stated that "if we are down five points or less in the polls by election time, we're going to win."[15] According to Roberts, hidden anti-black sentiment among voters would swing a close election to Deukmejian. Bradley thought the comments were an insult to all the people of California. Five days after Robert's comments, Deukmejian accepted his resignation. At this point, Deukmejian's campaign seemed to be falling apart. Remarkably, at the same time, Bradley's lead in the polls shrank from 14 to 7 percent.[16] The reasons for his decline are not clear.

Pollsters generally believed that race would not be a significant factor in this election. While admitting the difficulty of obtaining accurate information on racial attitudes they apparently felt the responses they received were accurate. Two pollsters went so far as to state that Bradley's race would help him more than hurt him.

A Teichner Poll in late September found that 10 percent would vote for Bradley because he was black, while 12 percent favored Deukmejian because he was white. Teichner decided to stop asking this racial question because it did not seem to be an important factor in the campaign.[17]

I. A. Lewis, director of the *Los Angeles Times* Poll, asked six questions aimed at measuring "anti-black" attitudes. After subtracting "pro-black" attitudes, Lewis found a shift from Bradley to Deukmejian of about 7 or 8 percent, "presumably" caused by race. Lewis was quick to point out that the *Times* Poll "shows that factors other than race are far more influential in the current campaign."[18] He concluded that Bradley's party affiliation and the economy would benefit Bradley more than the issues of crime and race would aid Deukmejian.

In an article about an unscientific series of interviews with whites in San Jose, Democratic pollster Peter Hart stated that Bradley would benefit because he is "a non-threatening black whose values, background, and demeanor seem to be correct."[19] According to Hart, instead of the traditional backlash, whites would vote for Bradley because they wanted to do the right thing.

The most widely reported poll on racial attitudes was conducted in early October by *The California Poll*. Poll director Mervin Field found that 5 percent of all potential voters stated that they would not be inclined to vote for a candidate who is black. On the other hand, Field reported that 12 percent of the votes said they would be disinclined to vote for a candidate of Armenian descent. Since Deukmejian is Armenian, Field took this to mean that Deukmejian's background could potentially act as a greater drag to his chance of becoming Governor than being black works against Bradley.

Field's findings are not without their problems. Among the 5 percent who would not vote for a black man, 1 percent did favor Bradley. On the other hand, among the 12 percent who said they would not vote for an Armenian-American, 5 percent intended to vote for Deukmejian. One might guess that these contradictory findings either mean that 1 percent and 5 percent respectively of those polled did not know the ancestry of the candidate or that they were voting for him despite their prejudice or because of greater prejudice toward the other candidate. Indeed, most concede that Bradley's race was far better known than Deukmejian's ethnicity. Moreover, when pited against each other it is likely that the anti-black prejudice would be more intense than anti-Armenian prejudice. The same poll, for example, found that 16 percent of the voters were not inclined to vote for a lawyer. Yet since both major candidates were lawyers, it is unlikely that this anti-lawyer prejudice prevented all those polled from voting for one of the major candidates on election day.

In short, Field was the only pollster to suggest that ethnic prejudice against Deukmejian could possibly outweigh Bradley's race. Given the well-known problems in obtaining accurate data on racial attitudes, Fields' suggestions are ill-advised at best.[20]

Bradley, of course, was aware that his campaign was historic. His campaign made no mistakes comparable to the Robert's incident. He avoided controversial issues, appealed to powerful interests, and did not give the appearance of making special appeals to minorities or liberals. In fact, his image was so moderate that the United Farm Workers did not endorse him nor did the California League of Conservation Voters. Despite his pro-business, pro-development views, corporate campaign contributions went almost entirely to the Republican candidate. For example, the oil industry favored Deukmejian in contributions by a 5-1 margin. As a Standard Oil of California official stated, "both are good candidates, but Deukmejian fits the bill a little better than Bradley."[21] Thus, Bradley's moderation did not pay off in terms of support for major business and agricultural interests.

A little noted but nonetheless significant use of race was injected into the campaign by Bradley himself. In a subtle way Bradley attempted to persuade voters that voting for him was comparable to voting for the American Dream. He wanted voters to prove that the sky was unlimited in California, that a poor black sharecropper's son could become governor of the nation's largest state. This Horatio Alger theme appeared in campaign literature and in Bradley's public statements. In a speech to the Commonwealth Club of San Francisco, the Democratic candidate said, "If I could have the optimistic outlook that I've enjoyed all my life—when there wasn't really any hope or any real promise that it was going to work—why can't we of this state have that same kind of optimism? . . . When I was a youngster and talked in these almost pollyannish terms, there were some people around me who said 'you're out of your mind. Nothing good can ever happen to you, or us'."[22]

Perhaps the most dramatic instance of this attempt to use race in a positive manner came in the last televised debate between the two major gubernatorial candidates on October 26. In his two-minute concluding statement, Bradley stressed his experience and ability to get people to pull together. Then he told the story of a little Hispanic boy who sent Bradley four dollars that he had earned cutting grass. According to Bradley the boy gave him the money because he hoped to be governor someday and saw Bradley as a hero to be emulated.[23] (Thus, in one dramatic moment Bradley became not only the role model for aspiring blacks but also Hispanics and all those who believed in the American Dream.) Bradley was endorsed by the Mexican-American Political Association and by his Chicano primary election opponent Mario Obledo.

Deukmejian was not averse to using his own humble roots to appeal to immigrants. Speaking to the Republican Asian-Americans in San Francisco, he recited the "European immigrants creed" to an audience which included members of a successful first generation with Korean, Japanese, Indonesian, Indochinese, Filipino, Chinese, and Russian backgrounds.[24] Yet Deukmejian's forays into the minority communities across the state were relatively rare. The Los Angeles Times reported that Deukmejian visited the Latino community only once during the campaign with Vice-President George Bush, who speaks Spanish.[25]

The Election

Tom Bradley's loss to George Deukmejian by less than 1 percent brought the race issue to the forefront. Given Bradley's lead in the polls, no other single issue seems to explain the outcome. One minute before the polls closed election night, pollster Mervin Field projected Bradley the winner by 10 points. Bradley held what seemed to be a victory dinner the night before at Chasen's in Beverly Hills. On election night his aides were already explaining his victory to Los Angeles television viewers.

Even as the returns came in the pollsters differed in their projections. When all three major networks projected Deukmejian as the winner, their San Francisco affiliates stuck with Bradley. The difference might be explained by their methods. The national television networks had extra people in key precincts actually counting the ballots. Local stations were relying on pollsters conducting exit interviews.[26] Apparently, a significant group of voters were saying one thing to pollsters but had, in reality, voted the opposite way.

After the results were in, Bradley's friends and aides began to examine the racial issue. Campaign chairman Nelson Rising said: "Maybe Bill Roberts was right. But it's still such a repugnant concept and I can't deal with it."[27] Media consultant Hank Morris suggested that Deukmejian sanctioned commercials designed to send out subtle reminders about Bradley's race. One such radio spot featured country actor Slim Pickens talking about how his "Daddy told me never to trust a skunk or politician."[28] *The Dictionary of American Slang* defines "skunk" as a derogatory term for a black. Another ad showed two senior citizens talking about how "California certainly has changed a lot."[29] An ad on crime featured a black behind bars and another breaking into the home of a white couple.[30]

Deukmejian's former campaign manager, Rising, has suggested that ads focusing on rape and electing a governor for ALL Californians, plus various statements by campaign directors, underscored the racial issue. While denying the racism charge in regard to campaign tactics, he agrees that racism was a favor in about 7 percent of the vote.[31]

Black friends of the Los Angeles mayor were more direct in their criticism. Assemblywoman Maxine Waters said, "He was the best of what a fair society could look for, and they rejected him."[32] State Senator Diane Watson added that "there is an element of racism in the electorate that you cannot factor into poll figures."[33] Former Congresswoman Yvonne Burke and A. M. E. Bishop H. H. Brookins also went on record in attributing the defeat to racism.

Thomas Pettigrew reports that along with subtle code words and an attempt to link Bradley with the far left and militant blacks, Deukmejian forces engaged in "dirty tricks." These included some racist leaflets in Spanish and another leaflet linking Bradley with atheism. Pettigrew also contends that some Democratic opposition groups were funded by the Deukmejian camp. In several cases Democratic candidates did not list Bradley on their campaign literature.[34]

Bradley, himself, was not willing to concede that race was a factor and may have been used against him. He carefully stated his position in a post-election interview:

> I always said I did not think there would be a significant racial element in the election. I wasn't saying there would be no degree of racial motivation.[35]

Some pollsters supported Bradley's position. Steve Teichner said his election day poll showed "no substantiation that race was an issue."[36] After reviewing pre-election survey data, election day exit polls, and official election returns, Mervin Field's *California Poll* concluded that "the late shift in the preference of white voters, who comprised 85 percent of the electorate, was the final element that Deukmejian needed to overcome Bradley's overall pre-election lead."[37] Election day surveys revealed that Deukmejian outpolled Bradley among white voters by 12 percentage points (55 percent to 43 percent). This 12 percent gap should be compared with Field's election day survey finding that 3 percent of Deukmejian's supporters actually stated that "they could not vote for a black man."[38] According to Field other factors contributing to Bradley's defeat were the low Hispanic and Asian turnout, Bradley's support of the handgun registration initiative, and the large absentee vote among Republicans.[39]

A CBS/*New York Times* poll also found that 3 percent of the electorate opposed Bradley on racial grounds. An exit poll for the *Los Angeles Times* found that 8 percent of the Democrats and independents who went for Deukmejian felt that government was doing too much for blacks and other minorities. On the other hand, of the Republicans who voted for Bradley, 5 percent said they felt the government was giving too little attention to blacks and minorities. Subtracting the pro-black votes from the anti-black votes leaves Deukmejian with a surplus of about 3 percent, or 200,000 votes.[40] Other political observers attributed the loss to various other phenomena. Some argued that gun-issue voters came out in record numbers to vote against Bradley. This argument was countered by those that believed that the nuclear freeze issue brought out more liberal voters. The anti-Brown backlash was seen by some as hurting Bradley. Others said Bradley lacked the charisma and organization to bring out large numbers of minority voters.

A post-election survey of voters conducted by V. Lance Tarrance and Associates reported that undecided voters broke six-to-four in favor of Deukmejian. This last-minute shift, which accounted for 16 percent of Deukmejian's support, was strongest in the Sacramento area and in southern California. The survey also suggested that several factors were responsible for undecided voters going to Deukmejian: (1) his tough stance on crime, (2) his statewide experience, and (3) Bradley's race.[41] Robert Staples reports that Bradley's own pollsters found that 10 percent of the whites they surveyed consistently said that they thought Bradley would do too much for blacks, while an additional 10 to 15 percent said they didn't know. In addition, 9 percent of those described as liberal voted for Deukmejian out of a personal dislike for Bradley.[42]

In summary the post-election surveys show a range of anti-black sentiment from 3 to 10 percent. The large undecided vote ranged from 7 to 15 percent and eventually favored Deukmejian. Historically, pollsters have attributed large numbers of "undecided" voters to hidden anti-racist feelings.

Analysis of the Election Returns[43]

In an effort to assess the influence of race as compared to other issues on the gubernatorial results we have analyzed the relationship between Democratic registration and the vote for the major Democratic candidates on a county-by-county level. Where the votes fall below the Democratic registration it has been labeled Democratic crossover. Two highly controversial initiatives—one supporting the registration of handguns (Proposition 12) and the other supporting a nuclear weapons freeze (Proposition 15)—have generally been seen as playing a role in the election results. We have introduced these issues as control elements in order to assess their impact on the Democratic candidates.

California Poll data from late October reveal that 39.1 percent of the registered Republicans surveyed supported handgun registration while 60.9 percent opposed such registration. Registered Democrats were in favor of handgun registration with 67 percent for and 33 percent against. Democratic support for and Republican opposition to handgun registration would seem to indicate that many of those Democrats opposing Bradley were doing so for reasons other than his support of Proposition 12. Moreover, the election of a Democrat who supported Proposition 12 (John Van De Kamp) as attorney general provides further evidence that Bradley's defeat may be dependent on factors other than gun registration. Proposition 15, the nuclear freeze initiative, found the Democrats also evenly split with 50.9 percent in favor and 49.1 percent opposed. Republicans, on the other hand, were decidedly anti-freeze with 65.3 percent opposed and only 34.7 percent in favor of Proposition 15.[44]

The mean crossover suffered by Bradley was compared to that of other Democrats in statewide races. These include the lieutenant governor's race which pitted Democrat Leo McCarthy against Republican Carol Hallett, the attorney general's race with Democrat John Van De Kamp opposing Republican George Nicholson, the Senate race matching Democrat Jerry Brown against Republican Pete Wilson and the nonpartisan race for superintendent of public instruction in which black incumbent Wilson Riles faced William Honig, a more conservative white challenger.

Using Democratic registration figures, Table 5.1 reveals that all three losing candidates suffered significantly greater Democratic defections than either McCarthy or Van De Kamp who won. Democratic voters appear most displeased with Jerry Brown (13.02%), followed by the two black candidates, Bradley (8.54%) and Riles (8.26%).

Table 5.2 provides further illumination of the crossover phenomenon. There is a stronger correlation between the Bradley vote and Democratic crossover than there is with the vote for any other candidate including Brown. The strong negative relationship indicates areas that gave the least support to Bradley had the highest crossover. This strongly suggests that it was not high Republican turnout, but rather Democratic defection, that caused Bradley the most difficulty. While this crossover also hurt the other candidates, its effect was less severe.

There is a significant negative correlation between the crossover vote against all five Democratic candidates and pro-handgun registration and pro-nuclear freeze vote (see Table 5.3). This relationship is strongest in the case of the Brown crossover and weakest in the school superintendent race. In this latter case one might expect issues related to education to be more salient to the campaign. However, it is important to note that Van De Kamp, the candidate for attorney general who favored the handgun initiative, was not as strongly affected by the pro-handgun registration vote as was Bradley and McCarthy.

Table 5.1   Democratic Crossover in Five Races in all Counties

Candidate	Mean	Standard Deviation
Bradley	8.54	7.32
McCarthy	3.52	5.02
VanDeKamp	4.00	4.88
Brown	13.02	6.44
Riles	8.26	6.93

Table 5.2   Democratic Crossover Correlated with
Vote for Democratic Candidates by County

Candidate	Pearsons Correlations[a]	Pearsons Correlations[b]	Pearsons Correlations[c]
Bradley	−0.72 (p=0.000)	−0.92 (p=0.013)	−0.74 (p=0.000)
McCarthy	−0.58 (p=0.000)	−0.88 (p=0.025)	−0.50 (p=0.000)
VanDeKamp	−0.48 (p=0.000)	−0.79 (p=0.055)	−0.48 (p=0.000)
Brown	−0.70 (p=0.000)	−0.96 (p=0.005)	−0.63 (p=0.000)
Riles	−0.66 (p=0.000)	−0.84 (p=0.036)	−0.72 (p=0.000)

[a]The vote for each candidate in all 58 counties.
[b]The vote for each candidate in 5 counties with a significant black population.
[c]The vote for each candidate in 53 counties with predominantly white populations.

The emphasis on race does not explain, however, the poor showing of Jerry Brown among Democrats. In Table 5.4, partial correlations are calculated controlling for the pro-handgun ban vote, the pro-nuclear freeze vote, and both votes combined (a second order correlation). Table 5.3 reveals that the Democratic crossover from Brown to his Republican opponent is primarily a function of the handgun issue and the nuclear freeze

Table 5.3   Crossover Vote in Five Democratic Races Correlated
with Pro-Handgun Registration and Pro-Nuclear Freeze Votes
in all 58 Counties

Candidate	Gun Vote (Pearsons Corr.)	Nuke Vote (Pearsons Corr.)
Bradley	−0.74 (p=0.000)	−0.74 (p=0.000)
McCarthy	−0.64 (p=0.000)	−0.72 (p=0.000)
VanDeKamp	−0.54 (p=0.000)	−0.44 (p=0.000)
Brown	−0.83 (p=0.000)	−0.80 (p=0.000)
Riles	−0.04 (p=0.000)	−0.13 (p=0.000)

Table 5.4   Partial Co-efficients of Correlations Between
Mean Democratic Crossover and the Percentage Vote
for Five Statewide Candidates in all 58 Counties

Candidate	Partial Corr.[a]	Partial Corr.[b]	Partial Corr.[c]
Bradley	−0.31 (p=0.010)	−0.26 (p=0.025)	−0.21 (p=0.074)
McCarthy	−0.33 (p=0.006)	−0.16 (p=0.109)[d]	−0.17 (p=0.111)[d]
VanDeKamp	−0.26 (p=0.026)	−0.33 (p=0.006)	−0.26 (p=0.024)
Brown	−0.12 (p=0.176)[d]	−0.14 (p=0.140)	−0.02 (p=0.429)
Riles	−0.66 (p=0.000)	−0.66 (p=0.000)	−0.64 (p=0.000)

[a]*Controlling on pro-handgun registration vote*
[b]*Controlling on pro-nuclear freeze vote*
[c]*Controlling on both handgun and nuclear freeze votes*
[d]*Not significant*

issue. When we control for these issues separately and together, we find that the mean Democratic crossover is no longer significantly correlated with the Brown vote. For Bradley, Riles, Van De Kamp, and to a lesser extent McCarthy, the mean crossover remains significantly correlated with their percentage votes when the two issues are controlled. Thus the explanation for the defeat of Bradley and Riles lies in the much larger crossover as revealed in Table 5.1, while McCarthy and Van De Kamp had fewer defections and won.

Election results indicate a turnout of 67.7 percent; state officials had predicted a 69.3 percent turnout. The average for the previous 20 years was 74 percent. Democratic San Francisco turned out at only a 62.3 percent rate, while Republican Orange County did a little better at 66.2 percent. Preliminary findings reveal that the turnout in minority areas was as high or higher than it was in white areas.[45] However, *The California Poll* suggests that the minority turnout was just 15 percent of the total vote, or 5 percent below the predicted level and was especially low for Hispanics.[46]

Official registration figure statewide indicate that 53.2 percent of those registered were Democrats, while 34.9 percent were Republicans with the remainder belonging to minor parties or independents. This 5-to-3 registration edge gave Democrats a majority in 55 of California's 58 counties. Despite that margin, Bradley managed to win only 14 counties. In Sacramento County, which Democrats were expected to carry, Bradley lost by 25,000 votes. Even in his home county of Los Angeles, Bradley won only 52 percent of the vote, while Deukmejian carried Orange County with 61 percent of the vote. This gave Deukmejian a surplus of 22,000 votes in two populous counties.

Perhaps the election results are most revealing when Bradley's totals are compared with those of his Democratic running mate for lieutenant governor, Leo McCarthy. McCarthy, a white state assemblyman, polled 52 percent of the vote compared to 44 percent for his Republican opponent. Twenty-nine counties gave McCarthy a majority as compared to the 14 won by Bradley. Even in heavily Democratic counties like Alameda (which includes Oakland), the liberal McCarthy won 63 percent of the vote while Bradley could only manage 59 percent. Democratic candidates for secretary of state, state controller, state treasurer, and attorney general also won by large margins. The election of the liberal Van De Kamp for attorney general by 11 percent over his Republican opponent is particularly significant given the claim that Deukmejian won as a result of his tough position on crime.

Discussion

The extraordinary nature of the 1982 gubernatorial campaign is given added significance when placed in historical perspective. Over the last 11 major elections from 1960 to 1972, two counties, Plumas and San Francisco, have placed in the top 10 Democratic counties in percentage of Democratic votes cast in 10 of those 11 elections. Bradley lost Plumas county. Following San Francisco and Plumas as those counties giving the highest percentage of Democratic votes cast in each of the major elections for the entire period are Shasta, Solano, Alameda, and Lassen counties in that order.[47] Among these six most Democratic counties in California, Bradley lost in Plumas, Shasta, Solano, and Lassen. Even in the highly urban counties of Alameda and San Francisco he trailed his white running mate by a significant margin. Table 5.5 shows the total percentage votes for Bradley and McCarthy in each of the six heavily Democratic counties.

Table 5.5   Total Percentages in Democratic Counties

County	Bradley	McCarthy
San Francisco	66.5%	77.9%
Plumas	42.4	51.6
Shasta	38.7	50.2
Solano	46.3	54.1
Alameda	58.9	63.4
Lassen	38.0	47.4

The statewide average for Bradley was 48.1 percent compared to McCarthy's 52.2 percent for a difference of 4.1 percent. In the six most Democratic counties the difference between Bradley and McCarthy averaged 8 percent.

While it seems clear that the Democrats did not do as well in rural counties like Shasta, Lassen, and Plumas as in the urban counties of San Francisco and Alameda, the Democratic crossover remains much greater for Bradley than McCarthy regardless of location.

Another measure that lends historical perspective to the 1982 election is an examination of the "most representative" counties over the 1960–1972 period. Eugene Lee states that Yuba, San Joaquin, and Los Angeles counties consistently voted the closest to the percentage division of the two-party total of the state vote for the winning candidate at each election. During the 12-year period Yuba's vote division was always within a range of 3.0 percent, San Joaquin's 3.3 percent, and Los Angeles, 3.6 percent. The ranges of all other counties exceeded 4 percent.[48] For the 1982 governors' race, Yuba's vote division was 4.5 percent above the state average for the winner, San Joaquin's was 10.8 percent above, and Los Angeles 3.4 percent below the state average. Only Los Angeles, then, remained consistent in regard to voting patterns in the election period from 1960 to 1972.

Whether we look at consistently Democratic counties, or simply consistent counties, the pattern remains the same. Bradley's vote totals are significantly lower than those given to other Democrats in 1982 and in the 1960-to-1972 period. These Democratic defections seem to occur in both rural and urban settings and in northern as well as southern California. Bradley won only one southern county—his home base—Los Angeles, which remained consistent with previous election averages.

The 10 years between 1972 and 1982 were a period of great growth in California. Increasing numbers of Asian and Mexican immigrants, as well as continued Anglo migration to California, have created a state political culture that is extremely diversified and constantly changing. To state that California may be categorized as a particular type of political culture is extremely risky. California's last three governors—Ronald Reagan, Jerry Brown, and Deukmejian—have been more ideological than most. Yet they have run the spectrum from very conservative to strongly liberal. Perhaps Bradley's pragmatic political style and moderate position on issues were incapable of rallying the necessary support. And maybe Bradley's attempt to construct a campaign modeled after his successful city campaign in Los Angeles ignored the complexity of a statewide race. At this point our knowledge of state political cultures provides little help in analyzing Bradley's defeat. Our knowledge of urban politics is helpful in predicting significant white Democratic opposition to Bradley although Bradley did better among white voters than all major city black mayors excluding himself.

Conclusion

Our analysis indicates that race was the major factor in Bradley's defeat.* Obviously, in an election decided by less than 100,000 votes out of a total of 7.5 million, a number of factors can be put forward. The anti-Brown vote did not appear to significantly affect the lieutenant governors' race despite the winner being a liberal who led the state assembly for six of Jerry Brown's eight years in office. The handgun issue did not prevent the liberal, John Van De Kamp, from winning a position formerly held by Deukmejian as attorney general. Our data reveal that the handgun initiative and nuclear freeze issues affected all candidates and especially Jerry Brown. However, race had an independent effect that caused the defeat of Bradley, and by extension, Wilson Riles.

Given the unreliability of survey data on voter motivations and attitudes in regard to race, we have attempted to assess indirectly the impact of such attitudes by examining the conduct of the campaign, the views of professional pollsters, and the Democratic crossover vote. In addition, a look at the other controversial issues on the ballot and the vote in historically Democratic counties seem to strengthen our contention that race was exceptionally significant in the gubernatorial election.

Our survey of the literature on elections involving black mayors and the errors in previous pre-election polls in California demonstrate that Bradley's pre-election lead was unrealistically high. White voters, particularly Democrats, are often not willing to admit their opposition to Democratic candidates on racial grounds. In addition, one should not expect other racial minorities to turn out or vote for black candidates at the same level as black voters.[49]

Bradley's loss will have national repercussions. It is unrealistic to consider black candidates for major party national tickets until a black is successful in capturing a governorship. Bradley, as a mainstream candidate in a relatively liberal state, represented the best hope of reaching that milestone. While he almost made it, his defeat will make it more difficult for future black candidates to gain support. Eight million dollars is not a sum easily obtained. Bradley had given indications that he was thinking of national office. However, for now he is content with running for reelection as mayor of Los Angeles in 1986.

Black gubernatorial candidates cannot depend on high black voter turnout to push them to victory in predominantly white states. Neither can they rely on party identification to swing the results in their favor. They must run issue-oriented campaigns and forge new alliances on the basis of those issues.[50] Yet a black candidate running for the office of chief executive of

---

*Bradley also lost a 1986 election to Deukmejian by a 2-to-1 margin.

a state must also be exceptionally aware of the "politics of style." The candidate must maintain the interest of and support minorities while not alienating white voters. It is a task with no proven formula for success.

Notes

1. William E. Nelson Jr., and Philip J. Meranto, *Electing Black Mayors*, (Columbus Ohio: Ohio State University Press, 1977); Charles H. Levine, *Racial Conflict and the American Mayor*, (Lexington, Mass.: Heath, 1974), K. G. Weinberg, *Black Victory: Carl Stokes and the Winning of Cleveland* (Chicago: Quadrangle, 1968); Michael B. Preston, et al., eds. *The New Black Politics*, (N.Y.: Longman, 1982), Harlan Hahn, et al. "Cleavage, Coalitions, and the Black Candidate: The Los Angeles Mayoralty Elections of 1969 and 1973," *Western Political Quarterly* vol. 19, no. 1, 1976: 507-20; Robert M. Halley, et al. "Ethnicity and Social Class: Voting in the 1973 Los Angeles Municipal Elections," *Western Political Quarterly* vol. 29, no. 1, 1976: 521-30.

2. Nelson and Meranto, *Electing Black Mayors*; Levine, *Racial Conflict*; Yong Hyo Cho, "City Politics and Racial Polarization" (Presented at the annual Meeting of the Midwest Political Science Association, Chicago, 1972); Joseph McCormick, "The Continuing Significance of Race," (Presented at the Annual Meeting of the American Political Science Association, Washington, D.C., 1979).

3. Charles P. Henry, "Black Political Parties: The Politics of Race" (M.A. Thesis University of Chicago, 1971).

4. "Integrating Atlanta's Power Elite," *Business Week,* November 24.

5. Donald R. Kinder and David O. Sears, "Prejudice and Politics," *Journal of Personality and Social Psychology*, vol. 40, no. 3, 1981: 414-31.

6. Harlan Hahn, "Cleavage, Coalitions, and the Black Candidate"; Harland and Timothy Almy, "Ethnic Politics and Racial Issues: Voting in Los Angeles" *Western Political Quarterly* vol. 24 (1971); Hahn and David Klingman *Western Political Quarterly* vol. 29 (1976). Vincent Jeffries and J. Edward Ransford argue that racial prejudice cuts across class lines affecting both blue-collar workers and white-collar professionals; see "Ideology, Social Structure, and the Yorty-Bradley Mayoral Election," *Social Problems* vol. 19 (1972).

7. Halley, "Ethnicity and Social Class"; Alan C. Acock and Robert M. Halley "Ethnic Politics and Issues Reconsidered: Comments on an Earlier Study," *Western Political Quarterly*, vol. 28, no. 1 (1975): 737-38.

8. John O'Loughlin "The Election of Black Mayors, 1977," *Annal of the Association of American Geographers* vol. 70, no. 3 (1980): 353-70.

9. John O'Loughlin reports that the 1977 turnout rate was 18 percent lower than the 1973 turnout rate in the Los Angeles mayoral election: see his "The Election of Black Mayors, 1977," 367.

10. I. R. McPhail "The Vote for Mayor of Los Angeles in 1969" *Annals of the Association of American Geographers*, vol. 61 (1971): 744-58.

11.   "California Poll September, 1978, and November, 1978" *Field Institute Survey Code Book, Data File Nos.*: fl7808–09 (1978).

12.   As a state legislator from 1963 to 1978, Deukmejian had focused his attention on crime. He authored the state's "use-a-gun, go-to-prison" law and other mandatory prison sentence laws. He was a leader in efforts to restore the death penalty and claims credit for over 180 laws designed to make California a "safer place to live." In 1978 he was elected attorney general, defeating a black congresswomen, Yvonne Burke.

13.   Tim Reiterman, "Deukmejian vs. Bradley: Their Records on Crime," *San Francisco Sunday Examiner and Chronicle*, June 13, 1982.

14.   William Endicott, "Bradley Win as Governor Would be Significant Event," *Los Angeles Times*, September 26, 1982.

15.   John Balzar, "Deukmejian's Denials," *San Francisco Chronicle*, October 19, 1982.

16.   "Deukmejian Cutting Bradley's Lead," *San Francisco Chronicle*, October 17, 1982.

17.   Carl Irving, "Pollsters: Being Black May Help as Much as it Hinders Bradley," *San Francisco Examiner*, October 24, 1982.

18.   I. A. Lewis, "The Race Vote Is There, But Not Hidden," *Los Angeles Times*, October 24, 1982.

19.   James Perry, "Bradley's Quiet Style Reassures Many Voters in California Campaign," *Wall Street Journal*, October 11, 1982.

20.   The attempt by pollsters to balance antiblack attitudes with prejudice against ethnics is reminiscent of the ethnic analogy. According to this view blacks are but the most recent of a long series of emigrants to America's urban centers. They are expected to work their way up the ladder of success as have the Irish, Italians, and Poles. The obstacles faced by these ethnics and now the Armenian-Americans are seen as comparable to the prejudice confronting black advancement. This analogy has been effectively rebutted in a number of works (Frank and Resnik, 1973; Bachrach and Baratz, 1970; Barnett and Hefner, 1976; Thernstrom, 1983). Critics generally point to the involuntary nature of black emigration during slavery, the slave experience, the permanent and visible badge of skin color, the long-standing rather than recent presence of blacks in urban America, and finally a limited economy as unique conditions that make the black experience different.

21.   Bill Boyarsky and Narda Zacchino, "Business Contributing Heavily to Deukmejian," *Los Angeles Times*, October 3, 1982.

22.   Larry Leibert "Bradley Tells the Story of His Success," *San Francisco Chronicle*, September 25, 1982.

23.   League of Women Voters, "Campaign '82 Debate," Televised Gubernatorial Debate, San Diego, October 26, 1982.

24.   Carl Irving, "Deukmejian Tells of Humble Roots" *San Francisco Examiner*, October 22, 1982.

25.   *Los Angeles Times*, October 31, 1982.

26.   John Balzar, "Why Pollsters Goofed," *San Francisco Chronicle*, November 4, 1982.

27. John Jacobs, "Bradley's Aides Find a Few Harsh Reasons for Unexpected Loss," *San Francisco Examiner*, November 11, 1982.

28. Nancy Skelton, "Bradley Says Loss Doesn't Narrow Political Options," *The Tribune*, November 21, 1982.

29. Jacobs, "Bradley's Aides Find a Few Harsh Reasons for Unexpected Loss."

30. John Balzar, "Voter's Biases Revealed," *San Francisco Chronicle*, November 14, 1982. Note that his videotape was prepared by Deukmejian in his role as attorney general and not as a campaign advertisement.

31. "Campaign Chiefs Review Election," *The Tribune,* August 27, 1983.

32. Richard Bergholz, "Recount a Possibility, Mayor Says," *Los Angeles Times*, November 4, 1982.

33. Ibid.

34. Lecture by Thomas Pettigrew, Institute for Social Change, Berkeley, California, October 27, 1983.

35. Nancy Skelton, "Bradley Says Loss Doesn't Narrow Political Options."

36. Jayne Garrison "Did Racism Cost Bradley the Election," *The Enterprise*, November 7, 1982.

37. Mervin D. Field "The Four Keys to Bradley's Election Defeat," *San Francisco Chronicle*, February 1, 1983.

38. Garrison, "Did Racism Cost Bradley the Election."

39. Field, "The Four Keys to Bradley's Election Defeat."

40. Richard Bergholz, "Anti-Bradley Vote Seen as Key Election Factor," *Los Angeles Times*, November 7, 1982.

41. "Last-minute Votes Gave Victory to Deukmejian," *The Tribune*, November 20, 1982.

42. Robert Staples, "Tom Bradley's Defeat: The Impact of Racial Symbols on Political Campaigns," *The Black Scholar*, Fall 1982: 37-45.

43. All data for this section are from the "Report of Registration" October, 1982 and from the "November 2, 1981 General Election Official Canvass" December 10, 1982, California Secretary of State, unless otherwise indicated. Means, Pearsons Correlations, and Partial Coefficients of Correlation for the five candidates and two issues are based on percent registered (Democratic) and percent of votes received in each of California's 58 counties. My thanks to Professor Percy Hintzen for his assistance with this section.

44. *The California Poll* data for late October 1982 (#8207) is for 1976 respondents including 764 who listed themselves as registered Republicans and 1009 who indicated they were registered Democrats. The party registration of these respondents was then cross-tabulated with Proposition 12 and 15.

45. Bergholz, "Recount a Possibility, Mayor Says."

46. Field, "The Four Keys to Bradley's Election Defeat."

47. Eugene C. Lee and Bruce E. Keith, *California Votes 1960–1972* (Berkeley: Institute of Governmental Studies, 1974).

48. Ibid.

49. As in his races for mayor of Los Angeles, Bradley did not do particularly well among Hispanic voters. The conservative *California Viewpoint* re-

ported that Deukmejian won about 150,000 Hispanic votes, twice the number Republicans traditionally gain statewide; see Jack Stevens, "Viva Duke!" *California Viewpoint*, November 1982:4.

50. In his successful bid for a Senate seat in Massachusetts in 1966, Edward Brooke witnessed a steady erosion of his pre-election lead in the months prior to the election. He chose to meet the racial issue head-on and the downtrend in his support was sharply reversed; see John F. Becker and Eugene E. Heaton, Jr., "The Election of Senator Edward W. Brooke," *Public Opinion Quarterly* 31 (Fall 1967).

PART TWO

Black Elected Officials and Political Participation

SIX

Black Political Progress in the 1980s: the Electoral Arena

Linda Williams

The impact of the civil rights movement, including the struggle for voting rights, has had a profound impact on American society. It has significantly altered disenfranchisement despite the continuation of many barriers. The following analysis, first, demonstrates that blacks have made substantial progress in exercising their voting rights since 1968; second, shows that there has been progress in the election of blacks to public office; third, summarizes major research findings on the benefits resulting from black political participation and the election of black elected officials; and fourth, concludes that thus far black electoral power has been unable to change significantly one major component of black subordination, economic deprivation, which still severely limits the rights won by the civil rights movement. Two critical questions confronting black Americans today are: 1) how to employ more studiously and creatively the ballot as a lever of power; and 2) whether political rights, however well exercised, are appropriate for bringing about basic economic change or whether a whole new set of structures and tactics is needed.

Context: The Importance of Voting

The goal of achieving progress in the electoral arena is often placed in the context of conventional wisdom that serves democratic theory. For example, the vote is said to be basic to all other rights and is perhaps the most precious right in any democracy. Through voting, it is said, groups can elect officials from their own group, who will serve their interests. Such statements, however, are rarely based on systemic empirical research. They are usually calculated to encourage action, but the role of electoral participation in helping citizens secure concessions from their government must still be one of the crucial questions for the study of democratic politics.

Addressing this fundamental question in 1940, black political scientist Ralph Bunche wrote:

> The vote has become a fetish with many Negroes, but there is little evidence that social problems anywhere in the world are solved by fetishism. . . . The great masses of whites, throughout the country, who have long been enfranchised, have been able to make but little progress toward solutions of many of their own problems with the ballot.[1]

However, by the 1960s Dr. Martin Luther King, Jr. concluded: "If Negroes could vote . . . there would be no more oppressive poverty directed against Negroes: our children would not be crippled by segregated schools, and the whole community might live together in harmony."[2]

Twenty years after the passage of the Voting Rights Act of 1965, few are as completely confident about the role of the vote in promoting equality in the socioeconomic realm as King was in the early 1960s. Yet most perspectives seem to fall into one of two broad categories typified by Bunche and King: political pessimism or political optimism. Both perspectives have been supported by numerous policy-oriented social scientists.

On the optimistic side, Campbell and Feagin have argued that the strong resistance of whites themselves to black voting belie the idea that there is no power to be gained by means of the electoral system. They contend that whites have recognized that influence and control come with political power and that this is:

> why white terrorist groups sought to drive white and black coalitions from office in the South during Reconstruction, in the disenfranchisement of blacks through the first fifty years of the twentieth century, and in institutional discrimination methods currently utilized to maintain electoral control.[3]

Andrew Greeley has argued that most militant action by blacks, violent or peaceful, has been "counterproductive while, on the contrary, the election of black mayors in several American cities with the help of white voters has established that a broad political consensus is not by any means impossible."[4] Levy and Kramer have not only contended that black Americans should get on with the so far successful business of expanding their power through electoral politics, but have also suggested that, though "far from its own goals the black use of electoral power is an example all ethnics should be following."[5]

The reasons for this optimism are diverse, but among them would be a view contrary to Bunche's, i.e., that the strategy of the ballot has in fact worked for many ethnic groups in the United States, the assumption that black Americans, once barriers to voting are fully removed, are likely to participate actively in electoral politics, and the faith that America's electoral-representative system can be made to work for black Americans.

However, these essentially optimistic views of the potential impact of black electoral participation are more than matched by the large number of pessimistic views. In the mid-1960s Matthews and Pronthro suggested that the benefits available to blacks through electoral politics often had been exaggerated, that talk of the vote as the key to racial equality was "political hyperbole."[6] Keech, in a study of black politics in two southern cities, concluded that it is questionable whether electoral successes could "eliminate the inequality with which three and a half centuries of discrimination had saddled the American Negro."[7] Piven and Cloward have contended that black political participation has resulted in leadership co-optation and few tangible benefits for rank-and-file blacks.[8] Jones maintained that black elected officials cannot reorder such priorities as housing, fair employment, consumer protection, police-community relations, and public education. He concluded that the "keys to black liberation lie somewhere external to electoral politics."[9] Walton contended that most black elected officials hold office in deprived areas and are powerless to effect change beneficial to blacks.[10] Greer found that few positive benefits had accrued to blacks since the election of a black mayor in Gary, Indiana.[11] Greenberg went even further, maintaining that electoral participation supported the racial status quo and was diversionary to the best interests of blacks.[12]

The reasons for these pessimistic views of black electoral participation are complex. There seem to be two schools of thought: a rationale on the left which is pessimistic because of the lack of political and economic resources among blacks,[13] the constraints of past discrimination, institutional racism, and the slow pace of change brought about through the electoral process,[14] and the hegemonic nature of capitalist power;[15] and a rationale on the right which is pessimistic because blacks are viewed as incapable of organizing politically in great enough numbers to be a strong voting bloc, unsophisticated in their use of the ballot and choice of party and candidates, and ignorant of the proper roles of the private and public sectors. The left rationale focuses on the system, the right rationale seems to blame blacks themselves.

This review has only begun to list the advocates and critics of black participation in electoral politics, and this chapter has no intention of trying to resolve this fundamental policy debate. But a critical point in its resolution is the standard of evaluation. Whether or not blacks are evaluated as successful in electoral politics doubtless depends on the criteria used. Small or inconsequential breakthroughs for some may be of great magnitude for others.

In spite of this policy debate, blacks are participating in electoral politics and winning political office in increasing numbers. It is this political phenomenon that is the explicit focus of this chapter. While account will be taken of the policy debate, the task here is basically a descriptive one; it also poses a few fundamental questions that must be answered before anyone can fully evaluate the link between black participation and electoral benefits:

1. What progress has been made in black voter registration and turnout over the last two decades?
2. What success have black voters had in electing blacks to office? What types of offices have blacks won and where have these offices been won?
3. Once in office, what, if anything, have black elected officials accomplished and what was has not been accomplished?
4. What options are available for greater accomplishments in the future?

The analysis which follows is exploratory, particularly in regard to questions (3) and (4). But it should provide the essential groundwork for further analysis on the critical question of the impact of electoral participation on the socioeconomic life-chances and present conditions of black Americans.

A Methodological Note

One of the problems involved in assessing the extent and significance of the inroads that blacks have made in American politics is that there are two methods of measurement. One method (the longitudinal) contrasts the number of black registrants, voters, and elective office-holders in the United States with the number who held office at some earlier period. A second method (the comparative) contrasts the number of black registrants, voters, and elective officeholders to white registrants, voters, and elective officeholders. Both methods will be applied in this chapter.

A second problem involves finding reliable data on black political participation. Data utilized in this study come primarily from three sources: the *National Roster of Black Elected Officials*, published by the Joint Center for Political Studies (JCPS); the JCPS/Gallup Survey conducted through personal interviews of 1300 whites and 900 blacks in May and June of 1984; and the U.S. Department of Commerce, Bureau of the Census, *Final Population and Housing Unit Counts* and *Current Population Reports*.

It has long been recognized that blacks and whites overreport voter participation in surveys. Recently, several political scientists have argued that voter validation checks show that blacks overreport voter participation more than do whites. (Voter validation checks involve checking the survey respondent with the voter registration lists.) These political scientists argue that black overreporting may result from a greater desire to give the socially acceptable response. In addition, blacks may be reluctant to admit they did not register or vote. Blacks have struggled to gain the franchise, and it may be difficult for many to acknowledge that they failed to exercise it. For example, Shuman and Presser, when comparing survey reports to voter validation checks, found that, in three out of four surveys, southern blacks were more likely to overreport voting than were blacks outside the South. But these authors admit that the possibility cannot be dismissed that some systematic biases in the voter validation process may have led to an underestimation of the relative level of black turnout:

> Maintaining registration lists is a local responsibility, and voter records may be maintained more accurately in more affluent white areas than in the poorer areas where blacks tend to reside. Records may be maintained better in the North than in the South, where a disproportionate number of blacks live.[16]

Thus Schuman and Presser admit that the relationship between race and overreporting may be artificial. Siegelman argues that this is likely, since he has discovered that "nonvoting voters" are more similar to validated voters than they are to respondents who acknowledge that they do not vote.[17]

Future students of black electoral participation will need to compare carefully acknowledged black nonvoters and blacks whose claim to have voted is not supported by the voter validation check, with blacks who are validated voters. The small number of blacks sampled in most national surveys makes such comparisons difficult.

Since the issue of whether blacks overreport and by how much is not settled and since the census provides the largest survey (thereby increasing its validity and reliability), there is no reason to believe that more blacks are overreporting today than in the past. For all these reasons the census survey reports are used in the following analysis to provide a rough standard for comparative and longitudinal change in voter registration.

Trends in Black Voter Registration

According to a recent poll conducted by the United States Bureau of the Census, 169,963,000 Americans were eligible to vote in 1984. Black Americans eligible to vote accounted for 10.8 percent or 18,432,000 of the total voting-age population.[18] Since most American national elections are won by 5 percent or less, blacks often have had the potential to be a significant force in deciding election results. In many state and local elections the black potential is even greater. For example, in Mississippi, South Carolina, Georgia, Louisiana, Alabama, and Maryland, blacks accounted for more than 20 percent of the voting-age population in 1984 (Table 6.1). To become a strong political force, however, blacks must transfer their numerical potential into voting strength.

Table 6.1　Registration and Voting by Race, for 20 States with Highest Black Proportions of the Electorate, 1984

State	Percentage of Total Electorate Black	Percentage of Voting-Age Population Reported Registered		Percentage of Voting-Age Population Reported Voting	
	Black	*White*	*Black*	*White*	*Black*
Mississippi	29.6%	81.4%	85.6%	69.2%	69.6%
South Carolina	29.2	57.3	62.2	47.9	51.4
Georgia	26.6	65.7	58.0	55.3	45.9
Louisiana	24.5	73.2	74.8	64.7	66.4
Alabama	23.0	77.2	71.4	62.8	54.8
Maryland	20.2	71.0	65.0	63.0	54.7
North Carolina	19.6	67.0	59.5	59.1	47.2
Virginia	17.5	63.7	62.1	57.8	55.0
Tennessee	14.9	70.2	78.5	56.7	64.7
Florida	14.6	64.1	57.3	55.5	43.2
Illinois	14.6	74.9	79.7	66.8	72.9
Arkansas	14.1	70.8	71.2	61.5	56.9
Michigan	13.2	74.3	75.1	62.6	65.4
New York	12.8	66.3	54.7	60.8	47.3
Texas	11.3	66.0	65.3	55.5	51.2
New Jersey	10.3	69.4	64.5	62.5	55.6
Ohio	9.3	69.5	73.4	62.3	64.9
Missouri	8.0	76.1	68.9	66.1	65.3
Connecticut	7.8	73.8	58.6	65.9	50.4
California	6.6	64.1	65.8	58.2	57.6

Source: U.S. Bureau of the Census, *Current Population Reports: Population Characteristics,* Series P-20, no. 397.

This task has not been a simple one, for disenfranchisement techniques developed at the turn of the century (such as the grandfather clause, the white primary, poll taxes, and literacy tests) have severely restricted black participation historically.[19] The 1944 *Smith* v. *Allwright*[20] decision in which the U.S. Supreme Court invalidated the white primary and other court cases struck down other disenfranchisement techniques, but it was not until passage of the Voting Rights Act of 1965 that major gains in black voter registration were made.[21]

Many voting rights analysts contend that blacks are still unable to cast an effective vote. Four related factors are cited as continuing barriers to black political participation: 1) minority vote dilution through sophisticated legal and administrative barriers such as at-large electoral systems, racial gerrymandering, candidate slating procedures, and runoff requirements;[22] 2) class barriers to participation such as poverty and lack of education;[23]

3) psychological barriers such as years of exclusions from voting, lack of civic training, fear, deference to whites, and apathy;[24] and 4) institutional obstacles such as the problem of inadequate information concerning voter registration and procedures, the often inconvenient place and time of registration, and the scarcity of black registration officials, especially in the South.[25]

Despite these barriers, the experience of blacks in politics since 1965 suggest that blacks have made progress relative to whites in political mobilization. A first level of mobilization is registering to vote, and here blacks have made substantial progress compared to whites. Based on the latest available figures, blacks nearly equalled the voter registration of whites in 1984 (Table 6.2). The gap between black and white voter registration rates was only 3.3 percentage points compared to a gap of 9.2 percentage points in 1968. In southern states the gap between black and white voter registration rates was an even smaller 2.2 percentage points in 1984 compared to 9.2 percentage points in 1968 (Table 6.3). Surprisingly, in several states (Mississippi, South Carolina, Louisiana, California, Illinois, Tennessee, Arkansas, Michigan, and Ohio) the percentage of blacks registered exceeded that of whites (Table 6.1).

The increase in black voter registration as compared with white voter registration seems largely due to increases in two groups: southern black votes (Table 6.3) and black female voters (Table 6.4). While blacks in the United States as a whole increased their voter registration rates by only 0.1 percentage points between 1968 and 1984, blacks in the South increased their rates by 5 percentage points in the same period. Similarly, as early as 1976 black women had higher voter registration rates than black men. Since 1976 this gap has widened; while black males increased their voter registration rates by 5.8 percentage points between 1976 and 1984, black females increased their voter registration rates by 9.5 percentage points. While the rate of increase between 1976 and 1984 in voter registration for black males and females was far higher than for white males and females, black females had the fastest rate of growth of all. By 1984 black female registration rates had topped the rates of both black and white males.

Finally, the categorization of blacks has markedly increased in many categories to a level greater than their social and economic status would indicate. For example, less well-educated, lower-income, and unemployed blacks vote at far higher rates than their white counterparts. Blacks with less than a high school education, household incomes of less than $10,000, or who are unemployed all registered to vote at higher rates in 1984 than did whites in these same categories (Table 6.5).

It is important to note that the black registration rate increased only minimally if one makes a longitudinal comparison of the black rate in 1968 and the black rate in 1984. This is the comparison that analysts use most

Table 6.2 National Registration and Voting by Race, 1964–1984

	1964	1968	1972	1976	1980	1984
Blacks						
All persons of voting age[a]	10,340	10,935	13,493	14,927	16,424	18,432
Number who reported registering[a]	NA	7,238	8,837	8,725	9,849	12,223
Percentage of voting-age population reported registered	NA	66.2%	65.5%	58.5%	60.0%	66.3%
Number who reported voting[a]	6,048	6,300	7,032	7,273	8,787	10,293
Percentage of voting-age population reported voting	58.5%	57.6%	52.1%	48.7%	50.5%	55.8%
Percentage of registered population reported voting	NA	87.0%	79.6%	83.4%	86.1%	84.2%
Percentage of total electorate	5.7%	9.0%	8.2%	8.4%	8.9%	10.1%
Whites						
All persons of voting age[a]	99,353	104,521	121,243	129,316	137,265	146,761
Number who reported registering[a]	NA	78,835	88,957	88,329	94,112	102,211
Percentage of voting-age population reported registered	NA	75.4%	73.4%	68.3%	68.6%	69.6%
Number who reported voting[a]	70,204	72,213	78,166	78,808	82,855	90,152
Percentage of voting-age population reported voting	70.7%	69.1%	64.5%	60.9%	61.1%	61.4%
Percentage of registered population reported voting	NA	91.6%	87.8%	89.2%	89.1%	88.2%
Black-white registration gap	NA	9.2%	7.9%	9.8%	8.4%	3.3%
Black-white voting gap	12.2%	11.5%	12.4%	12.2%	10.4%	5.6%

[a]*In Thousands*

Source: U.S. Bureau of the Census, *Current Population Reports, Special Studies*, Series P-23, no. 131 and *Current Population Reports: Population Characteristics*, Series P-20, no. 397.

Table 6.3   Percent Reported Registered
and Voting by Region and Race

	1968	1972	1976	1980	1984
NORTH AND WEST					
Registered					
White	77.2%	74.9%	69.0%	69.3%	70.5%
Black	71.8	66.0	60.9	60.6	67.2
Black-White Gap	5.4	7.9	8.1	8.7	3.3
Voting					
White	71.8	67.5	62.6	62.4	63.0
Black	64.8	56.7	52.5	52.8	68.9
Black-White Gap	7.0	10.8	10.4	9.4	4.1
SOUTH					
Registered					
White	70.8	69.8	66.7	66.2	67.8
Black	61.6	64.0	56.4	59.3	65.6
Black-White-Gap	9.2	5.8	10.3	6.9	2.2
Voting					
White	61.9	57.0	57.1	57.4	58.1
Black	51.6	47.8	45.7	28.2	53.2
Black-White Gap	10.3	9.2	11.4	9.2	4.9

Source: U.S. Bureau of the Census, *Current Population Reports: Special Studies,* Series P-23, no. 131 and *Current Population Characteristics,* Series P-20, no. 397.

frequently to support the view that blacks have made little progress in voter registration in the last two decades. Of course, it is extremely important that blacks increase their level of voter registration whether whites do or not. Yet, the comparative approach may be the most appropriate for assessing the success of black voter registration, since black Americans are affected by the same factors that determine general trends in electoral participation.

One of the ironies of American electoral politics is that more and more Americans have acquired the right to vote in recent years, but from 1960 to 1980 decreasing proportions of them have actually registered and exercised that right. The decline in registration and turnout has been linked to four major factors: 1) extension of the right to vote to 18-year-olds (since a disproportionate number of 18-to-20 year olds do not vote compared to persons 21 years old and over); 2) the erosion in the strength of political party identification of many Americans (which analysts feel results in less psychological involvement in politics); 3) the decline in a sense of political

Table 6.4   Percent Reported Registered and Voting by Race and Sex

	1964	1968	1972	1976	1980	1984
BLACKS						
Registered						
Males	NA	NA	66.5	56.6	57.2	62.4
Females	NA	NA	66.4	60.0	62.2	69.5
Male-Female Gap	NA	NA	−0.1	3.4	5.0	7.1
Voting						
Males	59.1	58.2	52.1	47.2	47.5	51.7
Females	58.0	57.1	52.1	49.9	52.8	59.2
Male-Female Gap	−1.1	−1.1	9	2.7	5.3	7.5
WHITES						
Registered						
Males	NA	NA	74.7	68.8	68.3	68.9
Females	NA	NA	73.1	67.8	68.4	70.3
Male-Female Gap	NA	NA	−1.6	−1.0	0.4	1.4
Voting						
Males	73.4	71.2	65.6	61.5	60.9	60.8
Females	68.2	67.2	63.4	60.5	60.9	62.0
Male-Female Gap	−5.2	−4.0	−2.2	−1.0	0	1.2

Source: U.S. Bureau of the Census, *Current Population Reports: Special Studies,* Series P-23, no. 131 and *Current Population Characteristics,* Series P-20, no. 397.

efficacy (over the years, fewer and fewer people have thought public officials cared about their opinions and/or have felt that as citizens they have any say about what the government does); and 4) the rise in public disaffection with the government's policies on issues such as race relations, Vietnam, and the Watergate scandals as well as a general feeling that government has failed to solve economic and social problems.[26]

Public opinion polls have demonstrated that blacks expressed lower feelings of efficacy and more disaffection than other groups throughout the 1960s and 1970s.[27] This suggests that the longitudinal decline in black voter registration rates between 1968 and 1980 was part of a general trend in voter registration rates. In sum, black registration rates followed general national trends. They went up in the 1960s, down in the 1970s, and up again in the 1980s; but after 1965 blacks made more gains in voter registration than whites.

In 1982 the Voting Rights Act was strengthened and extended. Nonetheless, complaints have persisted that the federal government is not actively enforcing it. In some areas black voter registration remains very low, and black voting rights are far from permanently secured. Indeed, there are

Table 6.5 National Registration and Turnout by Race, Education, Income, and Employment Status, 1984

	Registration			Turnout		
	White	Black	Black-White Gap	White	Black	Black-White Gap
Education						
Elementary: 0–4 years	32.7%	51.4%	18.7%	24.3%	41.1%	16.8%
5–7 years	51.1	64.1	13.0	40.1	51.0	10.9
8 years	61.5	64.2	2.7	50.4	54.5	4.1
High School: 1–3 years	54.6	60.0	5.4	44.2	48.4	4.2
4 years	68.2	65.8	−2.4	59.8	54.7	−5.1
College: 1–3 years	77.3	72.5	−4.8	69.1	63.2	−5.9
4 years	84.5	79.2	−5.3	79.4	72.7	−6.7
5 yrs/more	88.1	87.5	−0.6	84.1	82.5	−1.6
Family Income						
Under $5,000	47.1	58.7	11.6	35.8	43.3	7.5
$ 5,000 to $ 9,999	56.1	65.6	9.5	45.3	54.7	9.4
10,000 to 14,999	63.6	66.4	2.8	54.4	54.4	0.0
15,000 to 19,999	66.2	66.8	0.6	57.8	57.9	0.1
20,000 to 24,999	70.0	67.0	−3.0	62.1	61.4	−0.7
25,000 to 34,999	75.2	71.7	−3.5	68.1	53.0	−5.1
35,000 to 49,999	80.8	78.0	−2.8	73.9	70.6	−3.3
50,000 and over	83.3	79.4	−3.3	77.4	70.2	−7.2
Employment Status						
Civilian Labor Force	69.6	67.3	−2.3	61.7	57.6	−4.1
Employed	70.5	68.3	−2.2	62.8	59.1	−3.7
Unemployed	53.2	61.0	7.8	43.6	48.1	4.5
Not in Labor Force	69.8	64.5	−5.3	60.8	52.5	−8.3

Source: U.S. Bureau of the Census, *Current Population Reports: Special Studies*, Series P-23, no. 131 and *Current Population Reports: Population Characteristics*, Series P-20, no. 397.

approximately 6,209,000 unregistered blacks, more than half of these in southern states. Whether blacks can maintain and expand their rate of voter registration without strong federal support is questionable. However, as of 1984, blacks have made relative gains in voter registration, and they compromise sizable groups of registered voters in many states.

Black Voter Turnout

Increasing the number registered is an obvious requirement for black electoral success. Yet those registered must actually vote, and here progress has been made as well. In general, between 1968 and 1984 increases in black voting roughly parallel registration increases. Black voting as a percentage of registered voters has grown steadily since 1972 and was 84.2 percent in 1984 (Table 6.2). The rate of black voting is higher than the rate of white voting in the same states where registration rates are higher, except for Arkansas and California (Table 6.1). The percentage of blacks reported voting has grown faster in the South, although the rate of black voting in the South is still 5.7 percentage points lower than the rate of blacks voting in the North, and the gap between black and white voter participation rates is slightly larger in the South (Table 6.3). As with registration rates, black women report a higher rate of voter registration (Table 6.4); and less-educated, lower income, and unemployed blacks are reported to be voting at far higher rates than their white counterparts (Table 6.5).

The gap between black and white turnout rates narrowed dramatically in the 1980s, from 10.4 percentage points in 1980 to only 5.6 percentage points in 1984, the lowest gap ever recorded. Black voting increased from 50.5 to 55.8 percent, a gain of 5.3 percentage points, while white voter participation, like white registration, showed only a marginal increase (from 60.9 to 61.4 percent), a gain of only 0.5 percentage points. As a result, blacks comprised a larger share of the national electorate, exceeding one-tenth of the total electorate for the first time. (See Table 6.2).

What explains the growth in black registration and turnout between 1980 and 1984? Political scientist John Zipp has argued that although we know that various individual level factors are associated with voting and cannot be ignored, the fit between individuals and the options presented to them also needs to be incorporated into explanations of voting. According to Zipp, if one has a clear choice among candidates (one is not indifferent) and one's policy preferences are close to at least one candidate (one is not alienated), one is much more likely to vote.[28]

While the JCPS/Gallup survey data do not lend themselves to an empirical test of Zipp's thesis, they did produce findings that make his argument plausible. For example, blacks were clearly not indifferent to the choice between Ronald Reagan and Walter Mondale in the general election of 1984. Indeed JCPS/Gallup data reveal intense disaffection among blacks for Reagan: 83 percent of blacks interviewed felt that "Reagan's policies had been harmful to blacks"; a massive 94 percent of blacks disapproved of Reagan's handling of the "situation of poor people"; 72 percent of blacks believed Reagan was "prejudiced"; 62 percent did not view Reagan as a "strong leader"; and 85 percent said that Reagan did not "care about people" like themselves. Mondale, on the other hand, was considered not to be "prejudiced" by 62 percent of blacks surveyed; to "care about people" like themselves by 63 percent; and to be a "strong leader" by 62 percent. For blacks, then, Mondale and Reagan represented a clear choice, and alienation from Reagan may have generated much more interest among blacks in voting.

For example, the Gordon S. Black Corporation found in a survey conducted for *USA Today* (October, 1984)—which included an oversample of blacks—that 62 percent of blacks, as opposed to 44 percent of whites, said that they had increased their interest in politics since 1980. As a result, blacks were more likely than whites to have engaged in a variety of campaign activities such as attending a political rally (30 percent of blacks compared to 17 percent of whites), distributing candidate literature (17 percent of blacks compared to 8 percent of whites), and helping to register voters (30 percent of blacks compared to 9 percent of whites).[29]

Although comparable data to examine whether black participation in the primaries went up in 1984 do not exist, sketchy evidence suggests that it did. CBS/*New York Times* (June, 1984) exit poll data indicate that the number of votes cast in black precincts more than doubled in the New York primary, while black turnout increases ranged from 14 percent to 87 percent in the other states sampled. These surveys estimated that 3.05 million blacks voted in the Democratic primaries, representing 18 percent of the 16.94 million Democratic voters. Moreover, blacks accounted for a disproportionate share of first-time voters: 11 percent of black voters were casting a ballot for the first time, compared to only 7 percent among white voters.[30]

Again, Zipp's indifference-alienation model appears useful in explaining black voter turnout increases. In the primaries, the Jesse Jackson candidacy for the Democratic presidential nomination provided blacks with a clear choice and a candidate they felt closely represented their policy preferences. The JCPS/Gallup survey found that blacks felt Jackson possessed exceptional traits—e.g., 94 percent of blacks believed Jackson "cared about people" like themselves, and 89 percent thought he was a "strong leader." The National Black Electorate Study of the University of Michigan's Survey Research Center found that Jackson was so exceptionally popular with blacks that 57 percent said they would have voted for him as an independent in the general election.

In sum, the special circumstances of 1984—a primary candidate who generated great affection (Jackson), a candidate in the general election who generated great disaffection among blacks (Reagan), and a candidate who presented a positive choice (Mondale)—help explain the greatest surge in black voter turnout since the early 1960s. Additionally, registration groups such as the National Coalition of Black Voter Participation and the Voter Education Project as well as political departments of civil rights organizations such as the National Urban League and the National Association for the Advancement of Colored People were immensely influential in increasing black voter registration and turnout in the 1980s, especially in the South. The National Coalition alone reported that it registered 650,000 blacks in 1984 through its Operation Big Vote and Black Women's Roundtable programs.

Black Female Voters

Explaining the black female voter participation rate is more difficult. By 1984 the voter participation rate of black women was 7.5 percentage points higher than that of black men, and the gender gap had expanded to 11.3 percentage points among blacks under the age of 21. While the turnout of black men in the youngest age bracket increased by 4.1 percentage points during the last four years, the turnout of black women under 21 rose by 16.6 percentage points. Similarly, elderly black women have increased their turnout by 10.3 percentage points during the Reagan years. As a result, the male turnout "advantage" among blacks in that age bracket has shrunk to 2.9 percentage points.

It has been suggested that black women's slightly higher level of education and the distinctive distribution of the black female labor force, which is more white collar and less blue collar than the black male labor force distribution, explains their higher voter participation rate. However, black women display higher turnout rates than black men within the same occupation, income, education, and employment status groups.[31]

A second suggestion is that black women perceive discrimination on the basis of both race and sex, and thus both forms of group consciousness may stimulate the participation of black women more than racial consciousness alone among black men.[32] Indeed it is possible that feminist consciousness is a more potent determinant of political participation among black women then among white women.[33] Joint Center for Political Studies/Gallup Organization Survey (July, 1984) data reveal that more black women (33 percent) believe women have "too little influence in politics" than do black men (21 percent), white women (20 percent), and white men (14 percent). Similarly, slightly more black women (59 percent) believe blacks have "too little influence in politics" than do black men (52 percent). This would suggest greater gender and racial consciousness among black women than among white women or black men.

Another suggestion is that the programs cut by the Reagan administration disproportionately impacted black women and their children; thus black women may have felt more antipathy than any other group for the Reagan administration. JCPS/Gallup data also support this suggestion. For example, 74 percent of black women saw Reagan as prejudiced compared to 69 percent of black men; only 24 percent of black women felt Reagan was a strong leader compared to 36 percent of black men; 85 percent of black women disapproved of the way Reagan was handling his job compared to 78 percent of black men; and 74 percent of black women thought a Democratic administration would do more to help blacks get ahead than the Reagan administration, compared to 65 percent of black men. Thus black women may have felt more disaffection with Reagan than black men. Similarly, black women may have felt more affection for Jackson than black men. The Jackson campaign staff was disproportionately composed of black females; and black females contributed a majority of campaign finances.[34]

In sum, registration and turnout grew significantly between 1980 and 1984, but more among black women than black men. Finding out precisely what factors stimulated faster growth among black women and whether these factors can be used both to further stimulate black female and male voter participation should surely be one of the critical areas of research today.

The Effects of Voting: Black Elected Officials

The gains in voter registration and voting turnout have been paralleled by a substantial increase in blacks elected to office since 1965. When the Voting Rights Act was passed in 1965, it was estimated that there were fewer than 500 black elected officials in the United States.[35] In 1970, when the Joint Center for Political Studies began its annual survey of black elected officials, there were 1,469 black officials, By January 1985 blacks held 6,056 elective offices, an increase of 312 percent during the 15-year period since 1970 (Table 6.6). Yet, blacks still make up only a very small proportion of elected officials. While blacks comprise almost 12 percent of the American population, 10.8 percent of the voting-age population, and 10.1 percent of the 1984 national electorate, black elected officials represent only 1.2 percent of the total 490,770 elected officials in the United States.[36]

Where do black officials serve and what kinds of offices do they hold? Between 1970 and 1985 black Americans won at least one public office in every state except South Dakota. In 1985 there were no black elected of-

Table 6.6 Change in Number of Black Elected Officials by Category of Office 1970–1985

Year	Total BEOs N	% Change	Federal N	% Change	State N	% Change	Substate regional N	% Change	County N	% Change	Municipal N	% Change	Judicial/law enforcement N	% Change	Education N	% Change
1970	1,469	—	10	—	169	—	—	—	92	—	623	—	213	—	362	—
1971	1,860	26.6	14	40.0	202	19.5	—	—	120	30.4	785	26.0	274	28.6	465	28.5
1972	2,264	21.7	14	0.0	210	4.0	—	—	176	46.7	932	18.7	263	-4.0	669	43.9
1973	2,621	15.8	16	14.3	240	14.3	—	—	211	19.9	1,053	13.0	334	27.0	767	14.6
1974	2,991	14.1	17	6.3	239	-0.4	—	—	242	14.7	1,360	29.2	340	1.8	793	3.4
1975	3,503	17.1	18	5.9	281	17.6	—	—	305	26.0	1,573	15.7	387	13.8	939	18.4
1976	3,979	13.6	18	0.0	281	0.0	30	—	355	16.4	1,889	20.1	412	6.5	994	5.9
1977	4,311	8.3	17	-5.6	299	6.4	33	10.0	381	7.3	2,083	10.3	447	8.5	1,051	5.7
1978	4,503	4.5	17	0.0	299	0.0	26	-21.2	410	7.6	2,159	3.6	454	1.6	1,138	8.3
1979	4,607	2.3	17	0.0	313	4.7	25	-3.8	398	-2.9	2,224	3.0	486	7.0	1,144	0.5
1980	4,912	6.6	17	0.0	323	3.2	25	0.0	451	13.3	2,356	5.9	526	8.2	1,214	6.1
1981	5,038	2.6	18	5.9	341	5.6	30	20.0	449	-0.4	2,384	1.2	549	4.4	1,267	4.4
1982	5,160	2.4	18	0.0	336	-1.5	35	16.7	465	3.6	2,477	3.9	563	2.6	1,266	-0.1
1983	5,606	8.6	21	16.7	379	12.8	29	-17.1	496	6.7	2,697	10.0	607	7.8	1,377	8.8
1984ᵃ	5,700	1.7	21	0.0	389	2.6	30	3.4	518	4.4	2,735	1.4	636	4.8	1,371	-0.4
1985	6,056	6.2	20	-4.8	392	1.8	32	6.7	611	18.0	2,898	6.0	661	4.0	1,438	4.9

[a]The 1984 figures reflect blacks who took office during the seven-month period between July 1, 1983 and January 30, 1984.
Source: National Roster of Black Elected Officials, (Washington, D.C.: Joint Center for Political Studies), 1985.

ficials in North Dakota, South Dakota, New Hampshire, Idaho, and Montana. In other words, black elected officials served in 45 of the nation's 50 states in that year. A growing majority of them served in the South. In 1970, 48.0 percent of all black elected officials were in the South; by 1984, 63.1 percent of the total were in the South, and the proportions elected in other regions had declined (Table 6.7). Two southern states, Louisiana and Mississippi, now lead all other states in the number of black elected officials, with 475 and 444, respectively. Undoubtedly, one of the most important contributors to the growing proportion and actual number of black elected officials in the South has been the Voting Rights Act of 1965, as amended in 1975 and 1982. With the removal of many barriers to voting, blacks have been able to participate more and to elect blacks to public office. Table 6.8 shows the change in southern states covered by the act between 1970 and 1985. In the seven states originally covered by the act, the number of black elected officials increased from 407 in 1970 to 2,351 in 1985. This rate of increase was more than one and one-half times the rate of increase for the nation as a whole.

Table 6.9 presents data on changes in the number of officials over time by type of office. Since 1970 the number of blacks holding every type of office has increased. The great majority of black elected officials are municipal and education officials. In 1985, 71.6 percent of all black elected officials were in these two categories. The proportions of all black elected officials who fall into these two categories have stayed remarkably the same in the 15-year period since 1970. Impressive gains have been made especially in regard to county offices, with the number growing from 92 in 1970 to 611 in 1985, a more than 5-1/2 fold increase. In other categories, the growth rate has been slower, but even in these areas the numbers of officials have at least doubled in the 15-year period. The area of slowest growth, however, is in statewide offices.

In the rest of this section the growth and distribution of black elected officials at the federal, state, and local levels is examined. The section concludes by discussing the increases in black female elected officials at all levels of government.

Federal Officials

No blacks have served in the United States Senate since 1978 when Edward W. Brooke completed two terms as the Republican senator from Massachusetts. Between 1970 and 1985 the number of black members of the House of Representatives rose from 10 in 1970 to a high of 21 in 1984 and fell back to 20 in 1985. Nor surprisingly, all black representatives are from urban districts (Table 6.10). While they come from all regions of the country, the largest number (8) come from the Midwest.

Table 6.7 Black Elected Officials by Region

Year	South		Midwest		Northeast		West	
	Number	Percent[a]	Number	Percent[a]	Number	Percent[a]	Number	Percent[a]
1970	706	48.0%	396	26.9%	237	16.1%	132	9.0
1971	882	47.4	502	27.0	341	18.3	125	7.8
1972	1,067	47.3	589	26.1	422	18.7	179	7.9
1973	1,381	52.7	618	23.6	444	16.9	178	6.8
1974	1,609	53.8	691	23.1	497	16.6	194	6.5
1975	1,913	54.6	869	24.8	503	14.4	218	6.2
1976	2,301	57.8	937	23.5	514	12.9	227	5.7
1977	2,568	59.6	958	22.2	541	12.5	244	5.7
1978	2,733	60.7	966	21.5	529	11.8	274	6.1
1979	2,768	60.4	985	21.5	541	11.8	290	6.3
1980	2,981	61.0	1,041	21.3	570	11.7	298	6.1
1981	3,070	61.2	1,070	21.3	572	11.4	302	6.0
1982	3,140	61.4	1,090	21.7	577	11.5	308	6.1
1983	3,441	61.9	1,144	20.6	658	11.8	316	5.7
1984	3,498	61.9	1,137	20.1	688	12.2	331	5.9
1985	3,801	63.1	1,150	19.1	694	11.7	371	6.1

[a]Percent of continental United States only.
Source: National Roster of Black Elected Officials, (Washington, D.C.: Joint Center for Political Studies), 1985.

Table 6.8   Number and Percent of Black Elected Officials in Southern States Covered by the Voting Rights Act—1970 and 1985

| | 1970 | | |
State	Number of Elective Offices	Number of Elected Officials	Percent of Elective Offices Held by Blacks
Alabama	4,060	86	2.1%
Georgia	7,226	40	0.6
Louisiana	4,761	64	1.3
Mississippi	4,761	64	1.7
North Carolina	5,504	62	1.1
South Carolina	3,078	38	1.2
Virginia	3,587	36	1.0
Total	28,216	407	1.4

| | 1985 | | |
State	Number of Elective Offices[a]	Number of Elected Officials	Percent of Elective Offices Held by Blacks
Alabama	4,160	375	9.0%
Georgia	6,672	340	5.1
Louisiana	4,720	475	10.1
Mississippi	5,278	444	8.4
North Carolina	5,308	291	5.5
South Carolina	3,233	310	9.6
Virginia	3,043	116	3.8
Total	32,426	2,351	7.3

[a]Offices in 1982
Sources: Data on total number of elective offices are from U.S. Bureau of the Census, *1982 Census of Governments,* vol. 1, no. 2; data on black elected officials are from *National Roster of Black Elected Officials,* (Washington, D.C.: Joint Center for Political Studies), 1985.

State Officials

Currently no blacks hold the office of governor and only five hold important statewide executive offices. They are Henry Parker, treasurer of Connecticut; Roland Burris, comptroller of Illinois; Richard Austin, secretary of state of Michigan; Douglas Wilder, Lieutenant Governor of Virginia, and Julio Brady, Lieutenant Governor of the Virgin Islands. In addition to the five statewide executive officials, 12 black judges have been elected statewide to courts of last resort. Undoubtedly, it is the small black proportion of the population in most states that has made winning statewide office extremely difficult for black candidates who still often must depend primarily on black votes to win.

Blacks have made more progress in being elected to state legislatures. In

Table 6.9   Distribution of Black Elected Officials by Category of Office
(in percentage)

Year	Federal	State	Substate Regional	County	Municipal	Judicial/Law Enforcement	Education
1970	0.7	11.5	—	6.3	42.4	14.5	24.6
1971	0.8	10.9	—	6.5	42.2	14.7	25.0
1972	0.6	9.3	—	7.8	41.2	11.6	29.5
1973	0.6	9.2	—	8.1	40.2	12.7	29.3
1974	0.6	8.0	—	8.1	45.5	11.4	26.5
1975	0.5	8.0	—	8.7	44.9	11.0	26.8
1976	0.5	7.1	0.8	8.9	47.5	10.4	25.0
1977	0.4	6.9	0.8	8.8	48.3	10.4	24.4
1978	0.4	6.6	0.6	9.1	47.9	10.1	25.3
1979	0.4	6.8	0.5	8.6	48.3	10.5	24.8
1980	0.3	6.6	0.5	9.2	48.0	10.7	24.7
1981	0.4	6.8	0.6	8.9	47.3	10.9	25.1
1982	0.3	6.5	0.7	9.0	48.0	10.9	24.5
1983	0.4	6.8	0.5	8.8	48.1	10.8	24.6
1984	0.4	6.8	0.5	9.1	48.0	11.2	24.1
1985	0.3	6.5	0.5	10.1	47.9	10.9	23.7
Growth from 1970 to 1985							
Number	10	227	32	519	2,275	448	1,076
Percent	100.0%	144.3%	—	564.1%	365.2%	210.3%	297.2%

Source: National Roster of Black Elected Officials, (Washington, D.C.: Joint Center for Political Studies), 1970–1985.

1970, 31 blacks were state senators and 137 were state representatives. Black state senators increased by 59 between 1970 and 1985, and black representatives increased by 165 over the same period (Table 6.6). Blacks have not won proportional equality, however, in any of the state legislatures. As Table 6.11 reveals, they have made the greatest proportional gains in the Alabama senate (5 of 35 members) and House (19 of 105 members). Overall black state senators constituted 4 percent of the nation's 2,362 state senators. The black House members comprised 6 percent of all 5,076 state representatives. When the history of black-white relations in the U.S. is considered, these gains in state legislatures, especially in the 11 ex-Confederate states, seem more impressive. As of January 1985, all of the 11 ex-Confederate states had at least one senator, and each of these states had at least four black representatives. Blacks were at least present in the legislative bodies which for nearly a century had acted to segregate them and subsequently to ignore them as citizens. Yet clearly, black electoral victories in state legislatures are still at rudimentary levels.

Table 6.10   Congressional Districts Represented by Blacks, January 1985

State, Region, and Representative	Party	District	Central City	Percent Black	Percent Hispanic
California (W)					
Dellums	Dem.	8	Oakland	24%	6%
Dixon	Dem.	28	Los Angeles	42	26
Hawkins	Dem.	29	Los Angeles	46	28
Dymally	Dem.	31	Compton	31	22
Distict of Columbia (S)					
Fauntroy	Dem.	At-large	Wash., D.C.	66	3
Illinois (MW)					
Hayes	Dem.	1	Chicago	90	1
Savage	Dem.	2	Chicago	66	7
Collins	Dem.	7	Chicago	60	4
Maryland (S)					
Mitchell	Dem.	7	Baltimore	70	1
Michigan (MW)					
Conyers	Dem.	1	Detroit	66	2
Crockett	Dem.	13	Detroit	67	3
Missouri (MW)					
Clay	Dem.	1	St. Louis	46	1
Wheat	Dem.	5	Kansas City	20	2
New York (NE)					
Towns	Dem.	11	Brooklyn	47	34
Owens	Dem.	12	Brooklyn	78	9
Rangel	Dem.	16	Manhattan	49	25
Ohio (MW)					
Stokes	Dem.	21	Cleveland	58	1
Pennsylvania (NE)					
Gray	Dem.	2	Philadelphia	76	1
Tennessee (S)					
Ford	Dem.	9	Memphis	51	1
Texas (S)					
Leland	Dem.	18	Houston	39	27

Source: *Congressional District Factbook,* (Washington, D.C.: Joint Center for Political Studies), 1984.

Regional Officials

Regionalism, a collaborative approach among units of local government within a specific geographical area to solve common problems, is now a prominent feature of government. It involves a wide variety of structural arrangements ranging from special-purpose regional or area-wide bodies to unified regional governments. Every state except Alaska has formed special districts to provide to substate regions specific services such as fire protection, transportation, conservation, or recreation.[37]

Table 6.11 Blacks in States Legislatures, January 1985

State	Number in Legislature		Number of Percentage of Elected Blacks			
	Senate	House	Senate	Percent	House	Percent
Alabama[a]	35	105	5	14.3%	19	18.1%
Alaska	20	40	—	—	1	2.5
Arizona	30	60	—	—	2	3.3
Arkansas[a]	35	100	1	2.9	4	4.0
California	40	80	2	5.0	6	7.5
Colorado	35	65	1	2.9	2	3.1
Connecticut	36	151	3	8.3	7	4.6
Delaware	21	41	1	4.8	2	4.9
Florida[a]	40	120	2	5.0	10	8.3
Georgia[a]	56	180	6	10.7	21	3.3
Hawaii	25	51	—	—	—	—
Idaho	35	70	—	—	—	—
Illinois	59	118	6	10.2	14	11.9
Indiana	50	100	2	4.0	6	6.0
Iowa	50	100	1	2.0	—	—
Kansas	40	125	1	2.5	3	2.4
Kentucky	38	100	1	2.6	1	1.0
Louisiana[a]	39	105	4	10.3	14	13.3
Maine	33	151	—	—	—	—
Maryland	47	141	5	10.6	19	13.5
Massachusetts	40	160	1	2.5	4	2.5
Michigan	28	110	3	7.9	14	12.7
Minnesota	67	134	—	—	1	0.8
Mississippi[a]	52	122	2	3.9	18	14.8
Missouri	34	163	3	8.8	12	7.4

State						
Montana	50	100	—	—	—	—
Nebraska (Unicameral)	49	—	1	2.0	—	—
Nevada	21	42	1	4.8	2	4.8
New Hampshire	24	400	—	—	—	—
New Jersey	40	80	1	2.5	6	7.5
New Mexico	42	70	—	—	—	—
New York	61	150	4	6.6	16	10.7
North Carolina[a]	50	120	3	6.0	13	10.8
North Dakota	53	106	—	—	—	—
Ohio	33	99	2	6.1	10	10.1
Oklahoma	48	101	2	4.2	3	3.0
Oregon	30	60	1	3.3	2	3.3
Pennsylvania	50	203	3	6.0	15	7.4
Rhode Island	50	100	1	2.0	3	3.0
South Carolina[a]	46	124	4	8.7	16	12.9
South Dakota	35	70	—	—	—	—
Tennessee[a]	33	99	3	9.1	10	10.1
Texas[a]	31	150	1	3.2	13	8.7
Utah	29	75	1	3.5	—	—
Vermont	30	150	—	—	1	0.7
Virginia[a]	40	100	2	5.0	5	5.0
Washington	49	98	1	2.0	2	2.0
West Virginia	34	100	—	—	1	1.0
Wisconsin	33	99	1	3.0	3	3.0
Wyoming	30	64	—	—	1	1.6
Total	2,362	5,076	90	3.8	302	6.0

[a]Ex-Confederate States

Source: National Roster of Black Elected Officials, (Washington, D.C.: Joint Center for Political Studies), 1985.

Members of most substate regional bodies are either appointed or elected to office, with the largest number being appointed. In 1977 the U.S. Census Bureau identified 25,962 special districts, 15,853 of which were authorized to elect their officials; they were served by 72,377 elected board members. Very few blacks hold regional elective office. The 32 who did in 1985 comprised a mere 0.4 percent of all elected regional officeholders and are located in the Virgin Islands and only three states (California, Illinois, and North Carolina).

County Officials

There are 3,042 organized county governments in the United States. The only states without county governments are Connecticut and Rhode Island. Officials elected to county offices typically serve as members of county governing bodies, county coroners, tax assessors, clerks, election commissioners, attorneys, judges, and law-enforcement officers.

Of special interest is the number of black elected county commissioners. Black elected county commissioners increased from 64 in 1970 to 534 in January 1985 (Table 6.6) and are disproportionately located in the states of the Deep South. In the South county commissioners have considerable authority. Among other things they set the county budget, have taxing authority, handle county finances, and dispense public services such as welfare. In rural areas, commissioners are usually the most important local officials. For this reason black gains in this category are particularly important.

Municipal Officials

Impressive gains have been made in regard to municipal offices with the number skyrocketing from 623 in 1970 to 2,898 fifteen years later (Table 6.6). City council members comprise by far the largest number (2,189) of all black elected officials, but blacks have also made enormous progress in winning mayoral offices. In 1970 there were 48 black mayors; by 1985 there were 286. A large number of these mayors are in small towns, as Table 6.12 shows. There are 107 black mayors in towns with populations of under 1,000, 37.4 percent of the total number. Another 81 black mayors serve in towns with populations of 1,000 to 4,999. Thus more than 3 out of every 5 black mayors are serving towns with populations less than 5,000. Yet a number of blacks have won mayoralties in larger cities. Black mayors now represent four of the nation's six largest cities: Harold Washington, Chicago; Thomas Bradley, Los Angeles; W. Wilson Goode, Philadelphia; and Coleman Young, Detroit. As Table 6.12 indicates, 23 black mayors held office in cities of 25,000 to 49,999, and another 27 black mayors held office

Table 6.12   Distribution of Black Mayors by Population

Population of Town or City	Number	Percentage of Total Number
Under 1,000	107	37.4
1,000 to 4,999	81	28.3
5,000 to 9,999	20	7.0
10,000 to 24,999	20	7.0
25,000 to 49,999	23	8.1
50,000 and above	27	9.4
Unincorporated and/or Data Unavailable	8	2.8
Total	286	100.0

Source: William O'Hare, "Places with Black Mayors," (Washington, D.C.: Joint Center for Political Studies, forthcoming).

in cities of 50,000 and above. Almost 2 out of every 10 black mayors, therefore, was in a city with a population greater than 25,000.

Other black elected officials at the municipal level include 67 members of municipal governing boards and 235 members of neighborhood advisory commissions. While the success of blacks at the municipal level is laudable, it should be noted that black municipal officials make up only 1.3 percent of all elected officials in municipalities and townships.

Judicial and Law Enforcement Officials

In the area of law enforcement blacks have also made progress in getting elected to public office, although the rate of growth is smaller than for county, municipal, and education officials (Table 6.9). There were 367 black judges in 1985, an increase from 114 in 1970. These judges were 55.5 percent of the 661 black law enforcement officials. Dramatic progress has been made especially in the South. In 1970 the South had only 21 black judges; by 1984 the South had elected 92 black judges. Still, in January 1985 several southern states had no black judges (Delaware, South Carolina, and Virginia) and other southern states had only one or two (Arkansas, Kentucky, Mississippi, Oklahoma, and West Virginia). The 230 black justices of the peace, constables, and magistrates comprised 34.8 percent of all elected officials in the law enforcement category. These offices ordinarily involve modest authority but can provide services otherwise unavailable for blacks. The 37 black sheriffs and marshalls are particularly significant for their black constituents in many areas. They are important symbolically to blacks, particularly in the South where the white sheriff has often been viewed as an active enforcer of the racial status quo. A black sheriff represents a dramatic change. In 1985, 31 of the 37 black sheriffs and marshalls (84 percent) were elected in southern states. Still, the number of black southern sheriffs is proportionately small; even in the 102 predominantly black southern counties, blacks comprise only 4.7 percent of the total number of sheriffs.

Education Officials

Black elected education officials serve at the state, county, and municipal levels of government. They hold office as administrators and members of various education boards. There were 1,438 blacks in education offices in 1985, 966 (222 percent) more than in 1971. Although these education officials comprise almost one-fourth of all black elected officials, they constitute only 1.4 percent of the total number of elected education officials in the United States.

The distribution of black education officials among various offices is as follows: 10 are members of state education agencies; 44 are members of university or college boards; 1,368 are members of local school boards; and there are 16 others who serve in positions such as superintendents of schools.

Black Female Elected Officials

There are currently 1,359 black women holding elective office in the U.S. (Table 6.13). In 1975 (the first year separate statistics were compiled) there were 530. While the pattern of growth and distribution of black females elected to office follows that of black elected officials as a whole, the number of black female officeholders, comprising 22.4 percent of all black elected officials, continues to increase at a faster annual rate than all black elected officials combined. For example, between 1984 and 1985 the number of black elected officials rose from 5,700 to 6,056, representing an annual increase of 6.2 percent. Women experienced a higher growth rate. Their number increased from 1,259 to 1,359, for an annual gain of 7.2 percent.

Given the far greater voter registration and turnout rates of black women, the higher annual rate of increase of black female elected officials is less impressive. Moreover, the absolute number of black female elected officials added in 1985 trailed the number of black males badly—100 new black female elected officials compared to 256 new black male elected officials. Moreover, more black female elected officials are elected to lower office than black male elected officials. While 81.4 percent of all black female elected officials are municipal and education officials, 68.8 percent of black male elected officials are in these categories.

Many have argued that black women are making substantial progress in getting elected to office when compared to white women. Data to demonstrate this advantage are virtually unavailable. The data that do exist

Table 6.13 Numerical and Percentage Change in Female Black Elected Officials, 1975–85

Year	Number	Number Change	Percent Change	Percent of All Black Elected Officials	Federal	State	Regional/ County	Mayors	Municipal	Law Enforcement	Education
1975	530	—	—	14.7	4	35	31	9	203	34	214
1976	684	154	29.1	17.2	4	38	49	11	300	39	243
1977	782	98	14.4	18.1	4	46	48	12	368	41	263
1978	843	61	7.8	18.7	4	46	53	11	396	45	288
1979	882	39	4.7	20.5	2	57	55	8	396	51	313
1980	976	94	10.7	19.9	2	60	66	13	437	59	339
1981	1,021	45	4.6	20.3	2	64	76	22	450	60	347
1982	1,031	60	5.9	21.0	2	65	91	27	477	63	356
1983	1,223	142	13.1	21.8	2	73	77	31	547	76	417
1984	1,259	36	2.9	22.1	2	75	78	19	573	78	424
1985	1,359	100	8.0	22.4	1	73	92	35	613	86	458

Source: National Roster of Black Elected Officials, (Washington, D.C.: Joint Center for Political Studies), 1970–1985.

indicate that this may be a false conclusion. For example, for at least three offices (mayors, state legislators, and members of the U.S. Congress) white and black women comprise roughly the same proportion of elective officials for their race. White women comprised 4.9 percent of all white members of Congress, 15.6 percent of all white state legislators, and 10.2 percent of all white mayors in cities with populations over 30,000 in 1985. Black women similarly comprised 5 percent of all black members of Congress, 18.9 percent of all black state legislators, and 3.7 percent of all black mayors in cities with populations over 30,000.[38]

For the most part, black elected women are distributed by region of office in much the same way as all black elected officials. Consequently, the South has the greatest number (54.8 percent) and the West the least (7.9 percent). Yet the distribution pattern of black women compared to black men demonstrates that the South has elected fewer black women proportionately than the other regions of the country.

Assessment

While the number of black elected officials has grown substantially since 1970, blacks still comprise less than 1.5 percent of the total number of elected officials, and the rate of growth in black elected officials has slowed dramatically. The 1970 to 1975 period was one of substantial increases in the number of black elected officials. Each year there was an increase of between 14.2 and 26.6 percent or an average of 407 additional black elected officials. Beginning in 1975, however, the rate of increase began to decline. While the rate of increase for 1970 to 1975 was 138.5 percent, it was only 40.2 percent for 1975 to 1980 (an average of 282 additional black elected officials each year), and the growth rate was only 23.3 percent for the period 1980 to 1985 (an average of 229 additional black elected officials each year) (Table 6.14).

Many reasons have given to explain this rapid decline.[39] Perhaps the best two are the following:

1. Continuing political and economic barriers make it difficult for blacks to register and vote, or to run for and win public offices. While the rate of growth of black elected officials peaked during the same period black median income gains relative to whites peaked may be coincidental, it suggests that the vote may not have an influence over the distribution of advantages that is separate from the influence of those social and economic factors that are associated with minorities exercising the vote and running for public office in the first place. Thus the fact that black economic well-being, black voting, and the rate of growth of black election to office all declined simultaneously appears to indicate an important relationship.
2. Between 1970 and 1975 blacks rapidly filled elected offices in jurisdictions

Table 6.14   Number and Rate of Change
of Black Elected Officials, 1970–1985

	Number Added and Rate of Change		
	1970–75	*1975–80*	*1980–85*
United States			
Number	2,034	1,409	1,144
Percent	138.5%	40.2%	23.3%
Regions			
South			
Number	1,207	1,068	820
Percent	171.0%	55.8%	27.5%
Midwest			
Number	474	171	80
Percent	119.7%	19.7%	7.5%
Northeast			
Number	266	66	125
Percent	49.5%	13.1%	22.0%
West			
Number	87	79	73
Percent	64.9%	36.1%	24.5%

Source: National Roster of Black Elected Officials (Washington, D.C.: Joint Center for Political Studies), 1970–1985.

with substantial black populations, thereby creating an artificially high rate of increase. As more and more predominantly black jurisdictions elected black officials, the numbers of newcomers declined.

This second reason appears to be extremely likely. While there is still ample opportunity to expand the number of black elected officials by simply electing blacks in the remaining black majority places (e.g., O'Hare found 339 places nationwide with a black population majority but without a black mayor),[40] there is little doubt that there are fewer and fewer such places especially at higher levels of office. What is not running out is nonblack constituencies in an 88 percent nonblack nation. It is likely then that for attaining higher offices and expanding rapidly the number of black officeholders, black candidates must be able to attract more votes from other ethnic groups in the future.

While lingering racism continues to reduce political (and other) options for blacks, some rudimentary progress is being made in this direction. The most highly publicized example of such progress in 1985 was the election of L. Douglas Wilder as Lieutenant Governor of Virginia, a state with a long segregationist history, formerly the capital of the Confederate South.

Blacks make up only 12 percent of Virginia electorate, but Wilder won by securing 99 percent of the black vote and 46 percent of the white vote. There are other examples of whites voting for blacks as well. The Massachusetts electorate is less than 5 percent black. Yet in 1966 and again in 1972 the state sent Republican Edward Brooke, a black, to the United States Senate. Similarly, the huge California electorate is less than 10 percent black. Yet in 1974, Californians elected a black man—Mervyn Dymally—lieutenant governor. Black mayors in such cities as Philadelphia (where Wilson Goode got about 20 percent of the vote in predominantly white neighborhoods) and Charlotte, North Carolina (where Harvey Gantt got 41 percent of the vote in such Charlotte neighborhoods) may be the harbingers of the black candidate to come.

Already, approximately one-third of all black mayors have been elected in cities with black populations of less than 50 percent.[41] Some are cities like Chicago, where blacks were a near majority, but others are cities like Los Angeles and Spokane, where blacks comprise only 17 percent and 2 percent of the total population, respectively. Additionally, 9 of the 20 black members of the U.S. House of Representatives were elected in districts where blacks are in the minority. Seven of these nine come from districts composed primarily of blacks and Hispanics, but two, Ronald Dellums of California and Alan Wheat of Missouri were elected in districts where whites comprised 70 percent of the population.

Although progress is being made, racial voting patterns are still closely tied to the election of black officials. Most black elected officials represent majority black constituencies. Thus the geographic distribution of black elected officials has consistently followed closely the distribution of the black population.

What then can be said by way of summarizing the current status of black electoral politics in the United States? Walton has provided a useful perspective to assess the developmental status of black politics. He contends that group politics develop through four stages: (1) nonparticipation. In this stage blacks are excluded from electoral participation either through local restrictions or lack of interest in politics; (2) limited participation. Minimal black participation by a selected few is the rule; (3) moderate participation. At this level more than 50 percent of the black population in a political unit participates in politics. Blacks creating pressure for more participation are able to attain selected goals and elect some political officials; and (4) full participation. Here blacks have not only the avenues to power, but control a proportionate number of offices, enough to make an impact in many areas where they desire changes.[42] The material examined in the preceding sections of this Chapter—voter registration, turnout, and black elected officials—indicates that blacks in the national arena have reached the stage of moderate participation, but clearly blacks are still very far from full participation—equitable representation among public servants. Correcting this inequity is essential if blacks are to be part of a genuinely representative system of government. Such an objective should therefore be a higher priority for the country and particularly for blacks. Continued protection by the federal government of black voting rights in areas where they have been threatened historically is a must.

The Benefits of Moderate Participation

Americans have often sought redress for social and economic problems through electoral politics, and it is not surprising that blacks have tried to utilize the same channels. That black political participation is working, at least compared to the past, is the most important point to be derived from the preceding sections. During the first half of the 1970s blacks came to public office in unprecedented numbers, and in the 1980s blacks have begun to vote again in unprecedented numbers. But have black officials been able to benefit their black constituents?

This chapter began by pointing out the ongoing debate in the literature on the impact of black voting and black elected officials. On one side, there are those who argue that black political participation and the election of black officials have produced few substantive benefits, and on the other, there are those who argue that some substantial changes have occurred as a result of black political participation and the election of black officials. This section does not seek to settle that debate, but rather to summarize briefly the implications of the evidence to date.

To establish a causal relationship between black political participation, the election of black officials, and benefits to blacks is empirically difficult. One reason is that there are two central questions. One asks how successful black elected officials have been in reordering the priorities of their governments and persuading them to seek novel solutions to outstanding problems, particularly those salient to black Americans, e.g., economic equality. A second asks how successful have black elected officials been in garnering for the black community a more equitable distribution of existing services and benefits provided by their governments. Those who analyze the first question generally conclude that black elected officials have had little or no success. Those who analyze the second usually find modest success.

A second problem in assessing the impact of black elected officials involves choosing the appropriate level of analysis. Blacks elected to higher levels of government have performed useful functions. For example, blacks in state legislatures have formed state black caucuses, which have met with executive officials to voice the interests of blacks; at times, they have held the balance of power between Republicans and Democrats on certain bills, e.g., on Virginia's open housing law, the first in the South. Many have held seniority long enough to win important committee chairmanships and have been influential in writing legislation favorable to black interests.

Similarly, in the U.S. Congress, the members of the Congressional Black Caucus now hold important chairmanships. For the first time in the history of Congress, blacks now chair five standing committees and two select committees: the Budget, Education and Labor, Standards of Official Conduct, Small Business, and District of Columbia committees, and the select panels on Hunger and Narcotics Abuse and Control. Blacks also chair 16 subcommittees, including one on the Armed Services Committee and two on the tax-writing Ways and Means panel. This gives black authority at least the potential for power, if not always power, itself. Recently the Caucus has been credited with spearheading legislation through the House on economic sanctions against South Africa because of its apartheid policies, getting more money for social programs than the original House and Senate budget plans called for, and other similar endeavors.

Clearly there is a limit to what 20 members of a 535-member body (the U.S. House and Senate) and/or the small number of black state legislators can do. It may be that many more black state legislators and members of the U.S. Congress must be elected before a useful analysis of the impact of black elected officials at the state and national levels of government can be made. As Mayor Richard Hatcher of Gary, Indiana observed:

> Blacks still do not control the real power centers in this country. . . . Our major gains so far have been limited to local government. Here we do indeed control terrain that was formerly beyond our groups.[43]

Several analysts have explored the impact of black political participation in general and of black elected officials in particular. Most of the major studies of the relationship suggest that electoral participation does make a difference. For example, black voting power produced a more equitable distribution of public services, more black public employment and appointments and the passage of civil rights ordinances in Durham, North Carolina and Tuskegee, Alabama. Similarly, black leadership created and sustained opportunities for black employment in municipal jobs in 40 cities.[44] Further, white legislators responded to greater black electoral power with policy payoff in Mississippi;[45] the election of blacks produced an expansion of public employment, greater federal grants and private foundation support, and a betterment of black living conditions in Greene County, Alabama,[46] and Fayette, Mississippi;[47] the election of a black mayor changed police practices in Gary, Indiana;[48] the election of black mayors and city council members increased social expenditures and intergovernmental revenues in cities over 25,000;[49] and black elected officials enforced affirmative action and minority set-aside policies more rigorously than their white counterparts in 12 cities in California.[50] Clearly, black electoral power has had an impact.

While impressive, this impact has been limited in distributive benefits and short-lived redistributive benefits. Most of the distributive benefits identified in the literature are favorable only to one segment of blacks, the middle class. For example, Eisinger found that the most striking employment gains in city work had occurred at the professional and managerial levels and that the proportion of blacks in low-level jobs had decreased. He concluded that "the increasing professionalization of the black municipal workforce appears to be part of a general formation of a larger black middle class."[51] Similarly, stronger enforcement of affirmative action and minority set-aside programs benefit primarily the black middle class.

Redistributive benefits which affected primarily the poor (e.g., larger grants for poverty programs and expanded services) depended, to a degree that seems to have been unappreciated at the time, on support from a pro-spending national elite. As the national economy became less bouyant and many local economies fell into serious decline, political resources and public policies also shifted.[52]

President Carter began the shift and upset traditional Democrats with his fiscally conservative leanings. President Reagan has gone even further, coming to office on a clear Republican program of reducing taxes and cutting spending. Congress and state houses similarly shifted toward fiscal conservatism with the election of more Republicans and conservative Democrats, and fewer liberal Democrats. While black citizens continued to express preferences for more government spending in many areas, many black elected officials remained fiscally liberal in principle, but felt pressured toward more conservative policies by forces like the taxpayers revolt.[53] As Kenneth Gibson put it, the solution to fiscal problems was "not living beyond your means."[54]

At the heart of the problem is an historic example of gigantic mistiming. Just as rural blacks reached the big cities when the industrial jobs that had uplifted other ethnic groups began to wane, so urban blacks today have reached city hall precisely at the moment when the real power to deliver jobs, money, education, and basic services is migrating to higher levels of government and the private sector.

For example, in many cities (such as New Orleans, Louisiana or Gary, Indiana) mayors cannot impose or increase a property tax, let alone tap any state surplus. In Washington, D.C., the mayor cannot tax the biggest landowner in the city, the U.S. government, but must rely on Congress to decide how much that government will pay the city in lieu of taxes. In Birmingham, Alabama, the black mayor cannot choose his own police chief. In Detroit the mayor spends a good part of his time working to win tax breaks for major corporations in order to keep them from moving out. In short, city government, as it is constituted in America today, simply does not provide the opportunities for blacks that control of city hall did back in the days of the white ethnic machines.

In sum, at the local level, urban changes and fund cuts have limited the impact of black elected officials. The growing fiscal limitations on city governments, along with other important changes in urban life, are forcing a major revision of black hopes, strategies, and electoral expectations. The changes raise some disturbing questions about the ultimate success of the black "revolution" in electoral politics.

Increasingly the question hanging over black elected officials is the same one that haunts compassionate white elected officials. Can any elected officials make government work for the poor at a time when both public interest in real reform and the funding and power of public institutions seem so inadequate for the task?

Moreover, the demographic factors that permitted even such fragile black political successes are changing. "White flight" long ago ceased to be a major trend; now the returning white middle class settlers and the new immigrants are displacing blacks in some cities. Borderline cities like New Orleans may well become majority white again, and cities like Cleveland that once seemed destined to have majority black populations may never do so. This means that black elected officials will have to generate not only massive black support for black candidates but a respectable percentage of the white vote as well. As the demographic base shifts, black mayors' constituencies will also change. The black groups that helped put many black leaders into office declined over the 1970s. Civil rights organizations lost much of their membership and support, at both the national and city levels. As organized groups became less influential, black candidates turned their appeal to broader electoral constituencies, including whites and middle-class blacks, who were less visibly united with poor blacks than a few years earlier. This appeal to individual citizens often meant a decline in racial saliency. Black officials increasingly resembled their white counterparts, as they confronted, day-by-day, the harsh problems of meeting constituents' demands with limited means. Debates emerged about the black middle class, its rapid economic gains, materialistic life styles, and waning civic involvement. While many blacks remained poor, poverty seems to have declined as a key national issue.

But remember that these changes occurred simultaneously with dramatic increases in the numbers of black elected officials. Ironically, as blacks grew more politically important, racial politics and reordering governmental priorities in the interests of the black poor declined as salient factors in the American political environment. Programs for the poor were cut back, and even gutted, whether the local officials were black or white.

Thus, for many blacks, two decades of increasing black success in elec-

tive politics have failed to bring any meaningful change in their lives. Political participation, higher education, and other changes may have resulted
in important changes for middle-class blacks, allowing them to do markedly
better than 20 years ago. However, the one-third of blacks below the poverty line, especially the 2 to 3.5 million chronically poor blacks,[55] are facing
deteriorating conditions, and there seems to be little or not improvement
in sight. Economic deprivation is now the severe and critical problem
plaguing the national black community.

Summary and Conclusions

It has been suggested that minority groups in American politics can maximize their political effectiveness where there is: (1) a large number of minority voters; (2) high voter registration; (3) substantial voter turnout; and
(4) maximum cohesion of voters.[56] This paper has presented considerable
evidence that blacks have made important gains in regard to registration
and turnout and some evidence of important gains in regard to cohesion.
Black mobilization in the mid-1960s is a clear trend.

Since blacks are registering and voting at higher rates, it is not surprising
that blacks are being elected to once-forbidden city, county, law enforcement, education, legislative, statewide executive, and congressional offices.
Although these new black officials are circumscribed by a variety of hand-
icaps in the present political and economic climates, they have brought new
and important benefits to some segments of their constituencies.

However, black voter participation and the election of black officials
have been unable to change significantly one major component of black
subordination—economic deprivation—which still severely limits the progress of many blacks. Two striking economic facts are: the unemployment
rate of blacks has remained at least twice as high as that of whites since
World War II; and the median family income of blacks in every region of
the country except the West compared to whites has been steadily declining
since 1975. As of 1984 the national median family income for blacks was
only 55.7 percent of that for whites; it was 55.1 percent that of whites in
1965.

An earlier quotation reflected King's early optimism about the powers
of the ballot. By 1968 this optimism had changed to realism, perhaps. King
remarked to an aide less than a week before his death:

> Truly America is much, much sicker, Hosea, than I realized when I first began
> working in 1955. We can now see ourselves as the powerless poor trapped
> within an economically oriented power structure. Our insight into the struc-
> ture of American society teaches us that the right to vote or to eat in any
> restaurant, while important, does not penetrate the "power plant" and there-

fore does not actually effect conditions of living. The whole structure of American life must be changed.[57]

Whether political rights and black elected officials are sufficient to bring about basic economic changes or whether a whole new set of structures and tactics is needed is unclear. It may be that only black self-help economic strategies, more black attempts at entrepreneurship, and more leadership of poor blacks by the black middle class will generate economic progress for all blacks. Alternatively, it may be that economic changes are likely to occur not through traditional politics or traditional economic ventures, but through creative social protest and disruption. Perhaps only the complete fulfillment of political rights, the complete testing of the real possibilities for accomplishing black gains through the mechanisms of electoral politics, the election of many more blacks at higher levels of government, the fullest efforts of these officials in adopting programs for serving black needs—in sum, the exhaustion of the possibilities of the electoral-representative system in the U.S. will make clear what is needed next and propel black American another leap forward.

The struggle for voting rights and the experiences of black voter participation and black elected officials in the last 20 years suggest some basic lessons regarding the prospects for future change: first, blacks must recognize the importance of maximizing their voting potential, of electing blacks to offices at all levels, of making black concerns felt in elections in which there are no black candidates, and of becoming more involved in the formulation and implementation of public policies that affect their lives; second, a successful struggle for economic progress will require combining the quest for electoral power with, in the words of King, "creative tension," i.e., the tension created by exposure of injustice; third, if a successful struggle for economic justice is to occur, it will require a high level of internal organization that uses all the resources of the black community; and finally, indigenous black leaders will have to devise creative tactics and strategies appropriate for bringing about economic change. Past struggles have proven King was correct when he concluded: "We know through painful experience that justice is never voluntarily given by the oppressor. It must be demanded by the oppressed."[58]

Notes

1. Ralph Bunche, *The Political Status of the Negro in the Age of FDR*, ed. Dewey W. Grantham (Chicago: University of Chicago Press, 1973), 87–88.
2. *New York Times*, February 2, 1965, 1.
3. David Campbell and Joe R. Feagin, "Black Electoral Victories in the South," *Phylon*, XLV, no. 4 (1985): 333.

4.   Andrew Greeley, *Why Can't They Be Like Us* (New York: E. P. Dutton, 1971), 14.

5.   Mark R. Levy and Michael S. Kramer, *The Ethnic Factor* (New York: Basic Books, 1972), 44–45.

6.   Donald R. Matthews and James W. Prothro, *Negroes and the New Southern Politics*, (New York: Harcourt Brace and World, 1966), 481.

7.   William R. Keech, *The Impact of Negro Voting* (Chicago: Rand McNally, 1968), 109.

8.   Francis S. Piven and Richard Cloward, *Poor People's Movements: Why They Succeed and How They Fail* (New York: Random House, 1977).

9.   Mack Jones, "Black Officeholders in Local Governments of the South: An Overview" (speech before the American Political Science Association, Los Angeles, California, September 6–12, 1970).

10. Hanes Walton, Jr., *Black Politics: A Theoretical and Structural Analysis* (New York: J.B. Lippincott, 1971), 200.

11. Edward S. Greer, *Big Steel: Black Politics and Corporate Power in Gary, Indiana* (New York: Monthly Review, 1979).

12. Edward S. Greenberg, Neal Milner, and David Olson, *Black Politics: The Inevitability of Conflict* (New York: Holt, Rinehart, and Winston, 1971), 15.

13. Michael Preston, "Limitations of Black Urban Power: The Case of Black Mayors," in Louis Masotti and Robert Lineberry, eds., *The New Urban Politics* (Cambridge, Mass.: Ballinger, 1976).

14. Keech, *The Impact of Negro Voting*.

15. Greer, *Big Steel*.

16. Howard Schuman and Stanley Presser, *Questions and Answers in Attitude Surveys: Experiments on Question Form, Wording, and Context* (New York: Academic Press, 1981), 151, 154.

17. Lee Siegelman, "The Nonvoting Voter in Voting Research," *American Journal of Political Science*, 26, no. 4 (1982):47–56.

18. U.S. Bureau of the Census, *Current Population Reports: Population Characteristics*, Series P-20, no. 397 (1985).

19. J. Morgan Kousser, "The Undermining of the First Reconstruction," in Chandler Davidson, ed., *Minority Vote Dilution* (Washington, D.C.: Howard University Press, 1984), 27–46.

20. *Smith* v. *Allwright*, 32 U.S. 649, 64 S.Ct. 757, 88, L.Ed. 987 (1944).

21. Chandler Davidson, "Minority Vote Dilution: An Overview," in *Minority Vote Dilution*.

22. Ibid.

23. Matthews and Prothro, *Negroes and the New Southern Politics*, 3.

24. Lester M. Salamon and Stephen Van Evera, "Fear, Apathy, and Discrimination: A Test of Three Explanations of Political Participation," *American Political Science Review* (December 1973): 1288–1306.

25. Penn Kimball, *The Disconnected* (New York: Columbia University Press, 1972), 3.

26. Paul Abramson, John Aldrich, and Dave Rhode, *Change and Continuity*

in the 1980 Elections (Washington, D.C.: Congressional Quarterly Press, 1982), 41.

27.   Ibid.

28.   John F. Zipp, "Perceived Representativeness and Voting: An Assessment of the Impact of 'Choices' vs. 'Echoes,' " *American Political Science Review*, 79 (March 1985): 50–61.

29.   Thomas Cavanagh, *Inside Black America* (Washington, D.C.: Joint Center for Political Studies, forthcoming).

30.   Adam Clymer, "The 1984 National Primary," *Public Opinion*, 17, no. 3 (1984): 3.

31.   U.S. Bureau of the Census, unpublished data, 1985.

32.   Sandra Baxter and Marjorie Lansing, *Women and Politics: The Visible Majority*, rev. ed. (Ann Arbor: University of Michigan Press, 1983).

33.   Cavanagh, *Inside Black America*.

34.   Conversation with Donna Brazile, Executive Direction of the National Political Congress of Black Women.

35.   Williams, "Black Political Progress in the 1970s: The Electoral Arena," in *The New Black Politics: The Search for Political Power*, eds. Michael Preston, Lenneal J. Henderson, Jr., and Paul Puryear (New York: Longman, 1982), p. 75.

36.   Ibid., p. 76.

37.   Ibid., p. 90.

38.   Compiled from data from Joint Center for Political Studies, *National Roster of Black Elected Officials* 1985 and National Women's Political Caucus, *National Directory of Women Elected Officials* 1985.

39.   For a full list of reasons, see Williams, *The New Black Politics*, p. 75.

40.   William O'Hare, "Places with Black Mayors," (Working Paper, Joint Center for Political Studies, forthcoming).

41.   Ibid.

42.   Walton, *Black Politics*, 12–16.

43.   Quoted in Terry N. Clark and Lorna C. Ferguson, *City Money: Political Processes, Fiscal Strain, and Retrenchment* (New York: Columbia University Press, 1983), 174.

44.   See Keech, *The Impact of Negro Voting*; and Peter Eisinger, *Black Employment in City Government, 1973–1980* (Washington, D.C.: Joint Center for Political Studies, 1983).

45.   Gary Brooks and Williams Claggett, "Black Electoral Power, White Resistance, and Legislative Behavior," *Political Behavior*, 41, n. 3 (1981): 49–68.

46.   David Coombs, M. H. Alsikafi, C. Hobson Bryan, and Irving Webber, "Black Political Control in Greene County, Alabama," *Rural Sociology*, 42, no. 1 (1977): 398–406.

47.   Campbell and Feagin, "Black Electoral Victories in the South," 141.

48.   Greer, *Big Steel*.

49.   Albert Karnig and Susan Welch, *Black Representation and Urban Policy* (Chicago: University of Chicago Press, 1980).

50.   Dale Marshall and David Tabb, *Minority Participation and Political Payoffs in California* (New York: Basic Books, 1985).

51.   Eisinger, *Black Employment in City Government*, 49.
52.   Clark and Ferguson, *City Money*, 177.
53.   Ibid.
54.   Ibid., p. 184.
55.   Milton Coleman, "Fifty Six Percent of Blacks Find Reagan Racist," *Washington Post*, January 20, 1985, 1.
56.   Joe R. Feagin and Harlan Hahn, "The Second Reconstruction: Black Political Strength in the South, *Social Science Quarterly*, vol. 47, no. 3 (1974), 42–43.
57.   Quoted in David J. Garrow, *The FBI and Martin Luther King, Jr.* (New York: Penguin Books, 1981), 207.
58.   Martin Luther King, Jr., "Letter from Birmingham Jail," *American Visions*, 1, no. 1 (1986), 53.

PART THREE

Urban Politics
and Public Policy

SEVEN

The Election of Harold Washington: An Examination of the SES Model in the 1983 Chicago Mayoral Election

Michael B. Preston

The Election of Harold Washington

In Chicago the chief sport is politics. It is a game that captures the imagination of young and old alike. Anybody engaging in Chicago politics learns how to play the game of hardball, or retires early. The point of the game is power. Those that have it, want to keep it; those that don't have it, are always trying to figure out a way to get it. The game for years was dominated by white Irish Democratic machine politicians; black politicians played supporting roles. Harold Washington's election has "modified" the "rules of the game." It has also introduced new players.

One needs to emphasize "modified" because it is not yet clear how successful he will be in reforming a city that most Chicagoans believe is not ready for reform. Whatever the outcome of this struggle, the election of Harold Washington as mayor will be remembered as one of the most exciting elections in Chicago's long and illustrious political history.

Harold Washington's victory in the 1983 Democratic mayoral primary and general election surprised some and shocked others. Indeed, only the true believers predicted a Washington victory in the primary. The group most surprised by the results of the primary was the Democratic organization. Its members simply did not believe that Washington was a serious threat until a week before the election. The news and broadcast media also never took the Washington candidacy seriously, and the major political analysts and pollsters all favored Richard M. Daley, the son of former Mayor Daley. Thus the average white citizen and voter was led to believe that the race was really between the incumbent Mayor Jane Byrne and States Attorney Richard M. Daley.

The basic question that arises here is how all of these groups could hold such a faulty perception; what prevented them from seeing the warning signals that had been flashing for quite some time?

One explanation is that for over 20 years black voters in Chicago were not taken seriously by the Democratic organization. They were predictable as well as controllable. Their turnout was usually low and overwhelmingly favored the regular Democratic candidates—both black and white. However, by the time of the 1979 mayoral election, black voter attitudes and voting turnout had undergone a rather remarkable change. Black voter dissatisfaction with machine policies and programs led them not only to become more antimachine but more independent voters as well. *Indeed, in an unusual twist of events, blacks instead of whites became the leaders of the independent political movement in Chicago.*

In 1979 blacks gave reformist candidate Jane Byrne over 63 percent of their votes. And when Jane Byrne was elected but turned out not to be a reformer, they not only helped defeat her choice for states' attorney, Edmund Burke, but subsequently went on to defeat a black alderman whom she had supported in a special election.

By the time of the 1982 Illinois gubernatorial election, black voter registration and turnout had increased substantially. Black votes not only almost helped defeat a popular Republican governor, Jim Thompson, but for the first time blacks outvoted whites on a statewide basis, 64 percent to 54.2 percent. What is remarkable about all of this is the fact that the Democratic organization never really took the changes in black voting behavior seriously. They considered them aberrations rather than permanent changes. In other words, they refused to accept the fact that "a new black voter" had emerged in Chicago. And what white Democratic party leaders also failed to realize is that the new black voter has shifted the emphasis from the civil rights revolution to the electoral revolution.

The new black voter may be categorized into two groups: previously registered voters who have developed a stronger sense of political efficacy and group consciousness or newly registered voters who now see some linkages between political process and product. Charles Hamilton has called this the "P" paradigm, i.e., when *process* (political activity however defined) leads to a *product* (more jobs, better schools, ethnic pride, or conversely negative outcomes), then *participation* is likely to increase.[1] The newly registered black voters are significant because they represent the groups that have been the least likely to register and vote: the young, poor, women, and the elderly. They have come to believe, like many of their middle-class brethren, that they can make a difference. This is especially true when the choices presented call into question their ethnic pride or group identity, or when oppressing forces are seen as hostile to black interests.

A key factor in the resurgence of black voting in Chicago and elsewhere has been the emphasis placed on voter registration and mobilization. Indeed, in a recent analysis of the failure of the SES model to explain the rise in black voter turnout, Nie and Erbring argue that the factor linking the civil rights movement and electoral and economic participation and contributing to their actual or potential success is organization. They note that:

> In countries with strong traditions of collective organizations among, or encompassing, lower socio-economic strata, "group" identification and mobilization tend to redress the imbalance of individual resources, at least at the polls. Either way, of course, it appears as though in the political as in the economic domain, organization is the weapon of the poor.[2]

The increase in black voter participation raises a question about whether traditional models of voter participation can adequately explain past as well as present voting trends of the black electorate. Thus we begin our analysis by examining the theoretical literature on voting behavior. Second, we shall also look at historical black voting trends in Chicago by analyzing voting participation data for the 1975 through 1979 Chicago mayoral elections and comparing them with the outcomes of the 1983 mayoral election. Third, we will examine the linkages between Harold Washington's election and his political impact on black voter turnout. Fourth, we will discuss how the 1983 election in Chicago deviated from the traditional voting behavior literature. Indeed, we shall show how the traditional gap in turnout between predominantly white and predominantly black wards was significantly reduced in spite of substantial differences in median income between these wards. Finally, we conclude by discussing whether the black voter turnout in 1983 is likely to be sustained in the 1987 Chicago mayoral election in which Harold Washington is expected to seek reelection.

Theories of Participation

Prior research has offered a myriad of explanations for why people participate in the political arena. Sidney Verba and Norman H. Nie contend that citizens participate in the political arena to influence the selection of governmental personnel and policies.[3] They continued their analysis by asserting that political participation is justified because it can help reduce social and economic inequalities. Those of lower status—workers, poor blacks, and new immigrants—can maximize their political influence through participation. Ultimately they may induce the government to carry out policies beneficial to them, pressure the administrative body to equalize opportunities of participation, and remove the legal and social restraints upon them.[4]

However, opening opportunities does not necessarily equalize participation rates. All may receive equal access to participate in a formal sense—that is, suffrage is universal and the right to petition is guaranteed by all and all can join in campaign activity.[5] But, that participation is voluntary.

Obviously some will take greater advantage of opportunities than others. And most studies of active participation (including that by Verba and Nie) reveal that those with higher status occupations, higher incomes, and higher education levels participate more. In short, whites participate more than blacks.

Verba and Nie posit a socioeconomic model which states that participation is largely the produce of an individual's income and occupation. The higher a person's status or class dimensions, the more likely it is that he or she will participate in the political arena. According to their analysis, social class affects voting through an intervening set of variables; one such variable is "civic orientation." This orientation includes: 1) a psychological involvement in politics—i.e., a sense of having a stake in the political system and its outcome; 2) the feeling of political efficacy—i.e., the belief that one's participation has or could have some effect on the outcome of the political process; 3) the quality of political information possessed which varies with education; and 4) the commitment felt toward one's community.[6]

Other scholars argue that apathy is the reason why some people vote less than others. They specifically contend that blacks, in particular, do not engage in political activities at the same level as whites because they are not as interested in politics as whites.[7] This theory implies that blacks have a low sense of civic obligation, i.e., a lower sense of duty about participating in public affairs. This theory also suggests that blacks do not have a clear understanding of politics and the importance of voting.

Another commonly advanced explanation offered by Erickson, Luttberg, and Tedin suggests that:

> The well-to-do participate because they have a greater stake in political outcome (the protection of their advantaged position) . . . this upper-class bias would certainly seem to operate in a fashion likely to lessen the political influence of the more disadvantaged classes.[8]

Many political scientists and other researchers point out that participation is greatest among those who are high in socioeconomic status, that is, among the most educated, the wealthy, and those with prestigous occupations.[9] Certainly, there seems to be linkage between social status and political participation. We turn once again to Erickson, Luttberg, and Tedin who state:

> Blacks participate less than whites; women participate somewhat less than men. . . . These differences can largely be explained by differences in socioeconomic status and placement in the life cycle. According to a U.S. Census survey, 71% of whites voted in the 1976 *presidential election* compared with only 49% of blacks. This gap reflects the fact that blacks generally participate less than whites.
>
> At one time, low black participation was the result of overt discrimination, particularly in the South. Today, . . . the gap is basically due to socioeconomic differences between the races. . . . When the voting rates for blacks and whites are compared at the same level of education and income, the differential declines to a mere 2% (percentage) points. Blacks actually participate more than whites when this sort of comparison is extended to activities beyond voting.[10]

Verba and Nie also shed some light on the impact of race as well as class as determinants of mobilization and participation in electoral success. They suggest that socioeconomic status is closely related to race. It is interesting to note that Verba and Nie's data indicate that consciousness of race (either as a problem or a basis of conflict) appears to bring blacks *up to a level of participation equivalent to that of whites*. For example, in their measurement of group consciousness, 64 percent of their black respondents mentioned race spontaneously in response to a question about group consciousness and political participation, and 24 percent mentioned race more than once.[11] In comparing the rates of participation of blacks at varying levels of group consciousness with the average participation of whites, the key variable in the group consciousness model tended to be group consciousness itself.[12] This awareness on the part of blacks tends to *overcome the socioeconomic disadvantages* of blacks and makes them as active as whites. In a more recent analysis, the importance of "group consciousness" is particularly evident in Nie's recent empirical analysis of the correlation between wealth and voter turnout in elections from 1922 to 1966. In contravention to what the SES model would predict, turnout among low-wealth votes was as high as and often higher than turnout of high-wealth votes from 1922 to 1950; only from 1956 to 1966 is there a strong positive relation between wealth and voter turnout. They explain this result by stressing the importance of political machines as an organizational force in the early years of the study (1922 to 1934), and then they stress the importance of an issue, the New Deal, drawing voters together. These same factors are contributing to the emergence of the new black voter.[13]

It seems clear then that the standard SES models cannot be used as a baseline to explain increases in black voter turnout. This is best explained by an increase in group consciousness, especially where a serious black candidate is running for a high political office and where the election is highly competitive.

According to Verba and Nie:

> If blacks participate more than one would expect of a group with a similar socioeconomic status (SES), the explanation may lie in the fact that they have, over time, developed an awareness of their own status as a deprived group, and this self-consciousness has led them to be more political than members of the society who have similar socioeconomic levels but does not share the group identity.[14]

This leads us to believe that blacks still participate less than whites but more than one would expect given their social and economic condition. Verba and Nie, while allowing for group consciousness in determining who participates, still maintain, like others who write on the subject, that socioeconomic difference is the baseline for analyzing who participates.[15] Obviously, the trend has been for the black electorate to participate less in local, state, and national elections and the reason stems from a lack of concern regarding political issues.

The fundamental question raised in this study is: How consistent and reliable is the present theory as the basis for interpreting Harold Washington's victory in the 1983 mayoral election? How do we account for the votes by citizens with low socioeconomic status? Moreover, how do we assess the political participation of the young adults who had very little education—who are identified as scoring very low on the political participation scale?[16] The traditional theories do not provide a sufficiently broad outlook into future occurrences which would help explain possible changes in the black electorate.

The work done by Sidney Verba and Norman Nie along with that of Ronald Terchek seems to be the most helpful for explaining Harold Washington's victory. In some ways Verba and Nie's study can be used as a source of reference for interpreting that victory, for they consider and emphasize black group consciousness as a factor in increased black participation. It is true that voter registration and participation by blacks did increase significantly in the 1983 mayoral election due to the fact that *black consciousness* was raised not only by the mass movement of people but also by the racist campaign of Washington's opponents. However, Verba and Nie's theory does not help explain the specific factors that led to the extraordinary participation of black voters. Nor do they explain whether these are likely to be patterned responses or just isolated responses to individual elections. And they do not specify under what condition group consciousness is likely to lead to higher participation.

Perhaps the most useful, relevant, and applicable theory stems from the work of Ronald Terchek. Terchek's theory supplements other theories because it incorporates the notion that incentives are helpful in determining who participates. We offer Terchek's theory as a basis for providing a more concrete analysis and interpretation of the Harold Washington victory. Although Terchek is willing, for the most part, to agree with other researchers on the subject, his findings reveal that three other factors must be considered: relevance of issues, symbolic importance of ethnicity to voters, and the expected competitiveness of an election. Terchek refers to these three areas as incentive structures and has found that their presence increases a group's participation.

1. With the introduction of more *pertinent issues* into local campaign, the incentive to participate should increase and result in a higher turnout.
2. The *symbolic* dimension of elections and candidates also provides an important incentive for participation. Ethnic affinity has long been an important symbolic component of American politics, and ethnic identification has often provided an incentive for otherwise inactive voters to vote for a representative of their ethnic community. The presence of a minority member on the ballot might be expected to increase minority group participation, particularly when the candidate is running for office that is considered important (such as *mayor* rather than clerk of courts), when the office has not been traditionally filled by members of the minority, and where the ethnicity of a candidate become an issue.
3. Relevant issues, ethnic identification, and the *competitiveness* of the election define the incentive structure for voting and should be coupled with Charles Hamilton's organization structure for minority group participation. Incentives and organization structures are not independent of one another. The very factors that make a candidate appealing to previously inactive voters also tend to generate other expressions of support, such as volunteer activity, money, and endorsement that serve to build an organization.[17]

Congruent with Terchek's discussion, Nie and Erbring's recent study finds it essential that more than one of these incentives be present.

> Organization must become the vehicle of a salient dimension of political conflict, with clear-cut partisan alternatives, if it is to mobilize voters. Yet a clear issue separation between parties alone appears to be equally insufficient to engage individual electoral participation, at least among lower-status voters, in the absence of organizational support.[18]

The most interesting aspects of the 1983 mayoral election and Harold Washington's victory can easily be identified with the incentive structures of which Terchek speaks; for example: 1) the long history of machine exploitation—a pertinent issue; 2) a mass movement of the people—group consciousness; Washington as a symbolic figure; 3) the amazing amount of racism that surfaced among white ethnics—competitiveness; and 4) the growth of individualistic as well as group selfishness that was later intensified by the fear of losing jobs, etc. or looking out for the possibility of a future position in the city. With the incorporation of all these items into the local campaign agenda, the incentive to participate in electoral politics at the local level increased and most definitely overcame what has been the normal trend among low socioeconomic status groups.

A close examination of the 1975 to 1983 mayoral elections shows that black political participation is strongly correlated with ethnic identity and awareness, that is, like other ethnic groups blacks are finally beginning to forge strong political ties based on race not class; and they are beginning to use those ties to wield political power.

A Note on Methodology

To analyze black voter participation in the city of Chicago during the period 1975 to 1983, we tried to devise a method of evaluating wards that would adequately reflect the character of our study. Since our particular concern is black voter participation, we tried to locate the most homogeneously black wards in the city. Thus, we call a ward that is more than 75 percent black a "predominantly black" ward and included it in our study. Likewise, in our brief analysis of white voter participation we used the same criterion for a "predominantly white" ward.

Unfortunately, it was not possible to determine the exact racial makeup of the wards in each election year. However, by looking at both 1970 and 1980 census data we were able to identify 14 black wards in 1975 and 1977, 15 in 1979, and 16 in 1983. There are now actually 19 predominantly black wards but the other 3 are less than 75 percent black. The increase in the number of black wards is due to two factors. The first arose as a result of a rapidly changing populace in the Ninth Ward. Although this ward was only 28.3 percent black in 1970, it was 89.1 percent black in 1980. Consequently, we assumed that the ninth ward was predominantly black by the 1979 election year and included it in our data from that year on. The other reason for the increase in the number of black wards was the melding of the populations in the Fourth and Fifth Wards to create two wards with black populations of 79 percent and 75 percent, respectively. The 16 predominantly black wards are: second, third, fourth, fifth (after 1980), sixth, eighth, ninth (after 1977), sixteenth, seventeenth, twentieth, twenty-first, twenty-fourth, twenty-seventh, twenty-eighth, twenty-ninth, and thirty-fourth.

We are hampered in our analysis by the lack of accurate income data for these 16 predominantly black wards. We decided, therefore, to measure wealth in terms of property values and rents on property as a substitute for yearly income flows during the 1977 to 1980 period. We feel that this is a good approximation of the relative prosperity of a community since the value of one's home and amount of rent are reasonably correlated with income and other measures of wealth. To do this, we first ranked the value of homes in these wards from 1 to 16; then we ranked the cost of rent in those same wards. On the whole, rents and the values of homes were positively correlated (higher rents in higher home owned wards). Then, using a combination of both rents and homes values, we were able to get absolute rankings for the wards (see Table 7.1).

In disaggregating our data by income (wealth) level we wanted to look at the lowest and the highest 25 percent of the wards. Unfortunately, we had to throw out the Fifth Ward (not a majority black ward until 1980) and use only the Eighth, Fourth, and Sixth Wards for our upper wealth wards. We were able to use all four of our lower wealth wards: twenty-fourth, sixteenth, twenty-seventh, and third.

The Data: 1975 to 1979

Theorists have been grappling with the question of why black voter registration and turnout have historically been significantly lower than among white voters. It was certainly true for Chicago in the elections between 1975

Table 7.1   Relative Wealth Ranking of Predominantly Black Wards

Absolute Rank	Ward	Home Rank	Home Value	Rent Rank	Rent Price
1	5	2	$69,899	1	$231
2	8	4	41,425	2	215
3	4	1	80,832	6	188
4	6	5	40,961	3	197
5	29	6	40,324	4	192
6	21	9	36,055	5	192
7	34	7	40,279	8	184
8	2	3	42,426	15	136
9	9	8	39,284	10	175
10	17	11	31,092	7	187
11	28	10	33,393	11	169
12	20	12	30,676	9	177
13	24	14	28,972	13	159
14	16	15	27,864	12	167
15	27	13	30,495	16	135
16	3	16	27,020	14	154

and 1979. Registration in predominantly black wards was consistently more than 5 percent below registration in predominantly white wards. In 1977 black ward registration (72.3 percent) was 6.4 percent less than in white wards (78.7 percent); and in 1979 it was 5.9 percent lower. In terms of votes in the political arena, a lower registration rate among eligible voters may not necessarily mean fewer blacks than whites were registered in each ward. However, on average, the black populace is younger than the white, meaning fewer people in black wards are eligible to vote. As a result, the total average white registration per ward in absolute value has been about one-third greater (34.6 percent in 1975 and 28.7 percent in 1977) than in black wards. During the period 1975 to 1979 black wards averaged only 26,700 registered votes per ward while white wards averaged 35,000 per ward.[19]

Much the same was true for turnout. Black turnout in the three elections averaged a disheartening 14 percent less than white turnout from 1975 to 1979: 58.6 percent for whites vs. 44.6 percent for blacks (see Table 7.2). It is interesting to note that both black and white turnout fell by substantial amounts during the 1975 general election and the 1977 primary. They also rose in unison in the 1979 primary; and instead of declining for the general election (as is usually the case), they both increased. This leads us to believe that some outside factors caused both black and white voters to stay away from the polls in the general election of 1975 and the primary of 1977. Whatever it was, it was stronger for black-ward voters since the turnout gap increased from 11.5 percent in the 1975 primary to 17.2 percent in the general election and 16.1 percent in the 1977 primary.

Given that the registration and turnout in predominantly black wards is consistently lower than that of predominantly white wards, we will now move on to our primary object of study; the predominantly black wards of Chicago. Looking closely at registration we see some intriguing facts. First, as noted before, mean registration in black wards was 72.3 percent in 1977 and then dropped to 64.2 percent in 1979. The black wards, however, were not homogeneous in their registration patterns. The three upper wealth

Table 7.2   Black vs. White Comparative Turnout: 1975 to 1979
(in percent)

	1975		1977	1979	
	Primary	*General*	*Primary*	*Primary*	*General*
Black wards	48.8	34.7	35.3	51.3	52.8
White wards	60.3	51.9	51.4	64.2	65.0
Differential	11.5	17.2	16.1	12.9	12.2

Source: Michael B. Preston, "Black Politics in the Post-Daley Era," in *After Daley,* eds. Samuel K. Gove and Louis Masotti, (Urbana: University of Illinois Press, 1982), pp. 97–100. Also see, Chicago Board of Election Commissioners.

wards tended to have higher registration than the mean; and the four lower wealth wards tended to be far below the mean (see Table 7.3). The differential between upper and lower wealth wards was amazing. In 1977 upper wealth ward registration was 15.3 percent greater than lower wealth wards; and in 1979 the differential was 12.5 percent. Although predicted to some degree by certain theorists, these findings are surprising, since they show a positive correlation between wealth position of a black ward and the registration rate within that ward.

Registration is one of the most important aspects of voter participation, yet registration alone does not elect a candidate. Those who are registered must turn out to have an impact on an election. As noted earlier, black turnout in the predominantly black wards has been consistently lower than that in predominantly white wards. Perhaps this phenomenon, like that of registration, can be seen as a function of wealth differentials. If turnout is positively correlated with wealth, then there should be a significant differential between turnout in the three upper wealth wards and the four lower wealth wards. However, the data do not support this (see Table 7.4). During all three election periods the upper wealth wards are extremely close to the mean: the differentials are not statistically significant except in the 1975 primary (2.9 percent deviation from the mean). Even more intriguing, turnout in the lower wealth wards was consistently higher than in the upper wealth wards, neglecting the 1975 primary. The average differential between lower and upper wealth ward turnout for the three specific elections (1975 general, 1977 primary, and 1979 primary) was 5 percent. Although registration in predominantly black wards in Chicago is positively correlated with wealth, it seems evident that there is no such correlation in terms of turnout.

For whom did blacks in predominantly black wards vote? Here, we only looked at the primary elections of 1975 to 1979. Because the overwhelming majority of blacks vote along Democratic lines, the primaries should yield the most salient facts. In the 1975 primary incumbent Mayor Richard Daley ran against a reform candidate, William Singer, and a black candidate, State Senator Richard Newhouse. Daley won the election citywide with the help

Table 7.3   Registration in Black Wards: Upper Wealth vs. Lower Wealth

	1977	1979
Mean % registration, all black wards	72.3	64.2
Mean % registration, three wealthiest wards	77.1	67.0
Mean % registration, four lower income wards	61.8	54.5

Note: Registration for the 1975 election could not be calculated from our data.
Source: Michael B. Preston, "Black Politics in the Post-Daley Era," in *After Daley,* eds. Samuel K. Gove and Louis Masotti (Urbana: University of Ilinois Press, 1982).

Table 7.4   1975 to 1979 Turnout in Black Wards:
Upper Wealth vs. Lower Wealth

	1975		1977	1979	
	Pri.	Gen.	Pri.	Pri.	Gen.
Mean Turnout % in Black Wards	48.8	34.7	35.3	51.3	52.8
Mean Turnout % Three Wealthiest Wards	51.7	34.7	36.3	50.0	52.3
Mean Turnout % Four Lower Income Wards	49.4	39.6	41.8	54.5	53.9

Note: Pri. means Primary Election and Gen. means General Election/1977 Special Elections Gen dat NA
Source: Michael B. Preston, "Black Politics in the Post-Daley Era," in *After Daley,* eds. Samuel K. Gove and Louis Masotti (Urbana: University of Illinois Press, 1982).

of a substantial black plurality, 45.7 percent. Singer and Newhouse respectively garnered 29.3 percent and 17.7 percent of the total black vote. Interestingly, the vote patterns in the upper wealth wards were significantly different than the lower income wards (see Table 7.5). Daley received 54.5 percent of the lower wealth ward vote, but only 43.7 percent of the upper wealth ward vote. Singer and Newhouse, however, had more support in the wealthier wards. Singer captured 32.6 percent and Newhouse 19.5 percent of this group's votes, while each received only 25 percent and 14.5 percent, respectively, in the lower wealth black wards.

The 1977 primary broke down in much the same manner as in the one in 1975. Once again there were three prime candidates: the machine candidate, Michael Bilandic; Polish ethnic candidate, Roman Pucinski; and black ethnic candidate, Harold Washington. Bilandic and the machine got 47.6 percent of the total black vote, Harold Washington netted 31.3 percent, and Roman Pucinski got some 12.5 percent. In this election the polarization between upper wealth and lower wealth wards was much greater than in 1975. In the fourth, sixth, and eighth wards Bilandic and Washington ran very close campaigns: Bilandic 40.3 percent, Washington 37.3 percent, and Pucinski 13 percent. Yet, in the Third, Sixteenth, Twenty-fourth, and Twenty-seventh Wards Bilandic (57 percent) more than doubled Washington's (23.8 percent) votes. Thus, we see that the machine seems to have had its greatest control in the poorest of the predominantly black wards.

These trends also hold for the 1979 primary in which Jane Byrne ran on a reform ticket and upset machine incumbent Bilandic. In this election the upper wealth wards almost completely left the machine: Bilandic received only 33 percent of their vote. Byrne, on the other hand, grabbed 64.3 percent of their votes. The low wealth wards were still the biggest backers of the machine, giving Bilandic 48.7 percent of their vote while only granting

Table 7.5 Black Candidate Selection: Upper Wealth vs. Lower Wealth

Electoral Position	1975			1977			1979		
	Upper	Mean	Lower	Upper	Mean	Lower	Upper	Mean	Lower
Machine	43.6	45.7 (Daley)	54.5	40.3	47.6 (Bilandic)	57.0	33.3	39.5 (Bilandic)	48.7
Independent	32.6	29.3 (Singer)	25.0				64.3	55.5 (Byrne)	44.6
Ethnic	19.5	17.7 (Newhouse)	14.5	37.3	31.3 (Washington)	23.8[a]			
Ethnic and Independent				13.0	12.5 (Pucinski)	11.9[a]			
Aggregated	52.1	47.0	39.5	50.3	43.8	35.7	64.3	55.5	44.6

[a]The 1977 election had no citywide independent challengers. Pucinski and Washington both ran ethnic campaigns.
Source: Chicago Board of Election Commissioners.

44.6 percent to Byrne. The Twenty-seventh Ward, which ranked as the second poorest, voted an amazing 63.9 percent in favor of Bilandic.

Analysis: 1975 to 1979

The data for 1975 to 1979 correlate positively with Sidney Verba and Norman Nie's socioeconomic model of voter participation. The figures reveal that upper wealth ward registration for the period was significantly higher than lower wealth ward registration. We should note that alienation from the political process and apathy are most likely to occur in lower income areas where the rewards of the political process are not readily observable.

In seeming contradiction to the above are the data for turnout in the predominantly black wards. If apathy is greater among lower income groups, then the lower wealth wards would have experienced much lower turnout rates. In fact, there was no positive correlation between wealth and turnout rate. However, other factors must be taken into account. Given that registration in the Third, Sixteenth, Twenty-fourth, and Twenty-seventh Wards is significantly lower, it is not meaningful to speak in turnout percentages. A more accurate assessment requires a look at raw votes in these wards. Lower wealth wards averaged a mere 9,904 voters per ward per election, representing only 74 percent of the upper wealth wards, which averaged 13,315 votes/ward/election. So, in terms of absolute numbers there is a positive correlation for the 1975 to 1979 election period between wealth and turnout.

Looking at the electoral position of many different candidates, there also seems to be divergence between the lower and upper wealth wards. We can categorically state that black upper wealth wards voted pro-independent and pro-ethnicity in the 1975 to 1979 period. This can be readily seen in the votes for independent candidates Singer and Newhouse in the 1975 election where they garnered a combined 52.1 percent of the upper wealth black ward vote. In much the same manner, Washington and Pucinski captured 50.3 percent in 1977. This majority would surely have been larger if Pucinski had run an independent campaign rather than a Polish-ethnic one. Finally, the overwhelming support of Jane Byrne in 1979 (64.3 percent) establishes that the upper wealth wards were growing more independent during that period.

One thing that is extremely confounding is the consistent support given by lower wealth wards to the machine. For example, the Twenty-seventh Ward, one of the poorest in the city, turned out 66.9 percent in 1977 and 63.9 percent in 1979 for Bilandic and the machine. Why would a ward that has received few, if any, benefits from the machine continue to support it so heavily? Given what we observed earlier concerning the actual number of voters, it is not difficult to explain this phenomenon. Essentially, in the lower wealth wards there is an extremely large pool of unmobilized and apparently apathetic non-voters with a few highly committed machine loyalists scattered throughout. Furthermore, we do not discount the possibility of large-scale corruption among a politically unsophisticated populace.

Underlying the analysis of candidate attractiveness for different segments of the black populace is one crucial point: None of the candidates from 1975 to 1979 were able to mobilize people who were not to some degree already politically active. Even Jane Byrne, running on a strong platform, was not able to motivate any significant number of blacks to take a few minutes to register and one-half hour to vote. It is generally assumed that the mayoral candidacy of Harold Washington did so motivate people. This assumption needs to be tested.

The 1983 Elections

The Democratic primary of 1983 saw a dramatic change in the scope of black political participation. Whereas over the 1975 to 1979 period registration in the predominantly black wards was consistently 5 percent below registration levels in predominantly white wards, in 1983 black registration jumped to phenomenal levels. In fact, the mean percent of registered votes in black wards (84.9 percent) was 12.8 percent higher than in white wards (72.1 percent). In absolute numbers, this translates into an average of 37,991 registered voters per black ward as compared to 34,252 registered voters per white ward. Similarly, black turnout percentages hit record levels in the 1983 primary—and were then surpassed in the general election. Mean turnout percentages across the 16 predominantly black wards was 74.2 percent. At the same time, however, white turnout approached 80 percent (79.6 percent). In other words, the same force was affecting black and white voters in a way that had never happened before.

Within the predominantly black wards, some extremely uncharacteristic patterns emerged. When we disaggregated by wealth level, we noted virtually no difference between upper and lower wealth wards. This completely breaks with the trend of the 1975 to 1979 period, where the differential between the two segments averaged 14 percent. Registration in the lower wealth wards in 1983 was 84.8 percent, while in the upper wealth wards it was 86.5 percent. Thus, in the 1983 election there was no correlation between the wealth position of a ward and its percentage of registered voters (see Table 7.6). This is consonant with Nie's recent suggestion that voting is a distinct form of participation:

> Unlike all other modes of participation, the exercise of the franchise is precisely not tied to differential personal resource endowments—at least, not by definition.[20]

Table 7.6   Registration and Turnout, 1983:
Upper Wealth vs. Lower Wealth

	Upper	Mean	Lower
Registration	86.5	84.9	84.8
Turnout	76.0	74.2	74.3

Turnout in the 16 predominantly black wards was also exceptionally high. In these wards 74.2 percent of all those registered voted. Differences in turnout between the upper and lower wealth wards was virtually nonexistent (1.7 percent), as was true for the 1983 registration figures. Lower wealth wards turned out at a rate of 74.3 percent, while the upper wealth wards had a 76 percent turnout rate.

In examining the candidates for whom the predominantly black wards voted in 1983, it is apparent that Congressman Harold Washington won the Democratic nomination as the result of overwhelming black support. The three candidates for office were incumbent Jane Byrne, independent Congressman Harold Washington, and Richard M. Daley. Washington received over three-fourths of the vote in the 16 observed wards (75.2 percent), Byrne attracted 12.9 percent, and Daley received only 4.2 percent. Support for Washington was exceptionally broad-based and cut across all income levels. However, upper wealth wards, historically more independent, turned out more favorably for Washington than did the lower wealth wards. The former gave Washington 79 percent of their vote, while the latter gave 70.3 percent of theirs, an 8.7 percent differential. Byrne managed to pull out only 10 percent of the vote in the three upper wealth wards and only 16.2 percent in the traditional machine stronghold of the Third, Sixteenth, Twenty-fourth, and Twenty-seventh Wards.

Another very interesting development, indeed a barometer of the new activism among black voters, can be found in the turnout rate of poor black residents in the Chicago Housing Authority (CHA) and how these residents voted. The CHA had long been a stronghold for the machine. The area is 85 percent black and a majority of its residents are below the poverty level ($4,600 is the average income).[21] In 1981 the CHA had 144,000 residents. Yet in the 1979 election Byrne received 45 percent of the vote, compared to 55 percent for Bilandic. This is the closest that any independent candidate had come to a machine candidate in about 14 years.

Byrne, the reformer, turned out not to be a reformer and in fact quickly became the leader of the machine. Her appointment of whites to control CHA plus other perceived insults to CHA residents caused some concern. But she also lived in CHA just before the election to show her support for residents who wished to rid themselves of gangs. One would think that this political theater would have helped Byrne in the primary. Instead, she won only 12 out of 52 CHA precincts. In the general election Epton, the Republican candidate, won only 7 of the 52 precincts. Washington won in an overwhelming percent of the precincts and an extraordinary percentage of the vote in the South Side.

It is clear that the candidacy of Harold Washington in the 1983 mayoral election had a substantial impact on black voter registration and turnout. The increase in registration among both lower and middle income blacks was phenomenal: Income did not seem to make a significant difference in the registration and turnout of black voters. In the next section, we briefly show how black voting patterns in the 1983 mayoral primary and general elections deviated from the expectations of the traditional voting behavior literature.

Median Income and Turnout Percentages of Black, White, and Hispanic Voters in the 1983 Mayoral Primary and General Elections[22]

An examination of the data on median income and turnout percentages of black, white, and hispanic voters yields some interesting findings. Table 7.7 displays the median income for 50 Chicago wards. The wards are grouped according to the predominant racial population of the ward. It is striking to notice the difference between the 24 predominantly white wards with an average median income of just over $22,000 and the predominantly black and hispanic wards, respectively, with average mean incomes of under $15,000. The ward with the highest median income is the predominantly white Forty-first Ward, while the ward with the lowest median income is the predominantly black Second Ward. The most prosperous predominantly black ward is the Twenty-first Ward with a median income of $22,311. The Twenty-first Ward would rank just twelfth among predominantly white wards in terms of median income and falls just below the white ward average median of $22,329.

Table 7.8 (appendix) presents changes in turnout between the 1979 and 1983 mayoral primary elections, respectively. The wards are grouped in terms of the predominant racial group in the ward. Turnout for the mayoral primary in 1983 was higher than turnout for the 1979 primary in 47 of Chicago's 50 wards. The predominantly white Eleventh Ward and the predominantly Hispanic Twenty-fifth Ward dropped two percentage points in turnout between 1979 and 1983, though it should be noted that the Eleventh's 83 percent in 1983 still ranked it first (along with the Thirteenth) among wards in turnout for the 1983 primary. The predominantly Hispanic Twenty-sixth Ward's turnout was unchanged from 1979 to 1983.

Table 7.7   Median Incomes of Predominantly[a] Black, White,
and Hispanic Wards, 1980

Black Wards		White Wards		Hispanic Wards	
Ward	*Median Income*	Ward	*Median Income*	Ward	*Median Income*
1	11,255	10	22,676	22	16,852
2	7,325	11	17,340	25	13,633
3	7,932	12	19,659	26	12,466
4	12,193	13	25,041	31	15,159
5	19,116	14	18,966	32	13,974
6	18,673	18	25,198	33	17,017
7	18,967	19	26,707	Mean	14,850
8	21,429	23	25,142		
9	17,920	30	20,653		
15	18,391	35	19,966		
16	10,897	36	23,862		
17	15,524	38	24,129		
20	10,116	39	23,906		
21	22,311	40	20,992		
24	10,232	41	27,309		
27	9,217	42	20,184		
28	11,038	43	29,698		
29	14,778	44	21,625		
34	20,938	45	24,802		
37	17,624	46	16,565		
Mean	14,796	47	19,644		
		48	16,975		
		49	19,439		
		50	24,512		
		Mean	22,329		

[a]*Predominantly defined as most numerous racial group in ward.*
Source: U.S. Census figures, 1980.

Turnout was up an average of 16 percentage points in the 20 predominantly black Chicago wards. The 24 predominantly white wards showed an average increase of 11.6 percentage points, while the 6 predominantly Hispanic wards showed an average increase of just 4 percentage points.

The 1983 turnout rate of 68.9 percent in the 20 predominantly black wards is all the more impressive when viewed in an historical context. Turnout for mayoral primaries in predominantly black wards prior to the Byrne-Bilandic race in 1979 had been as low as 36 percent in the 1977 special primary and had last topped the 1979 figure of 52.9 percent only in 1955 when 56.8 percent of the voters in the three black-majority wards turned out to vote in the mayoral primary. Turnout for the 1983 primary was thus as significant historically as it surely was politically.

Table 7.9 (appendix) compares mayoral primary turnout figures for 1979 and 1983 according to the candidate (Washington, Byrne, or Daley) that carried the ward in the 1983 mayoral primary. Washington-won wards showed an average increase in turnout of 16.5 percentage points compared to an average of 10 and 9.6 percentage points in the Byrne-won and Daley-won wards, respectively. Five wards won by Harold Washington (the sixth, seventh, eighth, seventeenth, and thirty-fourth) showed increases in turnout of 20 percentage points or greater. The only other ward in the city to show such an increase was the Byrne-won forty-fourth. It is significant to note that the five aforementioned middle-class Washington-won wards had median incomes greater than the average median income of all Washington-won wards. This provides evidence of the return of the black middle class to the Chicago electoral arena.

Table 7.10 (appendix) compares turnout for the 1979 and 1983 general mayoral elections for predominantly white, black, and Hispanic wards. Turnout was up in 1983 in all 50 wards. The ward with the greatest increase in turnout was the predominantly black twenty-ninth with a 1983 turnout of 80 percent, compared to a 1979 turnout of 49 percent. The ward with the smallest increase in turnout was the predominantly white eleventh with a turnout of 83 percent in 1979 and 84 percent in 1983. It is important to note that at this level of turnout, the eleventh is operating from a turnout "ceiling." It was in the predominantly Hispanic wards that turnout increases were far and away below the city mean. Indeed the ward with the lowest 1983 turnout percentage was the predominantly Hispanic twenty-second, which was ironically the Hispanic ward with the largest 1979 to 1983 change. The increases in turnout for the 1983 general election were even more dramatic than those for the 1983 primary (see Table 7.8 appendix).

General Election: 1983

Table 7.11 (appendix) presents turnout percentages for the wards carried by Washington and Epton, respectively, in the 1983 mayoral general election. The 22 wards carried by Harold Washington show an increase in turnout of 23.5 percentage points compared to 16.5 percentage points for the 28 wards won by Bernard Epton. Seventeen of the 22 Washington-won wards show increases in turnout of at least 20 percentage points. Two wards won by Washington showed increases of less than 10 percentage points, the predominantly Hispanic thirty-first (+2), and the predominantly black twenty-seventh (+9). The twenty-seventh recorded a turnout of 66 percent in 1979, but did so from a registered voting population of less than 20,000, compared to a city-wide average of approximately 28,500 registered voters per ward. Twelve of the 28 wards won by Epton increased their turnout by at least 20 percentage points. Five Epton wards showed increases of less than 10 percentage points.

Two major findings can be gleaned from Tables 7.8 through 7.11. First, tremendous increases in black ward registration, above and beyond the increases in white and Hispanic wards, are obvious for both the primary and general mayoral elections. This finding is reinforced by comparing turnout in wards won by the major candidates in both elections. Changes in registration for the general election in predominantly black wards were most significant (see Table 7.10 appendix).

Second, Tables 7.8 through 7.11 make an interesting point in terms of traditional voting behavior literature. The narrowing gap in turnout between predominantly white and predominantly black wards took place in spite of substantial differences in median income between these wards. Some of the most impressive increases in predominantly black wards took place in wards with higher median incomes (e.g. the Sixth, Eighth, and Thirty-fourth Wards) that previous to 1983 had been indistinguishable from the least prosperous black wards (e.g. the Second, Third, and Twenty-seventh Wards) in terms of turnout. This pronounced reassertion of the black middle class in Chicago mayoral politics along with turnout levels in black wards far above what would have been predicted from income levels alone were significant factors in Harold Washington's election in 1983.

The 28 Epton-won wards turned out an average of 81.6 percent of their registered votes compared to 77.9 percent in the Washington-won wards. *Washington's victory was thus not a matter of pure turnout, but also a product of the overwhelming support Washington received in the wards he won.* Table 7.12 (appendix) shows the percentage of the vote received by Washington and Epton, respectively, in the wards they carried in the general election. It is remarkable to note that Harold Washington received 90 percent or better of the mayoral vote in 16 of the 22 wards he carried. Ten of the 22 Washington-won wards were carried with at least 98.5 percent of the votes cast. This near unanimity in a majority of the Washington-won wards was enough to offset Epton victories in 28 wards, 6 of which came with more than 90 percent of the vote. Epton won eight wards with majorities of less than 60 percent compared to only one Washington-won ward (the predominantly Hispanic twenty-second) with less than 60 percent. Washington's victory was thus a product of huge increases in turnout in predominantly black wards, near-unanimous support in most of these wards on Election Day, and the ability to "hang-tough" in predominantly Hispanic wards (specifically the twenty-fifth and twenty-sixth) and predominantly white forty-sixth, forty-second, forty-eighth, and forth-ninth "lake-front wards."

Why It Happened

Traditional theories of voter participation cannot explain the victory of Harold Washington in the Chicago mayoral election of 1983. According to the thinking of people like Sydney Verba and Norman Nie, Harold Washington should not have won the election. The socioeconomic realities of Chicago had changed very little between the election of Jane Byrne in 1979 and the primary of 1983, so the participatory patterns in 1983 should have been similar to those of 1975–1979. They were not.[23]

While white registration and turnout was high in 1983, registration in predominantly black wards was over 10 percent greater than in predominantly white wards. At the same time, turnout among the two population groups was quite comparable. In absolute numbers of voter per ward there was an average of 27,269 votes per white ward and an average of 28,189 voters per black ward. Some part of the calculus in the Verba-Nie theory did not hold up in the 1983 election, at least as far as the black and white participatory patterns are concerned. This suggests that the factors important to the socioeconomic model are subordinate to some other force, i.e., organization. Nie and Erbring confirm our analysis of the weakness of the standard SES model:

> In effect, it [ethnic descent as an index of group political organization] reinforces an essential point in our perspective on the problem of electoral participation, by emphasizing the importance of group-level, organizational "top down" processes at the expense of individual-level, motivational "bottom up" processes as the driving forces.[24]

Also unexplainable in the framework of traditional theories is the convergence of registration and voting patterns among upper and lower income strata. As we saw for the 1975 to 1979 period, black registration was substantially higher in the upper wealth wards; and although turnout appeared to be similar across income level for the 1975 to 1979 period, we can explain that phenomenon as merely a function of the low registration rates in the lower wealth wards.

But in 1983 none of the trends or theories held up. Registration in the predominantly black wards was almost uniformly at extremely high levels (85 percent); and a turnout rate of approximately 75 percent cut across all income levels. Thus, the traditional theories of voter participation do not explain the sudden mobilization of the general populace that overcame the historical apathy of the black community.

Harold Washington's astounding victory can be explained by closely examining the factors which generate collective action. According to traditional economic and social theories, collective action rarely occurs because of the free-ridership problem; that is, we will never see groups uniting for a single cause so long as the possibility exists that one person can shirk responsibility (no internal control mechanisms). In the election campaign for Harold Washington the theory predicted that if voters believed their neighors were going to vote—diminishing the necessity of their individual vote—the incentive for any one person to participate approaches zero. But as our data reveal, free-ridership in the 1983 election was overcome: Chicago witnessed the largest black collective action since the Civil Rights movements of the 1960s.

For the first time in the history of Chicago politics, a viable black candidate ranked high on the agenda. To black Chicagoans, Washington embodied the hopes and dreams of centuries of struggle. Washington's movement cut across all socioeconomic classes; it reached the poverty stricken enclave of the Cabrini Green Housing Project as well as the gothic towers of Hyde Park. In these communities during the pre-election days and months, it was not uncommon to see the red, black, and green flag of black unity flying high with Washington's name displayed in bold print. This symbol of ethnic and black awareness, together with the highly emotional campaign, inspired over 600,000 black voters to register and to turn out. Undeniably, Washington's intellectual prowess and political sagacity were very important to the movement, but one cannot deny that in racially segregated Chicago, skin color was a fundamental issue.

In the primary, white registration, which had been on the wane, turned upward and turnout reached record numbers. Further, in the general election turnout in predominantly white wards reached an unprecedented 83 percent. For the first time in 50 years, a Republican candidate had a real chance to control City Hall. In the primary the entire Republican slate had received a mere 14,000 votes; in the general, after Washington had won the Democratic nomination, the Republican party and Epton got over 600,000 votes. White ethnic wards on the South and Northwest Sides, which had voted the straight Democratic ticket for decades, cast their ballots for Epton. White Chicagoans, like black Chicagoans, voted according to their commitment to race, not because of class and not much less than because of issues.

Finally, it should be pointed out that while Harold Washington won the election "fair and square," white democrats, led by Alderman Edward Vrdolyak, who is also chairman of the Cook County Democratic Party, have opposed him for over three years on almost all issues. They have held his appointments to various boards and commissions "hostage" so that he has been unable to appoint his own people; they took control of the city council in a coup right after Washington's election and formed the "Vrdolyak 29" in opposition to the "Washington 21." They kept control of the council from 1983 to 1986 and put their people in control of all committees.

In 1986, the courts ruled based on a suit filed by black and Hispanic claimants, (in which the author testified as an expert witness for black plaintiffs) that the ward remap for the city council done in 1980 discriminated against black and Hispanic voters; they subsequently ordered special elections in April of 1986. The Washington forces won four seats and thus the council had a 25-25 stand-off, with Mayor Washington eligible to vote to break a tie. Using his vote, he reorganized the council and put his people in charge of most committees and made them majorities on all committees. It seems as though Washington had, after three years, gained control of the council. However, that is not the case—yet.

The Vrdolyak group has sued and a circuit court judge has issued a curious (political) decision. He argues in effect that while the mayor and his majority has the legal authority to reorganize the council, he stayed the order until all appeals are heard or until the next election (the judge is up for election in 1987). Washington's group must now go back to court to get the stay removed if they are to control the council.

Thus we end this discussion as we started it. Politics is about power; white politicians in Chicago are fighting to keep what they have (by any and all means necessary) and the mayor and his people are fighting to expand their power. White politicians are desperate to "delay" and/or "sabotage" Washington's ability to govern and take control of board and commissions until the 1987 mayoral elections, which they hope to win. The 1987 mayoral election may well be the "last hurrah" for old line white machine politicians and one can expect the election to be as hard fought and bitter as the 1983 election. Desperate people do desperate things. Vrdolyak and his white colleagues on the council and in other political offices have made it clear that they will support a white Republican for mayor before they back Harold Washington (read a black mayor).

Harold Washington has found that the road to reform is littered with land mines set by his white opposition. If one could look into the future with any degree of certainty, one might predict that Harold Washington will still be fighting "council and racial wars" in 1987 and beyond.

Notes

1.   Charles V. Hamilton, "The New Black Politics," p. xix in *The New Black Politics: The Search for Political Power,* eds. Michael B. Preston, Lenneal J. Henderson, Jr. and Paul Puryear (New York: Longman, 1982), 126.

2.   Norman H. Nie, Lutz Erbring, and Edward Hamburg, "Electoral Participation in America: Looking Back" (Paper delivered at a conference on
Where Have All the Voters Gone? University of Chicago, April 26–28, 1984),
4.

3.   For a more detailed discussion of the main forms of political participation,
social status, and participation, see Sidney Verba and Norman H. Nie, *Participation in America: Political Democracy and Social Equality* (New York:
Harper and Row, 1972), 173. For the words of other scholars who argue
along similar lines see, for example, Robert Erickson, Norman R. Luttberg,
and Kent L. Tedin, *American Public Opinion: Its Origins, Content, and
Impact,* 2nd ed., (New York: John Wiley and Sons, 1980).

4.   Ibid., 12.

5.   Ibid.

6.   Ibid., 13.

7.   St. Angelo and Puryear, "Fear, Apathy and Other Dimensions of Black
Voting," 109 in *The New Black Politics: The Search for Political Power.*

8.   Erickson, Luttberg, and Tedin, *American Public Opinion,* 8.

9.   Ibid., 9.

10.   Ibid.

11.   Verba and Nie, *Participation in America,* 157–158.

12.   Ibid., 157–160.

13.   Nie, Erbring, and Hamburg, "Electoral Participation in America," 10–11;
also see appendix of their paper.

14.   Verba and Nie, *Participation in America,* 157.

15.   Ibid.

16.   Erickson, Luttberg, and Tedin, *American Public Opinion,* 8.

17.   Ronald Terchek, "Incentives and Voter Participation: A Research Note,"
Political Science Quarterly, vol. 94, no. 1 (Spring 1979): 135–136. See also
Penn Kimball, *The Disconnected* (New York: Columbia University Press,
1972), Chapters 3 and 8. In addition, see Harlan Hahn, David Klingman,
and Harry Pacton, "Cleavages, Coalitions, and the Black Candidate: The
Los Angeles Mayoralty Elections of 1969 and 1973," *Western Political
Quarterly,* vol. 29 (December 1976): 107.

18.   Nie, Erbring, and Hamburg, "Electoral Participation in America," 22.

19.   For a more extended analysis of the problem, see Preston, "Black Politics
in the Post-Daley Era," in *After Daley: Chicago Politics in Transition,* eds.
Samuel K. Gove and Louis H. Masotti (Champaign: University of Illinois
Press, 1978) 88–117.

20.   Nie, Erbring, and Hamburg, "Electoral Participation in America," 17–18.

21.   CHA *1981 Statistical Report* (Chicago, 1981).

22.   Some of these figures may be at variant with earlier figures because the data
presented here is based on more current census and election data.

23.   It should also be pointed out that some other theories or generalizations
about elections did not hold up here either. First, the incumbent, Mayor
Byrne, spent over $10 million in a losing effort in 1983—over $5 million
directed toward the primary. Of this sum, she budgeted at least $1.5 million
for T.V. advertising and $108,000 for radio. Richard M. Daley spent over

$1.97 million, and Washington a little over $400,000. Second, Washington won even though most black politicians (aldermen and state legislators) opposed him. He was opposed by 18 of the 23 black state legislators and 9 of the 15 black aldermen. Third, the campaign was in some cases poorly organized. Under these conditions, almost all of the traditional election literature would predict a defeat for such a candidate.

24.   Erbring, Nie, and Hamburg, "Electoral Participation in America," 17–18.

Appendix

Table 7.8   Turnout Percentages in Predominantly White, Black, and Hispanic Wards, Respectively, In 1979 and 1983 Primary, Change in Turnout, Median Income, and Predominant Racial Group

Predominantly White Wards (N=24)	Ward	Turnout 1979 Primary	Turnout 1983 Primary	Change 1979-1983[a]	Median Income	Percent White
	10	69	79	10	22,676	55
	11	85	83	−2	17,340	60
	12	66	76	10	19,659	67
	13	72	83	11	25,041	96
	14	68	78	10	18,966	65
	18	61	78	17	25,198	52
	19	64	78	14	26,707	84
	23	72	82	10	25,142	95
	30	59	74	15	20,653	80
	35	65	82	17	19,966	79
	36	67	77	10	23,862	96
	38	60	75	15	24,129	96
	39	63	75	12	23,906	76
	40	62	72	10	20,992	73
	41	61	73	12	27,309	97
	42	55	69	14	20,184	59
	43	62	74	12	29,698	82
	44	63	85	22	21,625	71
	45	68	78	10	24,802	95
	46	63	68	5	16,565	63
	47	64	75	11	19,644	71
	48	58	67	9	16,975	55
	49	68	72	4	19,439	70
	50	58	73	15	24,512	85
Mean		64.5	76.1	+11.6	22,329	75.5

Predominantly Black Wards (N=20)	Ward	Turnout 1979 Primary	Turnout 1983 Primary	Change 1979-1983[a]	Median Income	Percent Black
	1	59	66	7	11,225	45
	2	53	67	14	7,325	91
	3	57	63	6	7,932	99
	4	51	69	18	12,183	78
	5	58	73	15	19,116	75
	6	51	73	22	18,673	98
	7	49	70	21	18,967	57
	8	52	72	20	21,429	96
	9	55	72	17	17,920	89
	15	58	73	15	18,391	60

Predominantly Black Wards (N=20)	Ward	Turnout 1979 Primary	Turnout 1983 Primary	Change 1979-1983[a]	Median Income	Percent Black
	16	53	67	14	10,897	98
	17	51	71	20	15,524	99
	20	48	66	18	10,116	97
	21	56	74	18	22,311	98
	24	53	67	14	10,321	98
	27	58	64	6	9,217	88
	28	46	63	17	11,038	96
	29	47	66	19	14,778	87
	34	52	73	21	10,938	96
	37	53	70	17	17,634	61
Mean		52.9	68.9	+16.0	14,796	85.3

Predominantly Hispanic Wards (N=6)	Ward	Turnout 1979 Primary	Turnout 1983 Primary	Change 1979-1983[a]	Median Income	Percent Hispanic
	22	56	66	10	16,852	76
	25	67	65	-2	13,633	65
	26	69	69	0	12,466	59
	31	69	70	1	15,159	57
	32	66	71	5	13,974	46
	33	65	75	10	17,017	49
Mean		65.3	69.3	+4.0	14,850	59.0

[a]Change is positive unless indicated

Table 7.9 Turnout Percentages in Washington, Byrne, and Daley-Won Primary Wards, Respectively 1979 and 1983 Primary Turnouts, Change in Turnout, Median Income, and Black Ward Population

Washington-Won Wards (N=19)	Ward	Turnout 1979 Primary	Turnout 1983 Primary	Change 1979-1983[a]	Median Income	Percent Black
	2	53	67	14	7,325	91
	3	57	63	6	7,932	99
	4	51	69	18	12,183	78
	5	58	73	15	19,116	75
	6	51	73	22	18,673	98
	7	49	70	21	18,967	57
	8	52	72	20	21,429	96
	9	55	72	17	17,920	89
	15	58	73	15	18,391	60
	16	53	67	14	10,897	98

(continued)

Table 7.9 (*continued*)

Washington-Won Wards (N=19)	Ward	Turnout 1979 Primary	Turnout 1983 Primary	Change 1979- 1983[a]	Median Income	Percent Black
	17	51	71	20	15,524	99
	20	48	66	18	10,116	97
	21	56	74	18	22,311	98
	24	53	67	14	10,321	98
	27	58	64	6	9,217	88
	28	46	63	17	11,038	96
	29	47	66	19	14,778	87
	34	52	73	21	10,938	96
	37	53	70	17	17,634	61
Mean		52.6	69.1	+16.5	14,984	87.4

Byrne-Won Wards (N=22)	Ward	Turnout 1979 Primary	Turnout 1983 Primary	Change 1979- 1983[a]	Median Income	Percent Black
	1	59	66	7	11,225	45
	10	69	79	10	23,676	27
	14	68	78	10	18,966	7
	25	67	65	−2	13,633	15
	26	69	69	0	12,466	5
	30	59	74	15	20,653	0
	31	69	70	1	15,159	10
	33	65	75	10	17,017	2
	35	65	82	17	19,966	0
	36	67	77	10	23,862	0
	38	60	75	15	24,129	0
	39	63	75	12	23,906	1
	40	62	72	10	20,992	1
	41	61	73	12	27,309	0
	42	55	69	14	20,184	36
	43	62	74	12	29,698	8
	44	63	85	22	21,625	6
	46	63	68	5	16,565	14
	47	64	75	11	19,644	1
	48	58	67	9	16,975	15
	49	68	72	4	19,439	10
	50	58	73	15	24,512	1
Mean		63.3	73.3	+10.0	20,008	9.3

Daley-Won Wards (N=9)	Ward	Turnout 1979 Primary	Turnout 1983 Primary	Change 1979- 1983[a]	Median Income	Percent Black
	11	85	83	−2	17,340	21
	12	66	76	10	19,659	12
	13	72	83	11	25,041	0

Daley-Won Wards (N=9)	Ward	Turnout 1979 Primary	Turnout 1983 Primary	Change 1979-1983[a]	Median Income	Percent Black
	18	61	78	17	25,198	46
	19	64	78	14	26,707	15
	22	56	66	10	16,852	7
	23	72	82	10	25,142	0
	32	66	71	5	13,974	9
	45	68	78	10	24,802	0
Mean		67.6	77.2	+9.6	21,635	12.2

Table 7.10   Turnout Percents in Predominantly White, Black, and Hispanic Wards, Respectively, In 1979 and 1983 General Elections, Change in Turnout, Median Income, and Predominant Racial Grouping

Predominantly White Wards (N=24)	Ward	Turnout 1979 General	Turnout 1983 General	Change 1979-1983[a]	Median Income	Percent White
	10	60	84	+24	23,676	55
	11	83	84	1	17,340	60
	12	66	83	17	19,659	67
	13	75	90	15	25,041	96
	14	64	85	21	18,966	65
	18	61	86	25	25,198	52
	19	62	84	22	26,707	84
	23	73	90	17	25,142	95
	30	61	82	21	20,653	80
	35	69	79	10	19,966	79
	36	72	87	15	23,862	96
	38	65	86	21	24,129	96
	39	65	83	18	23,906	76
	40	60	80	20	20,992	73
	41	63	83	20	27,309	97
	42	58	79	21	20,184	59
	43	52	79	27	29,698	82
	44	67	80	13	21,625	71
	45	73	86	13	24,802	95
	46	69	83	14	16,565	63
	47	65	79	14	19,644	71
	48	59	75	16	16,975	55
	49	61	91	30	19,439	70
	50	60	80	20	24,512	85
Mean		65.1	83.3	+18.2	22,329	76

(continued)

Table 7.10 (*continued*)

Predominantly Black Wards (N=20)	Ward	Turnout 1979 General	Turnout 1983 General	Change 1979-1983[a]	Median Income	Percent Black
	1	58	76	18	11,225	45
	2	53	76	23	7,325	91
	3	50	76	26	7,932	99
	4	52	78	26	12,183	78
	5	59	81	22	19,116	75
	6	53	83	30	18,673	98
	7	52	77	25	18,967	57
	8	52	83	31	21,429	96
	9	57	79	22	17,920	89
	15	58	73	15	18,391	60
	16	50	78	28	10,897	98
	17	55	81	26	15,524	99
	20	51	78	27	10,116	97
	21	58	84	26	22,311	98
	24	50	79	29	10,321	98
	27	66	75	9	9,217	88
	28	46	75	29	11,038	96
	29	49	80	31	14,778	87
	34	53	83	30	10,938	96
	37	51	79	28	17,634	61
Mean		53.5	78.7	+25.2	14,796	85

Predominantly Hispanic Wards (N=6)	Ward	Turnout 1979 General	Turnout 1983 General	Change 1979-1983[a]	Median Income	Percent Hispanic
	22	56	67	11	16,852	76
	25	66	71	5	13,633	65
	26	67	71	3	12,466	59
	31	70	72	2	15,159	57
	32	63	71	8	13,974	46
	33	65	74	9	17,017	49
Mean		64.5	70.8	+6.3	14,850	59

Table 7.11   Turnout Percentages in Washington and Epton-Won General Election Wards, Respectively 1979 and 1983 General Turnouts, Change in Turnout, Median Income, and Black Ward Population

Washington-won Wards (N=22)	Ward	Turnout 1979 General	Turnout 1983 General	Change 1979-1983[a]	Median Income	Percent Black
	1	58	76	18	11,225	45
	2	53	76	23	7,325	91
	3	50	76	26	7,932	99

Washington-won Wards (N=22)	Ward	Turnout 1979 General	Turnout 1983 General	Change 1979-1983[a]	Median Income	Percent Black
	4	52	78	26	12,183	78
	5	59	81	22	19,116	75
	6	53	83	30	18,673	98
	7	52	77	25	18,967	57
	8	52	83	31	21,429	96
	9	57	79	22	17,920	89
	15	58	73	15	18,391	60
	16	50	78	28	10,897	98
	17	55	81	26	15,524	99
	20	51	78	27	10,116	97
	21	58	84	26	22,311	98
	22	56	67	11	16,852	7
	24	50	79	29	10,321	98
	27	66	75	9	9,217	88
	28	46	75	29	11,038	96
	29	49	80	31	14,778	87
	31	70	72	2	15,159	10
	34	53	83	30	10,938	96
	37	51	79	28	17,634	61
Mean		54.4	77.9	23.5	14,906	78.3

Epton-Won Wards (N=28)	Ward	Turnout 1979 General	Turnout 1983 General	Change 1979-1983[a]	Median Income	Percent Black
	10	60	84	+24	23,676	27
	11	83	84	1	17,340	21
	12	66	83	17	19,659	12
	13	75	90	15	25,041	0
	14	64	85	21	18,966	7
	18	61	86	25	25,198	46
	19	62	84	22	26,707	15
	23	73	90	17	25,142	0
	25	66	71	5	13,633	15
	26	67	71	3	12,466	5
	30	61	82	21	20,653	0
	32	63	71	8	13,974	9
	33	65	74	9	17,017	2
	35	69	79	10	19,966	0
	36	72	87	15	23,862	0
	38	65	86	21	24,129	0
	39	65	83	18	23,906	1
	40	60	80	20	20,992	1
	41	63	83	20	27,309	0
	42	58	79	21	20,184	36

(continued)

Table 7.11 (*continued*)

Epton-Won Wards (N=28)	Ward	Turnout 1979 General	Turnout 1983 General	Change 1979-1983[a]	Median Income	Percent Black
	43	52	79	27	29,698	8
	44	67	80	13	21,625	6
	45	73	86	13	24,802	0
	46	69	83	14	16,565	14
	47	65	79	14	19,644	1
	48	59	75	16	16,975	15
	49	61	91	30	19,439	10
	50	60	80	20	24,512	1
Mean		65.1	81.6	16.5	21,178	8.9

Table 7.12   1983 Mayoral General Election. Ward Voting Percentages for Washington and Epton

Washington-Won Wards (N=22)	Ward	Washington Percent	Epton Percent
	24	99.5	00.5
	6	99.3	00.7
	17	99.3	00.7
	3	99.3	00.7
	21	99.2	00.8
	20	99.2	00.8
	16	99.1	00.9
	28	99.0	01.0
	34	98.9	01.1
	8	98.5	01.5
	2	97.6	02.4
	9	94.1	05.9
	27	92.9	07.1
	29	92.9	07.1
	4	92.2	07.8
	5	91.0	09.0
	7	82.1	17.9
	37	77.0	23.0
	1	62.6	37.4
	31	60.6	39.4
	15	60.5	39.5
	22	52.2	47.8
Epton-Won Wards (N=28)	Ward	Washington Percent	Epton Percent
	25	49.3	50.7
	46	47.0	53.0

Epton-Won Wards (N=28)	Ward	Washington Percent	Epton Percent
	26	45.8	54.3
	42	45.6	54.4
	32	44.0	56.0
	18	43.8	56.2
	48	43.5	56.5
	49	43.1	56.9
	44	39.3	60.7
	33	37.9	62.1
	43	35.9	64.1
	10	34.0	66.0
	11	25.9	74.1
	19	20.1	79.9
	50	18.3	81.7
	47	18.1	81.9
	40	17.2	82.8
	14	16.1	83.9
	35	15.5	84.5
	12	15.4	84.6
	30	12.7	87.3
	39	12.4	87.6
	45	07.0	93.0
	41	06.8	93.2
	38	05.7	94.3
	36	04.9	95.1
	23	04.1	95.9
	13	04.0	96.0

EIGHT

Cleveland: The Evolution of Black Political Power

William E. Nelson, Jr.

The New Black Politics Revisited[1]

In the paper I produced for the first edition of this volume, I attempted to set forth the basic theoretical underpinnings of the new black politics. The fundamental objectives of the new black politics were summarized in the article in the following way:

> The new black politics looked inward to the reservoir of strength existing in the black community for the power required to move the struggle for black freedom to higher levels. Through the election of 'new breed' politicians to public office and the unification of the black masses through community based institutions, the social and economic position of the black community would be transformed. In places where they represented electoral majorities, blacks would take over local governments, and reorient policy priorities toward a concern for the vital needs of the black community. Wherever blacks existed in significant numbers, the prevailing power structure would be compelled to address itself to the welfare of black citizens. In this sense, the new black politics would become an instrument of social change, permanently eradicating obstacles to the upward mobility and continuing progress of the entire black community.[2]

Since the publication of my original article in 1982, additional evidence has come to light that allows us to comment more precisely on the impact of the new black politics on the social and economic transformation of the black community. This evidence suggests that the upsurge in the election of "new breed" black politicians to public office has been most effective in the promotion of the social and economic interest of upwardly mobile, elite sectors of the black community.

Relying heavily on their appointment powers and the existence of local affirmative action mandates, black mayors of major American cities have significantly expanded the representation of members of the black middle-class in public sector employment. One major study of this process notes that while the rate of increase in total black municipal employment in black mayoral cities has been important, the rate of increase in blacks in top civil service administrative and professional positions has been especially dramatic.[3] Black representation in administrative and professional positions in Atlanta, for example, increased from 41.5 percent in 1973 (the year Maynard Jackson became the first black mayor of Atlanta) to 60.7 percent in 1980.[4]

Apparently, black mayors have skillfully utilized the powers of their office and their broader political influence to strongly promote the recruitment of members of the black middle-class into major positions in local government. Detroit Mayor Coleman Young has appointed blacks to 51 percent of the city's department-head positions; under Young, they have also filled 41 percent of the top positions on municipal boards and commissions.[5] In his keynote speech at the annual meeting of the National Conference of Black Political Scientists in Columbus, Ohio in 1985, Mayor Harold Washington of Chicago spoke with pride of his efforts to "rainbow" Chicago government, appointing blacks, Hispanics, and women to major posts from which they had previously, by custom and tradition, been barred.

Strict enforcement of affirmative action mandates and residency requirements by black mayors has resulted in a significant penetration by blacks in lower echelons of municipal bureaucracies as well. Thus, over the decade from 1973 through 1983, black representation on the police forces in black mayoral cities like Detroit, Newark, and Atlanta increased dramatically. In Detroit, the increase was sixfold; in Newark and Atlanta it was threefold.[6]

Economic benefits flowing to the black middle-class have not been limited to public sector employment jobs. Black mayors have also substantially increased contracting and purchasing opportunities in local government for black business firms. In Detroit, the percent of city business flowing to minority business firms increased from 3 percent in 1973 to 20 percent in 1977.[7] The establishment of joint ventures between minority and majority contractors was a top priority of the administration of Maynard Jackson during his two terms as mayor of Atlanta. Aggressive action by the mayor's office on this issue led to the awarding of $70 million in contracts to minority firms in the construction of a $400 million expansion of the Hartsfield Airport Terminal beginning in 1975.[8] As mayor of Cleveland, Carl Stokes not only channeled city contracts into existing black businesses, but was responsible for the establishment of a number of successful black firms whose access to the resources of local government has continued to yield lucrative benefits. In recounting Stokes' role in this regard, one Cleveland respondent observed:

If you were to take the history of (Company X) you would not find any word that Carl founded that company. But he set these guys down in his office one day and said look, you five guys need to work together rather than apart so you can bid on a contract, not just in my administration, but in any administration. And that was the founding of (Company X). This is just one example. I could cite at least a dozen more. Chances are everytime you see a large Black company in Cleveland, it has some attachment to the Stokes administration.[9]

To what extent have the administrative accomplishments of black mayors satisfied the basic assumptions of the theoretical underpinnings of the new black politics? Clearly, large gaps remain between theory and practice. While black mayors have been modestly successful in increasing access to public resources by members of the black middle-class, they have been unsuccessful in significantly altering the social and economic position of the black community as a whole. Unemployment and poverty in black mayoral cities remain among the highest in the nation. Black governance of major American cities has not only failed to stem the tide of urban decay, but has precipitated policies of central city disinvestment by state and the federal governments, as well as private corporate interests.[10] These patterns have had a devastating impact on the economic position of high-cost black citizens heavily concentrated in cities governed by black mayors. Newark, New Jersey lost 50 percent of both its manufacturing jobs and its retail trade in the 10-year period between 1970 and 1980. Today one-third of its residents are poverty stricken and the official unemployment rate is well above 15 percent.[11] Blacks have constituted a commanding majority of Newark's population of over 300,000 for more than a decade.

The continuing economic crisis in black communities governed by black mayors sheds penetrating light on the limits of the policy consequences of the new black politics. A close examination of patterns of decision-making in black controlled cities suggests that the new black politics has not lead to a substantial alteration in the flow of major economic benefits at the local level. Elected on reform platforms that promised profound changes in the policy-making process, black mayors have almost uniformly embraced corporate-centered strategies that have virtually precluded the redistribution of major benefits to broad segments of the black community. In practical terms what this has meant is that in Detroit, Mayor Coleman Young has abandoned the anti-corporate philosophy he held prior to his election in 1973 in favor of policies that offer tax breaks and social investment subsidies to the business sector while reducing social consumption benefits to inner-city neighborhoods.[12] Liberal tax abatement policies in Detroit to attract corporate investment and promote downtown development have allowed the same corporate interests that dominated the budgetary process before the election of Mayor Young to maintain their premier influence; at the same time municipal revenues flowing into the black community have been reduced. As a substitute for the diminished services to neighborhoods provided by the city, the mayor has called upon citizens to provide voluntary contributions of income and labor.[13] Similar corporate center strategies have constituted the hallmark of the administrative programs of Andrew Young in Atlanta, Wilson Goode in Philadelphia, and Lionel Wilson in Oakland.[14] The upshot has been the perpetuation of old patterns of political influence within the formal framework of new politics symbolized by the expansion of black numerical representation in city government.

In short, black governance of central cities has not led to black control over the decision-making process. Control, at minimum, would require the building of independent organizations capable of mobilizing black votes in elections, and establishing ongoing functional linkages between black public administrators and the black masses.[15] One of the most salient aspects of black political life today is the virtual absence of these kinds of organizations. Black politicians, elected to public office on the back of quasi-independent, grassroots organizational efforts, have generally not sought to maintain these organizations as vehicles for the mobilization of black political influence in the policy-making process. It is, indeed, ironic that the new black politics has manifested itself most acutely in the context of traditional two-party politics. Once elected to public office, black politicians tend to become party men and to pursue their political goals on the basis of the rules and the norms of the political process they inherit.[16] The absence of independent formations to organize broad scale political influence means that black politicians are left extremely vulnerable to the blandishments of politically organized white elites. At the same time, politics in the black community, under these circumstances, tends to take on an individualistic character, with the pursuit of individual goals taking precedence over the achievement of benefits for the community as a whole.

The issues and problems discussed above underscore the difficulties inherent in the effort to use the electoral process as a new base of power for the black community. These problems have been played out in a dramatic way in Cleveland, Ohio since the election of Carl Stokes to the mayorship in 1967. The article I wrote for the first edition of this book analyzed these problems in the context of political conflict and development in Cleveland's black community in the 1970s. During the Autumn of 1985, I returned to Cleveland to collect information that would trace the evolution of black politics in Cleveland into the 1980s. The substance of this data is presented in this article. It is worth noting that the most recent research essentially supports and reinforces the themes emanating from the research undertaken in the decade of the 1970s.

The Rise and Fall of the Stokes Machine

Carl Stokes was swept into the mayor's office in Cleveland in 1967 on the back of a massive grass roots mobilization of the black vote. Stokes viewed the outcome of the 1967 mayoral contest not as a personal victory but as a mandate to fundamentally alter the subordinate social, economic, and political posture of the black community. A native of Cleveland, Carl Stokes had been an active participant in the militant struggle for social justice waged in Cleveland by civil rights activists in the 1960s. He represented a new breed of politician, consumed with visions of racial progress and committed to the proposition that creative social change could be achieved through the direct involvement of black administrators in local public policy-making.

As an experienced politician, Stokes clearly understood that he could not realize the social and economic goals of his administration without the creation of an enduring base of power in the black community. He viewed his election as the first black mayor of Cleveland as only the first stage in the campaign to forge a position of permanent power and influence for the community in the Cleveland political system. The second stage would have to entail the creation of a stable political organization capable of mobilizing broad scale support for the implementation of the social reform agenda put forward in both the public and private sector by his administration. During Stokes' first two-year term, efforts were made to lay the foundation for such an organization through the unification of black Democratic politicians under the banner of a separate black caucus. Shortly after his re-election in 1969, a formal decision was made to establish a new organization called the Twenty-first District Democratic Caucus.[17]

The Twenty-first District Democratic Caucus represented a determined effort on the part of Carl Stokes and his supporters to expand the arena of effective black political influence within the Democratic party. Members of the caucus found, however, that the leaders of the Cuyahoga County Democratic Party were not receptive to the notion of the exercise of influence over party policy by a separate black caucus led by Carl Stokes. Caucus demands for input into the selection of party candidates for public office were flatly rejected. In the wake of this rejection by the regular party, members of the caucus decided to withdraw en masse from the party and establish their own "independent" political organization.

The decision by the black caucus to withdraw from the local Democratic party established the political context for the formation of one of the most powerful political machines in the country. Operating as a non-partisan political instrument, the Twenty-first District Caucus began to take on the character of a formal third party. Rules and procedures of the organization called for the screening of candidates, the endorsement of candidates across party lines, and the fielding of an independent slate of candidates for public office. With the power of both black ward committeemen and black city councilmen under one central command, the caucus exercised firm control over the black vote in city, county, and congressional elections in the Twenty-first District. In several key elections held between 1969 and 1971, the caucus demonstrated its strength as a crucial political force in local elections. Although severely restricted in terms of experience and organizational resources, the caucus was not only able to elect its own candidates to public office, but to mobilize critical black support behind both Democratic and Republican candidates for public office. As mayor, Carl Stokes took full advantage of the political clout wielded by the caucus to quell opposition to his legislative programs in the city council, and to expand his managerial control over the police department and other troublesome components of the city bureaucracy.

The consolidation of political power in the office of the mayor, undergirded by the electoral strength of an independent black-controlled political machine, dramatically altered power relations between the black and white communities in Cleveland. The existence of a cohesive political power base extending beyond the office of mayor opened the door to the prospect that black political control would become institutionalized in Cleveland. Through shrewd bargaining and careful political organizing, leaders of the caucus would be in a position to wring major concessions from both of the regular political parties. In addition, black office holders would be able to exercise veto power over efforts by white city and suburban politicians to derail Mayor Stokes' agenda of social reform in the key areas of housing, transportation, education, and economic opportunity. Most importantly, a pivotal organizational foundation would be established so that future black politicians could build upon the gains of the current generation and political progress by the black community would be cumulative.

Central to plans for institutionalizing black control in Cleveland was continued black representation in the mayor's office and the maintenance of a cohesive, independent political organization in the black community. Prospects for achieving these objectives were seriously weakened by the announcement by Carl Stokes that he would not seek a third term in the 1971 mayoral contest. Efforts by the black community to maintain control over the mayor's office were negated by the defeat of Arnold Pinkney, one of Stokes' chief lieutenants, for the mayorship in 1971. The loss of the mayor's office to the Republicans, coupled with Stokes' departure to New York to work as a television journalist, dealt a crippling blow to the organizational activities of black leaders who wished to keep the caucus alive as an independent political organization. A number of black politicians began to succumb to pressure to return to the fold of the Democratic party where patronage could be found to keep their ward organizations alive. Unity within the caucus was further undermined by conflict between its three key leaders,

Arnold Pinkney, Councilman George Forbes, and Congressman Louis Stokes, over internal organizational procedures, the distribution of political benefits, and the construction of guidelines for the institutionalization of ongoing functional relations between the caucus and the Cuyahoga Democratic Party. Eventually, Pinkney and Forbes would break all formal ties with the caucus; their departure was followed by a mass exodus of black elected officials from the caucus back into the fold of the regular Democratic organization.[18] These events not only signaled the death of the caucus as a viable independent political machine, but the collapse of the broader organizational effort to institutionalize black control in Cleveland politics.

Ascendancy of the Forbes Machine

The decade of the 1970s witnessed a sharp transformation in the character and structure of black politics in Cleveland. During the Stokes era the fundamental goal of black politics was the redistribution of power in ways that would allow blacks to control their own destinies and share equally in the rewards of city government. The return of black leadership to the Democratic party fold after Stokes' departure changed the fundamental goal of black politics from community uplift to self-aggrandizement. Within the confines of the Democratic party the sense of common purpose that united black political forces across geographic, political, and class boundaries began to rapidly dissipate. Organizational structures committed to grass roots political mobilization in support of community-wide objectives began to disappear. What emerged in their place was a loose-knit political organization that took on the character and structure of traditional white-led political machines. The most salient attribute of this new organization was the heavy emphasis on the brokering of political influence in the service of the economic interest of a well-entrenched political elite. Black political leaders associated with this organization ceased to champion programs of social reform and community redevelopment, but embraced more pragmatic programs that would enhance their access to high levels of material benefits. This style of politics continued to grow in magnitude and influence in the decade of the 1970s; in the 1980s the basic pillars of traditional machine politics have remained firmly in place. Commenting on the character of black politics and the role of black political leaders in Cleveland at the present time one respondent observed:

> Today Black politics is looking more and more like white politics. In Cleveland, it does not have the kind of militancy or assertiveness it had in the 1960s. The political figures that have emerged as important in the Black community are those that sit on boards in the private sector. The only thing that distin-

guishes them from their white counterparts is the color of their skins. There is a traditional kind of politics existing here for the most part.[19]

Another respondent observed:

The name of the game in this city is politics and money. Black people are not in control of their destiny. Black politicians are in control. We give too much power and deference to our elected officials. When Black officials walk into the room Black people bow three times at the waist.[20]

Without dispute, the most powerful black politician in Cleveland (some say the most powerful politican period) is George Forbes, President of the Cleveland City Council. In the 1980s, Forbes has emerged as the acknowledged boss of Cleveland's black political machine.

Forbes' political career began in 1963 with his election to the city council one year after graduating from law school at Cleveland's John Marshall College of Law. Throughout most of the Stokes era, Forbes remained in the background as a loyal and faithful supporter of the mayor. In the aftermath of the decision by Stokes to retire from Cleveland politics and move to New York, Forbes surfaced as one of the chief participants in the negotiations designed to resolve differences between the Twenty-first District Caucus and the Cuyahoga Democratic Party. Under the initial terms of the agreement reached by the caucus and party leaders, Forbes was to be named cochairman of the county party organization. However, before this agreement could be sealed, Congressman Louis Stokes stepped forward, laid claim to the position, and served in this capacity for more than a year. In exchange for his agreement to step aside and allow Congressman Stokes to serve as party cochair, party officials promised to support Forbes in a bid to become President of the Cleveland City Council. Eventually Forbes was not only successful in his quest for the council presidency, but assumed the dual role of county party cochair in 1974 when Louis Stokes resigned the position to concentrate on his duties in Washington.

Forbes served as county party cochair for four years, leaving this position in 1978. As county party cochair, Forbes was able to amass an incredible amount of personal power. His party position gave him immediate and direct access to party patronage, a resource he used liberally to create a network of influence and support throughout city and county government.

It was in his role as president of the city council, however, that Forbes assembled the political contacts and formal power required to become boss of the new Cleveland machine. The foundation of his power base was his ability to collect "IOUs" by determining the distribution of public and private patronage to members of the city council. A skilled administrator and politician, he parlayed his control over committee assignments and budgets into a position of almost dictatorial control over the council.[21] Cleveland councilmen, both black and white, quickly learned that they could not gain access to the resources required to satisfy daily constituency demands without going through the council president. And the proposition was routinely accepted by everyone that major projects entailing the expenditure of millions of dollars of public funds required the endorsement of the council president before they could be introduced as items for councilmanic consideration. Forbes' capacity to manipulate his power as council president is cogently illuminated in the comments of the following Cleveland respondent:

> In Cleveland you have to understand that power is acquired through a process of collecting or moving on the weakness of other people. There has always been a confrontation between the city council and the mayor, even when Carl Stokes was mayor. But you have to remember that George being as shrewd as he is and having the mentor that he had, which was Charles V. Carr, really understood the application of power, he understands it more than anyone else. . . . There are a lot of people in council who I would describe as less than intellectual and who thrive on the notion that garbage is not being collected, dogs are running loose and they have a constituent they would like to get out of jail. That's the way they understand their role. George is perfectly content to allow them to fulfill that kind of role. He helps them do that. Here I'll give you an extra guy to help you answer those complaints. That allows him to curry favor with the council person at the same time he is able to take the IOU to get something else he might want.[22]

Through the manipulation of both external and internal resources, Forbes has been able to silence most of his critics on the city council. For example, councilwoman Fanny Lewis entered the council in 1979 as an outspoken critic of the council president. Eventually, she was compelled to solicit the council president's support for her effort to build a major federally subsidized housing project in the Hough area called Lexington Village. While Councilwoman Lewis and President Forbes do not see eye to eye on all issues, relations between the councilwoman and the council president are far less volatile than before.

Since becoming council president in 1973, the political position of George Forbes has been seriously challenged in the council in only two instances. In June 1980, a group of white councilpersons led by ninth ward councilwoman Barbara Pringle filed petitions to place on the election ballot a proposal to have the council president elected by citywide vote rather than members of the council itself.[23] Although Forbes was unable to prevent this measure from going before the voters, he was able to mobilize considerable support against it, and the ballot issue failed by a wide margin. A more serious threat to Forbes' power erupted in November 1981 when black councilman Lonnie Burten announced that he would run against Forbes for council president. Burten received the backing of 10 of 21 councilmen, including two black councilmen. Forbes considered the Burten challenge so important that he broke off a visit at his daughter's house in Washington, D.C. to return to Cleveland to whip up political support against it. Forbes received strong support in his efforts from the major black newspaper, *The Call and Post,* which denounced Burten's challenge as a front for racist whites.[24] The Burten revolt was broken when community pressure compelled one of the two black councilmen supporting Burten to renounce his support. When the vote was finally taken in the council, Forbes was nominated by Lonnie Burten, and received 16 of 21 councilmanic votes.

Forbes has built his base of political influence not only on his ability to exercise control over the council, but also on his extensive political ties with members of the business community. These ties were first firmly forged during the administration of Mayor Ralph Perk. At an early point in his career as council president, Forbes teamed up with Mayor Perk to push through the city council a redevelopment package designed to provide extensive incentives and benefits to the business community. The centerpiece of this redevelopment package was tax abatement, a policy that exempted major national corporations sponsoring construction projects in the downtown area from the payment of local revenue.[25] Forbes' participation in these efforts established for him a solid reputation as a friend of business interests. This reputation continued into the Kucinich administration where Forbes played a major role in blocking efforts by Kucinich to implement urban populism by taking away tax incentives from major corporations. In the final analysis, Forbes' relationship with the corporate sector has been mutually beneficial for both parties.

> George Forbes is a fabulous multiplier of power. He understands the operation of government. He has people in high places everywhere. The people you normally would think would know how to deal with him on a daily basis are in fear of him. I've seen the President of (X) Bank in awe over the fact he received a phone call from George Forbes. It's like everyone is a bunch of groupies. These rich old white men just cower to him because he'll call them a bunch of names in public, and hold up legislation on them. He knows how to take care of business. He's an example of the Willie Brown phenomenon.[26]

The concentration of power in the office of the council president through his relations with the business community has given Forbes a fantastic ability to punish his enemies and reward his acquaintances.

> George Forbes has a network of people everywhere. His closest confidants are running major white organizations or have considerable influence in them. When a contract for civil rights compliance comes down, the person who helps these companies to prepare to implement these requirements is one of George Forbes' closest confidants. He writes minority business enterprise programs for everybody. I don't know if there is an official connection but he

ends up writing most of them. I am sure this kind of expertise is shared by other attorneys in the field, but he's the one who picks persons to work on that kind of job.[27]

Black ministers have been major recipients of public funds passed down through the city council. Some respondents suggested a one-to-one relationship between the support by black ministers for black machine politics and their role as recipients of public funds to support their ongoing community related activities and church operating expenses.

> Almost every Black minister in Cleveland is the beneficiary of the largess of the city council president or the city council. Through the federal government we get block grant money and that block grant money is used for public feeding programs for youngsters or we get head start programs that are generally headquartered in churches. In these churches the minister has rent to pay; he has utility to pay; he has a large heating and air conditioning bill; and in the winter he has a gas bill. These monies supplement the monies given by the parishioners, by the congregation.[28]

Black churches are a part of a broader institutional web that locks vital elements of the black community into the dynamics of black machine politics in Cleveland (See Figure 8.1). In the final analysis, most major interest groups in the black community, including community associations and black businesses, must look to some facet of city government for fiscal and political support. The point should be underscored in this regard that over time George Forbes has extended the reach of his influence into high levels of city government beyond the city council. According to some observers, Forbes' influence in the Vonivich administration has been so great that he has, in effect, usurped a good deal of the mayor's decision-making authority.

> George Vonivich, as mayor, is a guy who wants to be known as the fairhaired boy. He's not interested in making waves. He's not interested in getting involved in small community disputes. He takes the high road while George does the battling and makes the decisions. As a consequence, George has been able to do what he pleases. He delivers what he wants, to whom he wants, when he wants to. The mayor just kind of sits back and says I am moving on to bigger and better things. George Vonivich has been trying to put himself on a path to higher office, while George Forbes has been content to stay there and take some of the trappings of government away from the mayor. Through this process, Forbes has been able to dictate who would do what, when and where.[29]

George Forbes has been able to cultivate strong rank and file black support for his role as "boss" of city politics by using the power of his office to write affirmative action requirements into city legislation and speaking out strongly against discrimination in key areas such as law enforcement

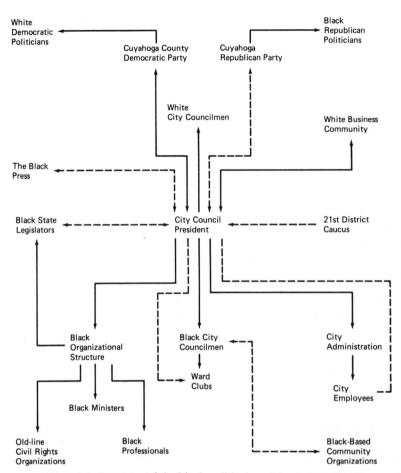

Figure 8.1 Structure of the black political machine in Cleveland.

and housing. Thus in March 1983, Forbes announced that he was taking steps to bring airlines operating at Cleveland Hopkins International Airport into compliance with the city's equal employment opportunity goals. One newspaper quoted Forbes as saying "one of the requirements for doing business in this city is that you have to have blacks working for you."[30] In support of black economic interests, Forbes has sometimes held up the city budget to force the police department to accept hiring quotas of blacks and executed a halt to city redevelopment plans until the impact of such plans on gentrification in the black community has been thoroughly examined. Speaking at a forum at the Cleveland City Club in 1983, Forbes strongly underscored his commitment to the achievement of social and economic justice for blacks in Cleveland:

> I made a commitment to myself long ago that I would spend the rest of my life in public office dedicated to the mediation of the problems and progress of my people. . . . I will fight the black fight. Black folks are mistreated, black folks don't have jobs. That's black women, black men and black children. I won't let black folks nor white folks deter me in my quest.[31]

Despite the allure of his image as a militant black activist, the general thrust of Forbes' political leadership has been toward the forging of strong links between the black community and the Democratic party, and the concentration of material benefits in the hands of party activists and their clients. In this sense, black politics in Cleveland has come full circle, from a politics of independence and community uplift, to a politics of subordination and self-aggrandizement. Clearly, the vision of a cohesive black political movement designed to assuage black grievances and establish a permanent base for community control in the public and private sectors has practically disappeared from the political landscape. It has been replaced with a focus on individual benefits and the concentration of power in the hands of a small political elite.

> The Forbes organization has the clout to make things happen. But the problem is that it always seems like these things are going in one direction to a small group. A hand full of people get the contracts. I am not sure the things he does filters down to the broad base of the black community. When the same people show up at the trough, I wonder if everyone is getting fed. Unquestionably, George Forbes is the most powerful political figure in this city. No one has the impression, however, of a black political organization rallying behind Forbes to right wrongs.[32]

That the ascendancy of the Forbes machine has not produced a corresponding increase in benefits for the black community is suggested by the small percentage of blacks holding key positions in the Vonivich administration, the extraordinarily high level of unemployment in the black community, and the continuing emphasis of Cleveland's urban redevelopment program on downtown development rather than the social and economic rehabilitation of central city neighborhoods.[33] Indeed, to the extent that the new machine in Cleveland is wedded to old machine politics, it operates as a crucial obstacle to the transference of major benefits from the public sector and private institutions to the black community.

The Dissipation of Black Political Mobilization

The success of Carl Stokes in elevating black political influence in Cleveland to new levels of authority was due primarily to the strong political mobilization of the black community as an independent force in local politics. This political mobilization was characterized by strong black-led civil rights protests, and a major upsurge in black registration and cohesive black voting in local elections. In the 1980s, black politics in Cleveland has been marked by the dissipation of black political mobilization. Respondents in this study agree that there is no visible or viable civil rights protest movement in Cleveland today. As institutions of social mobilization, traditional civil rights organizations in Cleveland like the Urban League and the NAACP are relatively ineffective. They have been unable to produce significant black political interest in explosive issues such as police brutality and repeated incidents of black hangings in suburban prisons. The issue of school desegregation has had a negative impact on black political mobilization, creating deep divisions among antibusing and probusing forces in the black community. With the passing of the black power era under Carl Stokes, blacks in Cleveland lost a great deal of confidence in their ability to meaningfully influence public policy through protest action. The results has been the virtual demise of the civil rights movement as an instrument of power in the black community.

> During the 1960s we as a nation talked about the revolution of rising expectations. I think that in some ways the 60s really did generate a kind of enthusiasm, idealism and commitment that generated political awareness and activity in the black community. Today these dreams have not been realized. Failed expectations have fed a growing apathy. There are no identifiable black issues to protest about. Even on something like South Africa, most of the protest leadership has come from the white community. You see blacks associated with that, but I think the leaders have come from the young white community for the most part.[34]

The demise of black protest activity has been accompanied by the decline in effectiveness of political organizations in the black community. Worthy of special note here is the continuing weakness of the Twenty-first District Caucus as an instrument of political power in Cleveland elections. Officials of the caucus contend that the organization maintains a financial membership of 4,000 persons. The number of active members in attendance at weekly meetings hovers in the neighborhood of 75. Although the caucus continues to screen candidates and to make endorsements, there is little evidence that an endorsement from the caucus carries significant weight in elections.

> How can an organization be effective when, for example, three years ago the caucus endorsed 12 candidates for 3 seats in East Cleveland. Three people were seeking election to the East Cleveland Commission. They endorsed 12 people. Now you tell me how you can be effective with an endorsement policy like that.[35]

The political power of the caucus has been undermined by its lack of patronage, the absence of a substantial war chest to finance campaigns, and the dual membership of most of its members in the caucus and the Democratic Party. Its most important electoral role involves grass roots campaign activities on behalf of its chairman, Congressman Louis Stokes. Between elections it seeks to play an important social service role by conducting workshops, providing assistance to individuals in trouble with the law, and participating in job search activities for the unemployed. One respondent explained the erosion of the Caucus' political strength in the following manner:

> You can build an organization, you can put it together tightly and keep it highly motivated, when there is one very clear cut goal you are trying to achieve—you want to elect a black mayor, etc. But as that organization begins to do the more traditional things, it sits there and candidates come in and ask for endorsements, and what they are doing does not look very different from what the Democratic Party is doing, endorsements begin to look very much alike, its clout begins to diminish. I don't think the caucus is a force any more, even in the black community. You would read about them a lot years ago. Now about the only time I see anything about them is around an election, you read a report and its on page 14B that here are the candidates the caucus has endorsed.[36]

Currently, there exists in Cleveland no viable, independently organized caucus of black politicians. The most logical group to form such an organization, black councilmen, are politically tied to the Forbes machine by patronage benefits and a single-minded concentration on the building of successful electoral organizations in their wards. At no time do these individuals meet to plan a community agenda or even a common legislative agenda. Commenting on this fact, one Cleveland councilman observed:

> People talk about agendas, but you'll find that the legislators never meet together. Not unless something happens to one of the hierarchy and they want everyone to come and support their efforts. But other than that they never sit down and talk about issues and we have 10 black councilmen in this city. We have black senators and congressmen in this city. Do you think they ever meet together. No. There is no black agenda, there are individual agendas, a push for themselves. But the little people out here, there is no agenda for the little people.[37]

At the community level, traditionally strong organizations such as the St. Clair Superior Coalition and the Buckeye Woodland Community Congress are bordering on the brink of dissolution due to a significant loss of government funding. The most serious danger is the loss of permanent staff; without permanent staff, these groups will be unable to serve as effective vehicles for political mobilization. The neighborhood movement in the black community has historically been slow to emerge because of the transient character of black residents. When new organizations have evolved, they have frequently been viewed as rivals to existing ward clubs by city councilmen. Sometimes councilmen have felt sufficiently threatened by the new structures that they have created new organizations of their own for the specific purpose of keeping the activities of independent political formations in line.

> The general strategy of the council people has been to ignore the neighborhood organizations if possible, and co-opt them if necessary.[38]

In the 1980s, the black community has not only witnessed the atrophy of effective black political organization, but the disintegration of its political leadership structure as well. With the exception of George Forbes, the cadre of political leaders that led the black community to majestic heights of power in the 1960s has virtually disappeared from effective roles in Cleveland politics. Carl Stokes, although active once again in Cleveland politics, has been hampered in his efforts to build a power base to challenge George Forbes by his role as a municipal judge. Conflict between Forbes and Stokes has periodically reached the level of public controversy. Stokes is clearly unhappy with the drift of current social policies in Cleveland. It is unclear at the moment whether or not he has the ability to summon sufficient strength to topple the Forbes-Vonivich coalition from power. Continuing conflict between Stokes and Forbes has produced an enormous amount of cross-pressure on many Cleveland political activists who are indebted to both individuals for their professional accomplishments.

> I think an awful lot of the tension between Forbes and Stokes centers on the issue, who is the leader of the black community. That carries over in part from the time when Stokes was mayor because a lot of people now in positions of influence in the black community got there because Stokes was mayor. Some of them are grateful and deeply loyal to Stokes for those opportunities. Some of those people also owe George Forbes a great deal because some of the reasons there are black faces in fairly important jobs down at city hall is because while they got there initially as part of the Stokes administration they have survived because of George Forbes' protection. There is the issue between the two of them of who's going to be top dog; but there is a lot of mixed, divided and conflicting loyalties among a whole lot of other blacks who in many instances are beholden to both of them.[39]

Presently, Carl Stokes is viewed as the only potential rival to Forbes. Arnold Pinkney's political influence has declined in the wake of his absence from the electoral process for several years, and his conviction on conflict of interest charges in conjunction with his service as a member of the Cleveland–Cuyahoga County Port Authority.[40] Because of his location in Washington, Congressman Louis Stokes has been unable to build a base of power in local politics to rival the influence of the Forbes organization. There is general agreement that Louis Stokes is an extremely popular congressman and will be able to hold onto his seat until he chooses to retire; Stokes' congressional strength offers him few advantages in the realm of Cuyahoga politics. Constituency work by a U.S. Congressman in Cleveland simply cannot yield the host of political benefits equivalent to those emanating from the entrenched position Forbes holds inside the Democratic and Republican camps. At the councilmanic level, Forbes eliminated one potential rival for power by negotiating the appointment of Councilman Michael White to a vacant seat in the Ohio Senate in Columbus.[41] Another major rival, Lonnie Burten, died of a heart attack. Virgil Brown, the first black politician to be elected to a countywide office, is burdened with the handicap of being a Republican in a Democratically controlled city.[42] While Brown is extremely popular in the black community, he does not have the complementary political support base required to effectively compete with the Forbes political organization. Finally, through the skilled manipulation of his powers to award and punish, Forbes has effectively prevented the emergence of young "turks" to challenge his power.

Thus, the responsibility for black political mobilization lies totally in the organizational and leadership hands of George Forbes and the Forbes machine. To date, the Forbes machine has shown no inclination to engage in the kind of broad scale electoral mobilization of the black community characteristic of the Stokes years. What is most striking about black politics in Cleveland today is the virtual absence of well organized "civic obligation" oriented registration drives.

> The Urban League says that a major registration drive is needed and it will do it. We are still waiting on the Urban League to act. In the meantime all we have are efforts by individual candidates to get people registered and to get them to turn out in their own elections. But there is not the kind of massive well organized city-wide or at least east-side-wide kind of drives reminiscent of the Stokes years.[43]

The absence of organized voter mobilization campaigns in the black community has resulted in a significant decline in black political participation since the heyday of the Stokes era. As Table 8.1 clearly shows, while the number of registered black voters since 1965 has greatly increased, the number of blacks participating in elections has significantly declined. The point should be underscored that while registration in black wards in the 1985 mayoral election was higher than registration in white wards (151,920 to 149,915), 65,703 voters turned out in white wards, while 53,720 voters turned out in black wards.[44] Clearly, a major facet of the black electoral problem in Cleveland is *turnout*. A close examination of the black vote reveals that the turnout problem is not a universal problem in the black community. In stable black neighborhoods with strong leadership, electoral participation tends to be fairly high. On the other hand, voting appears to

Table 8.1   Selective Summary of Cleveland's Mayoral General Elections in Black Wards, 1965–1985

	1965	1967	1975	1979	1985
Registered Voters	103,123	99,885	102,380	107,919	151,920
Turnout (N)	76,377	73,093	75,253	58,570	53,720
Turnout (%)	74.1	80.4	73.5	47.69	36.77

Source: Joseph P. McCormick, "The Continuing Significance of Race: Racial Change and Electoral Politics in Cleveland, Ohio. 1961–1977" (unpublished paper, Department of Political Science, Howard University, Washington, D.C.); Larry Brisker "An Election Analysis of the General Election, November 5, 1985, Cleveland, Ohio, (unpublished report, Pollmet, Inc., Cleveland, Ohio Cuyahoga County Board of Elections).

be an extremely difficult problem in neighborhoods typically occupied by a transient, highly mobile population. But regardless of the social character of the neighborhood, the secret to high mobilization and turnout is political leadership and organization. This fact is underscored by the comments of the following respondent:

> When I came to this ward (7) there were 6,000 registered voters. These are now 16,000. I work at making precinct committeemen do what they're supposed to do. I tell them they can't do less than I do. The average individual don't know who his precinct committeeman is. If the committeemen don't function you don't have a ward that's informed. I have to do it here because we don't have the wherewithal to do it on a wider scale. If we can demonstrate what can be done, its something that can be looked at elsewhere.[45]

While pockets of political strength in the black community still persist, the most salient feature of black political life citywide is the absence of effective black political leadership and organization. Extremely important in this regard is the failure of the Forbes machine to engage in across-the-board political mobilization. Like traditional political machines, the Forbes machine has concentrated on delivering the vote only for organization candidates; it has also resisted the temptation of activating more voters than those required to win elections. Completely removed from the political scene is the intensive grass roots political campaigning that succeeded in driving unprecedented numbers of blacks to the polls in the Stokes era. It has been replaced by a listless, issueless style of political campaigning that has discouraged broad scale participation by the black masses in the electoral process.

> You have to remember that every election focuses on the race at the top of the ticket. There has been no race of interest to black folks here for quite sometime. I believe that if we had a serious race blacks would turn out but I also believe George (Forbes) would do everything possible to prevent a se-

rious race from taking place. He told a person from Operation Big Vote he's for incumbents and incumbents do better when there are small turnouts.[46]

In the post-civil-rights era, the underlying stimulus for mobilization in the black community has been transformed into a deadly cynicism towards the electoral process:

> The reason for apathy in the black community is greater than in the white community. There is not much that the black community is going to be able to change even if it is united in terms of votes cast. Whites can change things because they constitute a majority of the citizens, the voting population. I think blacks are pretty well aware of the fact that, for the time being at least, they have as much power and are about as well served as they are going to be through the ballot box.[47]

The centralization of political authority in the black community has produced neither political unity or enhanced community-wide power. Young, independent candidates face a malestrom of political opposition in the black community in their bid for public office. One such candidate in 1985 was compelled to build her campaign on the back of volunteers from the Black Women's Leadership Caucus and a few courageous black ministers. Members of the black political establishment refused to embrace her campaign until the last minute when it was clear that she had an excellent chance of victory. The absence of a citywide organization to map strategies, groom candidates, and deliver votes has seriously undermined the impact of the black community as a center of power in the electoral process.

The 1985 General Election

The continuing political weakness of the black community was vividly revealed in the 1985 general elections for mayor and school board. In a city where blacks represent more than 50 percent of the registered vote, the black community was unable to mount serious opposition to the reelection of a white Republican Mayor, George Vonivich, in the 1985 General Election. The lack of black opposition to Vonivich was due in part to the fact that during his term of office, Vonivich had gone out of his way to court black support. Vonivich's public stand in behalf of the desegregation of the Cleveland Police Department was especially important in forging his image as a friend of the black community. Most critically, Vonivich was strongly supported by black political leaders who in turn discouraged the emergence of serious opposition to the mayor's reelection.

> George Forbes announced to the Cleveland community that he thought George Vonivich was doing a pretty good job and did not see why he needed any opposition. When George talks like that in public, that is sign language, that is code to his troops we are going to sit this one out.[48]

The only black candidate to step forward to challenge Vonivich for the mayorship was James Barrett. Although widely respected, Mr. Barrett was not viewed as a serious contender for the mayorship. His public experience consisted of service as a driver for Carl Stokes and Safety Director in the Kucinich administration. Running his campaign on a shoestring budget with no visible organization, Barrett's bid for the mayorship never got out of the starting block.

> He did not have a planner, a scheduler, no organizer, no money for phones. He had about 7 or 8 zealots who really believed that Cleveland deserved a Black candidate.[49]

The Barrett campaign was only a caricature of the robust effort that catapulted Carl Stokes into office nearly two decades before. Indeed, it is revealing that circumstances were far less favorable for the election of a black mayor in Cleveland in 1985 than in 1965.

Vonivich's close political ties to the leadership structure of the black community transformed itself into astonishing electoral strength in the black community. Table 8.2 reports the outcome of the 1985 General Election in the black community. This table indicates that Vonivich received 84.12 percent of the vote in black wards (1 through 10). His opponent, Gary Kucinich, received only 15.88 percent of the black vote. The percentage of Vonivich's vote in the black community was much higher than the percentage of the vote he received in the white community. In the white wards (11 through 21) Vonivich received 61.48 percent of the vote to 37.52 percent for Kucinich. Despite a lower turnout in the black community, Vonivich received 42,953 black votes to 39,716 white votes. Thus, in the 1985 General Election the black community was a major base of power for Vonivich. In a city where very few black Republicans reside, Vonivich's tremendous electoral appeal in the black community provided additional evidence of the near absence of organizational forces to mobilize black political resources behind a black developed and controlled social and economic agenda.

Additional light was shed on this matter by the outcome of the general election for the school board. When the 1985 race began, blacks held three of seven seats on the school board. Two black incumbents were up for reelection, Edward Young and Stanley Tolliver. Other major black candidates in the race were Cordi Stokes, the daughter of Carl Stokes, and Betty Jefferson, a spokesperson for black parents. They were challenged by several prominent white candidates, including James Carney, Jr., Joseph Tegreene, Benny Bonnano, Margaret O'Neill, and Alice Butts.

Several factors produced severe obstacles for the black candidates. One was the refusal of black political leaders to present a united front in support of the black candidates. Prominent black politicians publicly supported white candidates by posing in photographs with them and including them

Table 8.2 Summary of 1985 Cleveland Mayoral General Election in Black Wards

City Wards	Registered Voters	Voters	% Voter Turnout	Gary Kucinich	% Vote Kucinich	George Vonovich	% Vote Vonovich	Total
1	17304	7639	44.15	1183	16.21	6113	83.79	7296
2	14846	5277	35.54	948	18.78	4099	81.22	5047
3	17168	6978	40.65	944	14.25	5681	85.75	6625
4	15518	5271	26.84	800	15.90	4233	84.10	5033
5	14358	4165	33.35	700	17.96	3198	82.04	3898
6	14732	4789	32.77	661	14.53	3888	85.47	4549
7	15740	4828	37.29	635	13.97	3910	86.03	4545
8	15389	5870	31.70	725	13.12	4801	86.88	5526
9	14248	4878	28.25	581	12.61	4027	87.39	4608
10	12617	4025	57.13	823	21.51	3003	78.49	3826
Totals	151920	53720		8000		42953		50953

Source: Larry Brisker, "An Election Analysis of the General Election, November 5, 1985, Cleveland, Ohio" Pollmet, Inc.

on sample ballots.[50] These endorsements were troubling to many blacks because black school enrollment in Cleveland was nearly 80 percent. Because of this overwhelming black student representation in the school system, the belief was widespread in the black community that blacks should have a majority of the representation on the school board. This could only be achieved, however, through an extraordinary display of unity and discipline by black voters. Prospects for unity in the election were undermined by the enormous amounts of campaign funds several of the white candidates were willing to spread through the black community in return for political support.[51]

The electoral positions of several black candidates, especially the incumbents, was further weakened by the suicide of black School Superintendent Frederick Holliday. In his suicide note, Holliday suggested that he was deeply troubled by his running conflicts with school board members. Edward Young had emerged on the board as one of Holliday's strongest critics. Innuendoes began to crop up in the campaign that Young was chiefly responsible for Holliday's death. Eventually, Council President Forbes would enter the fray, expressing his personal opposition to Young's reelection. This move probably sealed the fate of Young's campaign for reelection.

The results of the school board race revealed a high degree of ethnic voting in the white community, and a less disciplined pattern of ethnic voting in the black community (see Table 8.3). In the white wards (11 through 21) black candidates received 2 to 4 percent of the votes cast. In the black wards (1 through 10) James Carney received 12 percent of the vote, Joseph Tegreene 10 percent of the vote, and Benny Bonnano 6 percent of the vote. This imbalance in ethnic voting led to the defeat of all the black candidates but one. Stanley Tolliver survived a strong challenge by Margaret O'Neill for his seat. Cordi Stokes came in sixth in the running and Edward Young came in a poor ninth. The top three candidates were James Carney, Jr., Joseph Tegreene, and Benny Bonnano, all white.[52]

Respondents in this study viewed the outcome of the school board race as a step backwards for the black community. In the absence of clear signals from black political leaders to vote a straight black ticket, black voters cast votes liberally across ethnic lines, giving critical support to white candidates while black candidates were being almost totally ignored in the white community.

> Black folks would say I've got two good Black folks now let me find two good white folks I can vote for. They diluted their vote. They did not bullet vote. That's because some people in the community had said, we're going to get Stan Tolliver and Ed Young back on the board, let's just vote for these two. Then we got to munching away at it. We've got two good ones, now

Table 8.3   Summary of 1985 Cleveland School Board General Election
in Black and White Wards

Black Totals		White Totals		Cleveland Totals
Benny Bonanno				
8,775	(6.19)	34,264	(15.34)	43,039
Alice Butts				
8,833	(5.85)	22,644	(11.80)	31,477
James Carney				
17,983	(12.71)	30,522	(15.06)	48,505
Mel Dimmer				
1,822	(1.26)	5,124	(2.50)	6,946
Neal Farrell				
2,025	(1.43)	8,291	(3.93)	10,316
Betty Jefferson				
11,110	(7.47)	9,932	(4.92)	21,042
James Omera				
3,041	(2.13)	11,780	(5.56)	14,821
Margaret O'Neill				
7,322	(5.16)	27,114	(13.08)	34,436
Cordi Stokes				
29,304	(19.98)	4,999	(2.61)	34,303
Joseph Tegreen				
15,342	(10.59)	32,973	(15.95)	48,315
Stanley Tolliver				
27,157	(18.58)	8,674	(4.37)	35,831
Edward Young				
12,772	(8.64)	8,319	(4.11)	21,091
Total				
145,486		204,636		350,122

Source: Larry Brisker, "An Election Analysis of the General Election, November 5, 1985, Cleveland, Ohio," Pollmet, Inc.; Cuyahoga County Board of Elections.

let's come back this week with another white man. And pretty soon that's what we had, all the Blacks voting for the good white man.[53]

The outcome of the 1985 school board race left deep tracks of discord, division, and dissension in the black community. Although it is difficult to predict in the long term what the direction of black political action in Cleveland will be, prospects for an immediate recovery from the debilitating impact of internal disunity do not appear to be very promising.

The Unfinished Agenda

The experience of black communities moving from protest to politics again requires that we raise serious questions concerning the basic assumptions of the new black politics. Specifically, the key assumption that the movement for social and economic freedom is always progressive has not been substantiated by the pattern of political activity occurring in many black communities over the past two decades. As Professor James Jennings has noted, political participation may either seek to achieve structural change in the distribution of wealth and power, or to maintain the status quo.[54] In the 1970s and 1980s, black political activities in local communities have been heavily weighted toward the maintenance of existing social, economic, and political arrangements.

New black politicians have been notable for their failure to produce a theory of social change that goes beyond the integration of the black community into the existing order.[55] These politicians are burdened by what Professor Manning Marable has called the "poverty of political practice," and the "poverty of theory and historical observation."[56] Theories of political independence and self-determination characterizing the quest for civil rights in the 1960s have been abandoned for a broad acceptance of the status quo in which the dominant priorities of the traditional power structure continue to function as the basic agenda of city politics.[57]

In Cleveland, Ohio, the black community, after two decades of struggle, remains caught up in the web of traditional politics. Despite significant gains in the community's access to key positions of authority, the progressive face of local politics has not materialized.[58] Black politicians do not consider themselves racial ambassadors, but administrative ombudsmen who seek to deliver patronage benefits in exchange for electoral support. Their vision of the political world does not encompass an understanding of the impact of external factors, such as international monetary policies, on the socio-economic status of their local constituents. The goal of political independence has been broadly rejected in favor of the goal of personal enrichment. Assessing the present political posture of black political leadership and organization in Cleveland one respondent observed:

> The people that could care and are knowledgeable have been bought. The people that need to care are too busy caring about where they are going to eat, where they are going to sleep and whether they will be warm. We lack a political arena into which we can coalesce our separate wants and needs and put them in a cohesive package and implement them.[59]

The need to establish progressive agendas and build independent black political coalitions remains an extremely urgent objective for blacks in American politics. There are signs on the horizon that the center of gravity in the black community may be moving in that direction. The mayoral campaigns of Harold Washington in Chicago and Mel King in Boston demonstrate that progressive black candidates still have the capacity to mobilize substantial support from the black masses in the electoral arena.[60] In both cities, progressive black political activists have come together to lead the way in the formation of independent political coalitions. These efforts represent hopeful developments; they must be replicated across the length and breadth of urban America if the promises of the new black politics are to be transformed into building blocks of progress for the black community.

Notes

1. I would like to thank Professor James Kweder, Professor Willa Hemmons, and Professor Larry Brisker for supplying a portion of the data used in this paper. I would also like to thank the College of Humanities and the Office of Research and Graduate Studies at The Ohio State University for providing financial assistance in support of this research. I am grateful to the citizens of Cleveland, Ohio who agreed to cooperate in this research endeavor.

2. William E. Nelson, Jr. "Cleveland: The Rise and Fall of the New Black Politics" in *The New Black Politics: The Search for Political Power* eds. Michael B. Preston, Lenneal J. Henderson, Jr., Paul Puryear (New York: Longman, Inc., 1982) 1st Edition, 188.

3. Peter K. Eisinger, "Black Mayors and the Politics of Racial Economic Advancement," *Readings in Urban Politics: Past, Present and Future* eds. Harlan Hahn and Charles N. Levine (New York, Longman, Inc., 1984) 2nd Edition, 251.

4. Eisinger, "Black Mayors and the Politics of Racial Economic Advancement," 252.

5. Richard Child Hill "Crisis in the Motor City: The Politics of Economic Development in Detroit" *Restructuring the City*, eds. Susan S. Fainstein, Norman I. Fainstein, Richard Childs Hill, Dennis Judd and Michael Peter Smith (New York: Longman, Inc., 1983), 108.

6. Eisinger, "Black Mayors and the Politics of Racial Economic Advancement," 251-252.

7. Richard Child Hill, "Crisis in the Motor City: The Politics of Economic Development in Detroit," 108.

8. James Curtis Smith, "Big City Black Mayors: Redefining the Dilemma of Governance," (Unpublished paper prepared for the 1986 annual meeting of the National Conference of Black Political Scientists, Chicago, Illinois), 28; Mack H. Jones, "Black Political Power in Atlanta: Myth and Reality," *Urban Black Politics, The Annals of the American Academy of Political and Social Science*, eds. John R. Howard and Robert C. Smith, vol. 439, September 1978, 111.

9. This quote is taken from a series of interviews conducted by the author in Cleveland, Ohio in the Fall of 1985.

10. Smith, "Big City Black Mayors: Redefining the Dilemma of Governance," 7–8.

11. Smith, "Big City Black Mayors: Redefining the Dilemma of Governance," 7.

12. Hill, "Crisis in the Motor City: The Politics of Economic Development in Detroit," 109–113; Betty Woody, *Managing Crisis Cities: The New Black Leadership and the Politics of Resource Allocation* (Westport, Connecticut: The Greenwood Press, 1982), 27–28.

13. Hill, "Crisis in the Motor City: The Politics of Economic Development in Detroit, 111–112.

14. Manning Marable, *Black American Politics: From the Washington Marches to Jesse Jackson* (London: Verso Press, 1985), 167–170.

15. Jones, "Black Political Power in Atlanta: Myth and Reality," 116; William E. Nelson, Jr., "Black Mayors as Urban Managers," *Urban Black Politics, The Annals of the American Academy of Political and Social Science,* eds. John R. Howard and Robert C. Smith, vol. 439, September, 1978, 64–67.

16. Jones, "Black Political Power in Atlanta: Myth and Reality," 116.

17. For a more detailed discussion of the formation of the Twenty-first District Caucus see William E. Nelson, Jr., "Cleveland: The Rise and Fall of the New Black Politics," 192–194.

18. On the conflict between Stokes, Forbes, and Pinkney see William E. Nelson, Jr., "Cleveland: The Rise and Fall of the New Black Politics," 195–200.

19. Cleveland interview, Fall 1985. op. cit.

20. Ibid.

21. Todd Swanstrom, *The Crisis of Growth Politics: Cleveland, Kucinich and the Challenge of Urban Populism* (Philadelphia: Temple University Press, 1985), 112.

22. Cleveland interview, Fall, 1985. op. cit.

23. "Forbes Enemies File Petition to Elect Council Leadership," *The Call and Post,* June 21, 1980.

24. "Burten Fronts Racist White Challenge to George Forbes," *The Call and Post,* November 28, 1981.

25. Swanstrom, *The Crisis of Growth Politics: Cleveland, Kucinich and the Challenge of Urban Populism,* 113.

26. Cleveland interview, Fall 1985. op. cit.

27. Ibid.

28. Ibid.

29. Ibid.

30. "Forbes Puts Airlines Into EEO Compliance," *The Call and Post,* March 20, 1982.

31. "Forbes Pledges to Fight for Blacks at City Club," *The Call and Post,* June 23, 1983.

32. Cleveland interview, Fall 1985. op. cit.

33. Swanstrom, *The Crisis of Growth Politics: Cleveland, Kucinich and The Challenge of Urban Populism,* 246–252.

34. Cleveland interview, Fall 1985. op. cit.

35. Ibid.

36. Ibid.
37. Ibid.
38. Cleveland interview, Fall 1985. op. cit. This respondent spoke candidly of the creation by one councilman of an organization called the Hough Area Panthers for Progress as a rival to an existing group called the Hough Area Development Corporation once it became clear that the councilman would not be able to exercise effective control over the latter organization.
39. Cleveland interview, Fall 1985. op. cit.
40. This controversial case received extensive news coverage in the local press. As penalty for his conviction, Pinkney was placed on probation and ordered to perform 60 hours of community work. The most serious penalty, however, was to his reputation as a community leader, and to his aspirations for future elective office. See, "Pinkney Placed on Probation," *Cleveland Plain Dealer,* July 6, 1985.
41. During his service on the council, White earned the reputation of being a skilled political organizer and a highly articulate spokesman for his constituents. Former student body president at The Ohio State University with a Masters in Public Administration, White is widely viewed as a potential candidate for mayor at the conclusion of the Vonivich era.
42. Mr. Brown was first elected to the Cuyahoga County Commission in 1980, and reelected in 1984.
43. Cleveland interview, Fall 1985. op. cit.
44. Larry Brisker, "An Election Analysis of the General Election, November 5, 1985, Cleveland, Ohio," (Unpublished research report prepared for Pollmet, Inc.), 1.
45. Cleveland interview, Fall 1985. op. cit.
46. Ibid.
47. Ibid.
48. Ibid.
49. Ibid.
50. See "Money Talks, Blackness Walks," *The Call and Post,* November 7, 1985.
51. Ibid.
52. Brisker, "An Election Analysis of the General Election, November, 1985, Cleveland, Ohio," 5-6. See Table 3.
53. Cleveland interview, Fall 1985. op. cit.
54. James Jennings "Black Politics in America: From Access to Power," in *From Access to Power: Black Politics in Boston* eds. James Jennings and Mel King (Cambridge, Massachusetts: Schenkman Books, Inc., 1986), 176.
55. Marable, *Black American Politics: From the Washington Marches to Jesse Jackson,* 175-179.
56. Ibid., 182.
57. Jones, "Black Political Power in Atlanta: Myth and Reality," 116-117.
58. For a discussion of the attributes of the "progressive" face of local politics, as distinct from the "traditional" face, see Jennings, "Black Politics in America: From Access to Power," 175-178.
59. Cleveland interview, Fall 1985. op. cit.

60.   On the Boston experience, see James Green, "The Making of Mel King's Rainbow Coalition: Political Changes in Boston, 1963-1983," in *From Access to Power: Black Politics in Boston,* 99-135; On the Chicago experience, see Marable, *Black American Politics From the Washington Marches to Jesse Jackson,* 191-246; See also, Abdul Alkalimat and Doug Gills, "Black Power vs. Racism: Harold Washington Becomes Mayor," in *The New Black Vote: Politics and Power in Four American Cities* ed. Rod Bush, (San Francisco: Synthesis Publications, 1984), 55-179.

NINE

Coleman Young and Detroit Politics: 1973–1986

Wilbur C. Rich

Cities in the Northeast and the Midwest have been electing black mayors since the 1960s. At first these elections were created with, in retrospect, rather unwarranted speculations about the future of the American city. Commentators in the media saw these elections as a rite of passage for blacks seeking their place in the leadership hierarchy of the political world. Social scientists, in general, were not sanguine about prospects for black leadership. They saw problems with the black succession to power in old cities with declining tax bases and fleeing white residents.[1] The success of blacks in the political arena raised the question: "What will they do with the newly acquired political power?" Would blacks use this power to open the city up to opportunities for all, or would they construct political machines like those of their ethnic predecessors? Would the new black politics look like the old white politics? Would the direction of urban politics be amenable to these new stewards?

Many white residents of Detroit responded to the 1973 election of Coleman Young with intense apprehensions and fear. Coming, as it did, only six years after the city's worst race riot since World War II, Young's selection was seen as the final chapter in the great liberal experiment begun by Mayor Jerome Cavanaugh and continued in less flamboyant fashion by his successor, Roman Gribbs. Would the Young victory be the starting point for the dismantling of Detroit's political-electoral reforms? Was it a harbinger of what Peter Eisinger calls the "politics of displacement"?[2] Were the new black politicians machine building in their quest for elective office? Two rather common but divergent interpretations have emerged from the three successive terms of office which Young has served.

The first interpretation is that Detroit blacks were clearly ahead of their time for the ethnic succession process. Hence, they will make all the mistakes of previous ethnic groups, plus others attributable to their lack of

experience. This argument also holds that the propensity for political mach-
ination is a natural response to the seductiveness of power and the actions
needed for political survival. An important part of this argument is that as
blacks join the middle class, the need for a machine will lessen.

The other interpretation is that blacks will capture control of elective
office, but will fail to consolidate an independent political power base. Since
they lack the organizational and political skills to move beyond capturing
political power, the development of an advanced organization will be impossible. The nurturing of a political organization will divert energies and
retard their penetration into upper economic realism. Lacking the financial
wherewithal, black leadership will serve as a facade for the white economic
elite, which will continue to dictate economic policy for the city.

This paper will first descibe the demographic changes taking place in
Detroit prior to the election of Coleman Young as mayor in 1973. Second,
we examine mayoral politics prior to Young; third, we analyze the election
and reelection of Coleman Young and attempt to assess his impact on the
politics and government of Detroit. Finally, we shall attempt to define the
emerging black politics which is likely to continue beyond, and perhaps
transcend, the incumbents' administration.

Detroit: A City in Transition

The decline of the American industrial empire has had serious implications
for Detroit. The domestic automobile industry, which has been the city's
fulcrum since the days of the Model T, is now hard-pressed by foreign im-
ports, tight money, and labor costs that continue to rise. Detroit, which has
been losing residents to the suburbs for decades, is now losing the metropolitan pool of skilled workers to other parts of the country.

Despite a 1980 population of 1,203,339 residents and a municipal public
employee roster of 19,600, the city has shrunk considerably. As the composition of the city's populace changed, formerly white-only neighborhoods
became integrated. Blacks today live in communities where they would not
have been permitted to purchase a home only 20 years ago. Indeed, some
of these neighborhoods have lost most, if not all, of their white population
since the 1980 census.

The flow of escaping white residents, which began in the 1960s with the
rise of racial tensions, approached a floodtide in the 1970s when both middle and working class whites began to move out. Detroit's white population
in 1970 was 838,877. By 1980 it had diminished to 444,730. Between 1970
and 1980 Detroit's black population had actually increased from 672,605
to 758,939 (see Table 9.1). This increase was primarily due to births, as there
has been a notable decrease in outstate black immigration to Detroit. De-

Table 9.1   Black Percentages of Detroit Population

Years	Total Population	Percentage Decline or Increase By Decade	Black Population	Percentage Increase By Decade	Black Percentage of Total Population
1940	1,623,452	—	149,119	—	9.2
1950	1,849,568	13.9	298,875	200.4	16.2
1960	1,670,144	−9.7	482,223	61.3	28.8
1970	1,514,063	−9.3	672,605	39.5	28.8
1980	1,203,339	−20.5	758,939	12.8	43.6

Source: U.S. Census 1940–1980.

clining in-migration thus is an important factor in the city's recent net population loss. Blacks are over-represented in the city welfare recipient population, as well as among its unemployed. There is now a significant movement of the black middle class to border-suburbs of the city. Together, these trends have produced a profound demographic transformation that has been accelerated by industrial decline.

An inevitable correlate of a declining population is the downsizing of local government services and employees. Since 1970 Detroit has lost approximately 600 city jobs. Today the city bureaucracy remains small for a city its size. Currently there are only 19,000 municipal employees. Most, if not all, Detroit civil servants are classified and protected by union contracts. Even the head of the personnel office (Chief Examiner and Secretary of the Civil Service Commission) was classified before the 1973 charter revision. That revision strengthened the mayor's administrative control of most city agencies. He now appoints directors for the mayoral agencies. The largest of these is the police department, with over 4,000 members (down from the high of 5,706 in 1976). The mayor also appoints the director of the Water and Sewerage Department, but its budget is derived from user fees.[3]

The mayor and the nine city council members are elected on a nonpartisan basis; the latter run as at-large candidates. Other elected offices are city clerk, members of the school board, and recorder's court judges. Each of these offices is independent of the mayor. The recorder's court and Wayne County Welfare Department are funded and administered by the state.

The imposition of a nonpartisan at-large election system on the city has inhibited the development of political parties. The 1918 charter revision eliminated the ward system, thus initiating the politics of personalities and every councilperson for him or herself. Although nonpartisan elections were imposed by the Republican party to stop the growth of machine politics it had the effect of accelerating the downfall of the GOP in city politics. The Republican party had almost disappeared as a force in mayoral politics.

The Democrats, despite the fact that they are in power, are anything but unified. One major problem is presented by the unions. In 1969 Greenstone concluded that the party had been coopted by labor union political action committees (PAC).[4] These PACs are active from the precinct to the state committee level and play a major role at every level of partisan elective office (from the university board of trustees to the governorship). However, despite nearly 40 years of involvement with the Democratic party, union PACs have not achieved political machine status. The unions have to negotiate policy with elected politicians and other interest groups. Complaints that labor's interest is being neglected are not uncommon. City politicians do have confrontations with union leadership but many have survived union-led purges.

The unions also have problems, chief among them a politically unreliable and inconsistent membership. Indeed, the disloyalty of the predominantly white membership is particularly baffling for many old-line labor leaders. The problems with the white membership started with their defection to the 1968 George Wallace presidential candidacy and was consolidated with the Reagan victories in 1980 and 1984. On the local level, the problem began with the leadership endorsement of Mayor Louis Miriani's 1961 reelection bid. White and black members failed to follow their lead and helped elect Cavanaugh. White members are now considered conservative voters.

An equally perplexing problem for the union is the alienation of their black members. Blacks in the union still remember the UAW support of Mel Ravitz over Coleman Young in 1973. Young has been supported by the unions in subsequent elections, but he has not needed their endorsement to win. Incumbency has made the mayor practically invulnerable. Greenstone's comments about Detroit politics still hold: "Detroit and Michigan politics rewards politicians in terms of their personal attributes."[5] Young is reelected because he is Coleman Young and performs well. Party and union endorsements are secondary considerations in his reelection. In fact, if the mayor needed a party organization to get reelected, then he would have problems.

The lack of an effective party organization serves to perpetuate disorganization and has had a ripple effect on black party activists. In many cases blacks are left to their own resources to organize for political action. The organizational problems for blacks are compounded by state law which divides party structure according to congressional districts.

The local district conventions, which are cornucopia of colorful political personalities, elected officials, and union leaders, mask the loose ties among the political actors. Although these conventions are representative of the political power structure, there is no direct linkage to various election districts of the city. The lack of accountability at the ward level discourages identification with particular citizen groups and promotes political entrepreneurship. Each candidate can build his own independent support group without much direction from the party. Hence the threat to withhold party support carries little weight with incumbents. City politicians view black political interest groups with slightly more respect.

Black interest groups have increased their role in city politics since the ascendency of Coleman Young. The Black Slate, the political arm of a religious organization known as the Shrine of the Black Madonna, still endorses candidates for local office. Candidates solicit the organization's support as they would any other civic or labor organization. The black church, fraternal organizations, and small businessmen organizations serve as a platform and source of support for black politicians. Yet none of these organizations, alone or in concert, could unseat an incumbent. This is not to gainsay the role of the black church as a political instrument. In fact, the success of the Shrine of the Black Madonna demonstrates the mobilization potential of the black church. However, no black interest group exercises enough economic power to dictate mayoral policy. The white corporate leadership structure and the mayor are the major players in the economic realm.

Various independent economic revitalization groups are also involved in economic decision making along with the city's Department of Community and Economic Development. Included among these are New Detroit, Inc., a prototype urban coalition agency which developed after the 1967 riots. Its purpose was to bring together business, labor, and community organizers. It focuses primarily on lobbying, public information gathering, and training. Detroit Downtown Development Corporation is basically an economic booster organization which sponsors and promotes development projects. The Economic Alliance of Michigan, a relatively new organization, is yet another business-labor lobbying group. Because these groups mainly consist of leaders of the business community, they play an important role in economic development in the city.

What is the significance of these groups? Jack Newfield and Paul DuBrul saw the proliferation of power groups in a sinister light. In their review of the 1975 New York City fiscal crisis they claim that "ultimate power over public policy in New York is invisible and unelected. It is exercised by a loose confederation of bankers, bond underwriters, members of public authorities, the big insurance companies, political fund raisers, publishers, law firms, builders, judges, backroom politicians, and some union leaders." The authors call these groups the *permanent government*.[6]

There is no functional equivalent of this type of fragmentation of power in Detroit. Some groups do exercise influence in city politics, but they are not a permanent government, and they do not control the city's politics. Kuo's observation about the centrality of mayoral initiative and decision making holds true for Detroit.[7] The mayor proposes and disposes. The various interest groups simply advise and consent. Once a decision is made, there seems to be little that any one can do to veto it. The city council rarely vetoes mayoral budgets or other policy decisions. It cannot effectively perform its oversight function because it has very little staff. The shift of power to the mayor has reduced the council role in policymaking. The council restricts its attention to casework, minor administrative hearings, and resolutions for distinguished citizens.

The concentration of decision making in the mayor's office parallels the transformation of the city's economy. Although diversification is the wave of the future, the corporate leaders will not abandon their automobile base, as the recent support for the construction of the General Motors plant in the newly-established Central Industrial Park indicates. In addition, the city is working to expand its service economy (see Figure 9.1). This new economy will be anchored to a downtown convention center. Originally, this was to focus on the futuristic Renaissance Center, but the city has recently added the Robert Millender Center, a hotel and apartment complex. Construction has also started on the expansion of the Cobo Hall Convention Center, making it the third largest convention center in the nation, and a people mover, which is currently being built, will be yet another tourist attraction. Finally there are plans for more residential apartments downtown to revitalize it as a shopping center.

These developments have not come about without controversy. The clearing of the Poletown area for the GM plant generated its share of bad publicity for the city. The people mover continues to have cost overrun problems that seem to defy the financial experts. The mayor himself has been criticized for developing the downtown area at the expense of the neighborhoods. Some mayoral critics argue that building downtown residential facilities will trigger uncontrolled gentrification. Other critics complain that the new service economy will create only low paying and low skilled jobs. Still others complain that corporations are deciding the city's future, not the residents.[8]

The shift to a service economy paralleled the weakening of political ties between the union leaders and members. The political fallout from these shifts has been a weakening of the labor movement in general and labor market dislocation specifically. The city's rate of poverty has increased and more black families are on welfare rolls. Accordingly, the classic conditions for an economically dependent population have become increasingly apparent in the political system. At the same time, the city's political arrangements preclude using the party or any other interest groups as leverage for change.

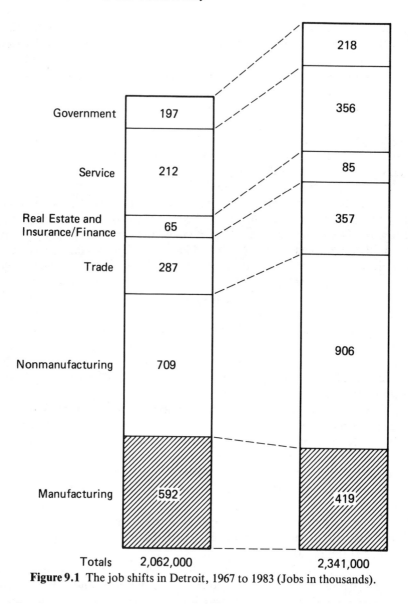

Figure 9.1 The job shifts in Detroit, 1967 to 1983 (Jobs in thousands).

Blacks, the victims of much of this economic dislocation, were also having problems with the liberal-labor coalition. It was not producing economically or politically. In order for blacks to win control of the city they had to rely less on the coalition and more on themselves. The beginning of the 1970s marked a turning point in black politics, and the 1973 Young candidacy became a testimony to the failure of the liberal-labor coalition to reciprocate for the support of the black voters.

Mayoral Politics Before Coleman Young

To understand the ascendency of Coleman Young it is necessary to review black mayoral politics in Detroit before 1973. In 1969 Richard Austin, a black politician who was very popular with both blacks and whites, ran a credible mayoral campaign against then Wayne County Sheriff Roman Gribbs. He lost by 1 percent of the vote (5,194 votes). A poll taken during the last week of the campaign and released one day before the election showed Austin leading Gribbs 42 percent to 39 percent, but there was also a significant percentage of "undecided" (18 percent).[9] Gribbs reacted to that poll by concentrating on white voter turnout and consolidation. The forecast of an Austin victory helped this effort. The poll watchers and commentators also assumed that Austin would have a record turnout among blacks.

In fact Gribbs received 6 percent of a less-than-overwhelming black vote. The black turnout was 70 percent of registered voters, down from the 80 percent that Detroit blacks had given Lyndon Johnson in 1964. Nonetheless, it was a substantial increase from the 50 percent turnout of black voters in the 1965 election. Despite his good showing among black voters and his increase in white voting percentages from the primary (from 9 percent to 18 percent), Austin simply could not overcome the high turnout among white votes in this election. The loss was chalked up as a setback for the emerging black political elite. The planning for 1973 began almost immediately.

Detroit's black political strategists spent the next four years determining who would be the "right" candidate. They envisioned a candidate who could excite that segment of the black community which is normally apathetic toward politics—the very poor. The goal was to get them to the polls at a rate of 80 to 90 percent of registered voters, and thereby to win these districts overwhelmingly. The candidate had to be clearly in favor of "law and order," knowledgeable about Detroit politics, and prepared to take on the task of rebuilding the city. Coleman Young emerged as the consensus choice.

The Election and Reelection of Coleman Young

Coleman Young had developed unusual credentials for a candidate for mayor of Detroit. He had been an automobile worker, then a visible labor leader and state legislator. As a labor leader, he had not hesitated to take problack and progressive positions, and defended his positions vigorously and with no mean degree of success. His record as a labor leader reflects his penchant for taking political risks; he often took on the white leadership of the unions. The union finally pushed him out in the 1950s. Accordingly, Young's ties with labor are personal and philosophical, not organizational.

Young was active in Detroit politics starting with the 1945 black attempts to win a seat on the Common Council. Then to the chagrin of his employer, CIO, Young became the state campaign director for Henry Wallace, the Progressive candidate for president in 1948. He was elected as a delegate to the Michigan Constitutional Convention in 1961 and subsequently to seats in the state House (1962) and Senate (1964). During his tenure in the Senate, he was elected to the National Democratic Committee. He also served as Democratic floor leader while a state senator. The Senate leadership position allowed him to prove both his capacity to stand up and fight, and to compromise and work with others. Young's role as a black radical in the labor movement was therefore followed by a political career characterized by a strong independent streak. Young's political campaign skills did not become well known until the 1973 mayoral election.

The 1973 Elections

The various candidates for the 1973 mayoral primary reflected the changing nature of the Detroit electorate. The major candidates were Edward Bell, a former judge and prominent black lawyer; John Mogk, a law professor at Wayne State University and specialist in housing; Coleman Young, state senator and former labor leader; Mel Ravitz, Wayne State University professor and president of the Common Council; and John Nichols, a former police chief. Ravitz and Bell faded during the campaign and received only 52,708 and 25,767 votes, respectively. Nichols won with a total of 96,767 votes. Young came in second with 63,614.

The runoff contest for the mayoralty was classic theater for Detroit politics. It pitted a liberal-labor leader with a reputation for radicalism against a "law-and-order" candidate with a 31-year affiliation with law enforcement. Many whites saw the race as the last stand before the takeover by the onrushing black majority. The 1970 census shows a dramatic increase in the number of black Detroit residents eligible to vote. At that time, most commentators were expecting a record turnout. Although whites were losing their edge in registration, few saw the need for a coalition with blacks. They supported Nichols because of his tough talk on crime. Senator Young's task was to present himself as a reasonable individual who was not attempting to drive whites from the community. His strategy was to shift the debate from crime to economic development. Although he was opposed to STRESS (Stop The Robberies, Enjoy Safe Streets), a police undercover squad, he had to validate a position as a "law-and-order" supporter.

The strategy of asserting a strong anti-crime posture, combined with a reform orientation, was effective. Young was able to characterize Nichols as a single-issue candidate with few economic plans for the city's future. According to *Detroit News* polls, Young led Nichols throughout the campaign.[10] In the first poll, taken in September (following the primary), Young led Nichols 46 percent to 33; in early October, the lead was 48 to 42. Just before the election the percentages were 48 to 43 among likely voters. The figures for all registered voters were 47 to 41, 50 to 39, and 52 to 40 percent. Among the undecided, Young held his own; he lost only 1 percent among likely voters and 3 percent among all voters. In the November poll it became clear that whites needed to turnout at a rate 6 percent higher than blacks to equalize the ballots, but the Nichols campaign was not generating that kind of interest among white voters. The problem was compounded by the growing increase in black registrants. It was believed that the 58,000 new registrants that fall were welfare recipients, mainly black, so Nichols faced an almost insurmountable task.

Table 9.2 shows the election results by district. Nichols and Young each had three districts in which they won over 90 percent of the vote. However, one of the districts in which Young achieved this was described as "mixed" (i.e., 10 to 50 percent white). It is important to point out that there were no districts in which a marginal win was scored by either of the candidates. The district which came closest to this was divided 59/41. Yet Young won by a citywide total of only 16,741 votes. The relatively narrow margin in the victory is explained by absentee votes. These distributed 24,529 to Nichols, as against 9,186 for Young. It is difficult to determine the composition of this vote, but it is quite unlikely that poor people or newly-registered voters would cast absentee ballots. The overall turnout (56 percent) was low in comparison with the 70 percent turnout in the Austin-Gribbs election.

The election results showed how much black politicians had learned since 1969. They now knew how to target their appeals. They had their main campaigns in white districts, even though there was as much chance of losing votes in those areas as of gaining them. This was more than a symbolic gesture, because it helped to show a commitment to both white and black voters that the candidate intended to conduct a fair administration. During and after the campaign, the newly-elected mayor reiterated his commitment to a 50/50 administration.

The 1977 Elections

By 1977, Mayor Young had a clear track record on which the electorate could evaluate him. He had abolished STRESS, appointed a black police chief, and launched an ambitious affirmative action plan. (The latter meant a minority increase from 11 percent to 32 percent in the police force in the

Table 9.2   1973 Election—Voting Statistics

District[a]	Raw Vote Totals		Percent Turnout	Winning Percentage	Ethnicity of District
	Young	Nichols			
3	9,117	3,154	43.1	74.2	white
4	3,867	15,084	49.8	79.5	white
5	1,758	21,182	56.0	92.3	white
6	1,689	22,349	58.6	97.4	white
7	5,869	10,415	50.3	63.9	black
8	16,068	1,209	53.6	93.0	black
9	10,133	3,035	48.0	76.9	black
10	7,361	2,724	49.1	72.9	black
11	5,499	3,025	36.7	64.5	black
12	13,319	1,774	48.9	88.2	black
13	12,411	8,318	57.0	59.8	white
14	14,954	5,445	52.9	73.3	white
15	23,404	3,025	36.7	64.5	black
16	4,485	17,506	47.4	79.6	white
17	5,781	15,275	53.5	72.5	white
18	1,379	18,635	48.5	93.0	white
19	5,984	13,396	53.4	69.0	white
20	18,939	1,927	54.4	90.0	white
21	15,274	5,055	53.0	75.0	mixed
22	17,622	975	52.8	94.7	black
23	15,632	910	43.3	93.9	black
24	6,451	2,600	47.3	71.2	black
25	1,907	11,910	52.2	86.0	white
26	5,567	2,755	55.6	66.8	mixed

[a]*District no. 1 is reserved for absentee ballots. There is no district no. 2.*
Source: Detroit Election Commission

period from 1970 through 1977). Throughout the first term there were police layoffs and recurrent budget problems. City residents had seen the mayor in action. However, the most important political change was demographic. Detroit had become a city with a black-majority population. With the change in population came a change in the issues; crime was replaced by economic revitalization as the most important issue. However, the most serious challenger in this election campaign was Councilman Ernest Browne, a black member of the Common Council.

Clearly, one of the underlying issues in the campaign was the hiring of black men and women under Young's Affirmative Action Plan. Browne and other candidates managed to get themselves labeled as moderates on this issue. Young was portrayed as an extremist. Brown also attacked Coleman Young's lifestyle. He blasted the mayor as a street-fighting man with gutter values, whose swinger lifestyle, Caribbean vacations, and eastside vocabulary were bad examples to the children of Detroit.

In the primary Coleman Young led 164,626 to Browne's 63,210 (which was only 404 votes short of Young's first primary total).

The 1977 mayoral election was heralded as the first black versus black mayoral race in the city's history. In 1973 Young had had only grass roots support; this time, he had the backing of the Detroit establishment and was endorsed by Henry Ford II, Coretta Scott King, the UAW's Wayne County Community Action Program Council, the Metropolitan Board of the AFL-CIO, and Michigan Teamsters Joint Council 43. His campaign contributors now included the whole spectrum of power in the city. The *Detroit News,* considered by some to be the most conservative of the city's two dailies, endorsed him for reelection.

Browne's campaign never developed a base. He was not successful in cultivating the image of some greater capacity for leadership in any of the contested issues. Young had already obtained the most impressive endorsements to go along with the developing national reputation as an effective mayor. He had been elected vice chairman of the National Democratic Party (1977 to 1981), and had become recognized as a friend of President Jimmy Carter, able to obtain favors, as well as give them. Detroit Democrats recognized Mayor Young as a significant pipeline to Washington, and former aides to the mayor were serving in the Carter administration.[11]

Browne was able to carry most of the absentee vote, just as Nichols had in 1973, but he completely failed to make serious inroads in Young inner-city support. While Browne won white districts 5, 6, and 13 handily, Young was competitive in 4, 7, and 19. Overall, Browne lost the election by 70,000 votes. However, the turnout (47.4 percent) was down from the Young-Nichols race, and was substantially below Young's prediction of a 65 percent turnout. In fact, the highest turnout in any district did not quite make 62 percent, and only occurred in one district (Detroit Election Commission, 1977). Despite this, the total spelled a convincing defeat for Browne, and added credence to the mayor's image of invincibility.

The 1981 Election: A Dearth of Candidates

During Coleman Young's second term as mayor, the city's fiscal situation deteriorated, a result of the nationwide economic decline and local revenue shortfalls. Population losses had begun to affect tax revenues, and the city was on the verge of its worst fiscal crisis since the Depression. The mayor's most visible response to the crisis was to establish a blue ribbon committee to review the city's financial situation. The Secret Committee predicted a deficit of $132.6 million. It recommended an increase in income taxes for both residents and nonresidents who worked in the city.

Many suburbanites who had fled the city to avoid the 2 percent income tax were furious. The proposal called for a 1 percent increase in the nonresident rate, to 1.5 percent. Although this was only half the new rate for city residents, it stirred many of the old claims of mismanagement in city government. Some claimed that municipal unions had gotten excessive pay raises for membership, and that the city was overextended in its expenditures. Now the city was asking the residents to bail it out of its difficulties. The unions helped by making wage concessions for 1982 and 1983. The mayor won the campaign to raise taxes, and residents voted to increase their taxes. If the 1977 election had left any doubts among local politicians about the mayor's invincibility, the vote on income taxes erased them, particularly in the minds of those who were interested in contesting him for the job. One of the most impressive features of the Detroit tax increase was that it took place during a time when most votes on tax rates resulted in decreases, rather than increases.[12]

Most Detroit politicians who harbored ambitions for the mayoral job decided to forego the 1981 campaign. The 1981 primary yielded Perry Koslowski, an unknown civil servant as the mayor's opponent. The result was a landslide victory for the mayor.

The real issue in the 1981 general election was whether a runoff was necessary. The major had won 71 percent of vote in the primary, against relative unknowns who were underfunded and could not generate issues of interest to the public. Perry Koslowski had little in the way of campaign funds or organization. His campaign strategy was to present himself as a management and finance expert. He blamed the major for the financial problems of the city, but his campaign soon became invisible. He only won the 4th, 5th, 6th, 18th, and 25th districts. Young got winning percentages in several white districts.

The 1981 election became a sideshow to the other issues on the ballot. In addition to supporting a proposal for an elected county executive and casino gambling, the mayor was supporting an opponent to incumbent City Clerk James Bradley. The mayor criticized Bradley for being out of town during the crucial income tax vote and also alleged general mismanagement of the election commission. Young preferred Shirley Robinson Hall, a young party activist and executive at a local utility company, who placed second in the primary and won the right to challenge Bradley. Ms. Hall received the political endorsement of the party regulars and the Black Slate, but she was no match for the veteran Bradley.

When the returns were in, the mayor won reelection by 63 percent of the vote, but he lost his other objectives: Bradley and public support for casino gambling in Detroit. On the subject of casino gambling, he was quoted as saying, "You win some, you lose some, and some you shoot craps or box-cars."

The 1985 Election: A Showcase for 1989?

As the 1985 primary approached, a series of problems emerged. Young was linked to two major scandals, and although there was no evidence that the mayor was involved, one of his appointees was convicted of bribery. The political picture was further confused when the mayor and his supporters became alienated from the state Democratic party organization. The latter accused the mayor of lukewarm support for the party nominee for governor. The two sides made up in time for the 1982 election, and the Democrats were able to win the governor's office. In the 1984 presidential primary the mayor supported Walter Mondale, the eventual nominee, against Jesse Jackson, a black civil rights leader. This caused some consternation among young black Jackson supporters, but the mayor stood by his decision. After the election the mayor returned to his downtown economic development plan, beginning the campaign to expand Cobo Hall and presiding over the completion of the Robert Millender Center. He also had amassed a large campaign fund for reelection. Political speculation started early, as some journalists wondered if the mayor would run again. Young was 67 years old, and a fourth term was unprecedented. The mayor further confused the situation by delaying his announcement. Even the veteran Erma Henderson, president of the City Council, misread the delay and filed for the mayoral race. She quickly withdrew after the mayor filed his papers.

The 1985 primary included a group of political amateurs and perennial minor candidates. The exception was newcomer Thomas Barrow, an accountant whose claim to fame was that he was a relative of the great boxing champion Joe Louis. The Barrow campaign spent most of its time achieving name recognition for the candidate. Barrow's campaign signs were all over town. He utilized every opportunity to make himself known to the voter. Nevertheless, Barrow came across as a young and inexperienced but articulate individual who was preparing for a future election.

In many ways, Barrow's race was a remake of Browne's 1977 race. Although he made an effort to appear thoughtful and balanced in his rhetoric, Barrow fell in the same trap as had Browne. He became known as the white voter candidate. In a *Detroit News* poll Young received 82 percent of the non-white vote to Barrow's 10 percent. Barrow received 51 percent of the white vote to Young's 23 percent.[13] If Browne was seen as the white hope of the 1977 election, then Barrow's campaign might be viewed the second coming of the white hope. In a city with a highly politicized black electorate any such characterization works against the candidate. Although a candidate can consolidate the anti-Young vote with this tactic, it practically dooms any serious penetration of the hard core of the Young support. As Koslowski's campaign had demonstrated earlier, the combination of the white vote and the anti-Coleman Young vote can yield approximately 35 percent of the total vote. This is not enough to win an election.

In the 1985 primary Young received 65 percent to Barrow's 28 percent. In order to defeat the mayor in the general election, Barrow had to hold his 28 percent and increase the remaining anti-Young vote by 16 percent. Barrow's only hope was to split the pro-Young voters, a feat no opponent had done in 12 years. A logical strategy in such a situation was to take the issue to the mayor and to create a debate.

Barrow adopted the perennial issues of crime, housing, and mass transit. One of his targets was the construction of the people mover, this proved to be a mistake because most of the anti-people mover sentiment was located in the suburbs; these are not Detroit voters. Moreover a *Detroit Free Press* poll conducted on primary day found that 68 percent of Detroit voters were in favor of the people mover. Barrow raised the issue of cost overruns but provided no suggestions for solving it. Meanwhile, the mayor concentrated his efforts on saving the project. Eventually he negotiated a city takeover of the South East Michigan Transportation Authority (SEMTA) project. The complicated negotiations involving the governor, U.S. Department of Transportation's Urban Mass Transit Administration (UMTA), and the mayor served to remind the voters of the mayor's reputation as a great negotiator.

Young also co-opted the crime issue. During the last days of the campaign the city was shocked by a series of teenage shootings in the public schools. Young seized the opportunity to promote the idea of metal detectors and random searches of students. He took on the local chapter of American Civil Liberties Union (ACLU) who had decided to file a suit arguing that such searches were a violation of privacy. These incidents provided yet another opportunity to show his constituency his law and order credentials.

Left with no clear issues, Mr. Barrow simply could not establish a base for his campaign. Barrow's problems were compounded by the mayor's decision not to debate his opponent, thereby denying the young candidate a platform.

The general election quickly became a referendum on the Young administration, and community attention shifted to the councilmanic campaign where some colorful characters were challenging the incumbents. The mayor continued his feud with City Clerk James Bradley. Young's candidate, Morris Hood, a former state legislator, who had been endorsed by the newspapers, the labor unions, and the activist community, was no match for the veteran Bradley. Bradley actually received 66 percent of the vote, a higher number of raw votes and a higher percentage than the mayor's 61 percent. At first glance it appears that Bradley is more popular than the mayor. Actually the city clerk is a very low profile office but the staff are among the most knowledgeable about city voting patterns. Bradley also benefited from being the incumbent. Detroit voters have a habit of returning incumbents and not being a part of mayoral purges.

Issues in Mayor Young's Election Campaigns

The classic work on voting behavior, *The American Voter*,[14] cites three tests for issue saliency for voters: the voter must be aware of the issues; indicate a preference, and perceive a difference between the parties and candidates on the issues.

In Coleman Young's first campaign, the issues were crime management and economic rehabilitation. The crime management issue was somewhat clouded because the public perceived crime prevention as somehow including racist sentiments. Thus many black voters interpreted Nichols' tough anticrime rhetoric as antiblack. They believed (with some justification) that STRESS was directly aimed at the black community. Young said that he would fight crime, but opposed the STRESS program as a vehicle. This was important because the black community felt they were not only more likely to be victims of crime but also victims of police violence stemming from the STRESS program. Coleman Young skillfully and effectively addressed those issues by promising that declines in crime rate could be accomplished by including more blacks on the police force and by instituting programs that relied on visible uniformed police presence, rather than television-style raids.

In the first reelection campaign, Young's opponent, Ernest Browne, tried to convince the voters that style was a legitimate factor; the effort failed.

In the mayor's third election campaign, the fiscal management of the city was the central issue. This, too, failed because of Young's successful bailout strategy. Candidate Koslowski was unable to show meaningful differences between his proposals and those implemented by the mayor. The fact that Koslowski, a political unknown, could get 37 percent of the vote tells us much more about the strength of the white voting bloc and the ABC vote (Anybody But Coleman) than it does about the challenger. This antivote often inflated opponents' totals beyond their real voting appeal.

In the 1985 election the mayor was again faced with an unknown with no experience in politics. The central issue in the campaign was the overall economic strategy of the city. However, Young's opponent, Tom Barrow, became sidetracked by such peripheral issues as the condition of mass transit, abandoned housing, and the people mover. Barrow mounted the people mover cost overrun issue before the city had control of that project. The mayor wisely spent the latter part of the campaign wrestling the project away from SEMTA, thereby defusing it as an issue. Barrow claimed that he would use monies that the city was getting for downtown development for other projects, which showed that he did not understand that most federal money cannot be used for purposes other than those legislatively prescribed. Barrow, like his predecessors, failed to show how he would conduct city affairs differently and more effectively than the mayor. He was only able to increase the opposition vote by 4 percent (39 percent) and won in only four election districts: fourth, fifth, eighth, fifteenth, and twenty-fifth. In the Eighth District the issue was whether the state should build a prison in the community. Barrow was against locating the prison in this area and his stand helped him win this inner city district. However, he was not able to replicate this feat elsewhere in the black districts. Although he did well in the Seventh and Seventeenth District, the turnout in these districts was low. Table 9.3 shows the results of that election.

The 1985 election was significant because it continued a trend of low turnout for city mayoral elections. Indeed only 37.7 percent of the registered voters bothered to go to the polls. This voter turnout was the lowest since 1951. None of Coleman Young mayoral elections have come close to the 70 percent turnout of the Austin-Gribbs race. Figure 9.2 shows turnout for mayoral elections since 1919.

The socioeconomic components of why people fail to vote have been the subject of various researchers. According to these studies, blacks have a low rate of political participation.[15] Nonvoting can signal satisfaction or alienation. Since the newspaper polls consistently find resident approval of the way the major handled his job, it is safe to assume that some nonvoters are satisfied with the mayor's performance. Many support Coleman Young, and if they were registered, they could be persuaded to vote for him. However, others are quite uninterested in city politics. Whether they represent a reservoir of votes which could be mobilized if needed remains to be seen.

It would appear that those who voted for Mayor Young—both black and white—were aware of the issues, but disassociated their support for the mayor from support for the issues he articulated. In 1973 he had won on the issues. By 1977 he had a track record, one which persuaded voters that he was a capable and effective incumbent. The separation of the issues from the man is quite evident in the 1981 election when the voters rejected the gambling proposal. A popular incumbent can often survive being at variance with the public on controversial issues.

A significant point in each election was the willingness of the average black voter to accept the mayor's word on issues such as fiscal management and economic redevelopment. This failed, however, when he tried to convince them to vote for the casino gambling proposal. Instead, they took the

Table 9.3   1985 Mayoral Election—Voting Statistics

District	Raw Vote Totals		Percent Turnout	Winning Percentage	Ethnicity of District
	Young	Barrow			
3	3,702	1,208	30.1	74.4	black
4	3,470	4,821	27.8	58.1	mixed
5	2,970	5,318	29.5	64.5	mixed
6	2,265	7,353	31.5	76.4	mixed
7	3,757	2,605	27.4	59.0	mixed
8	1,175	5,924	32.2	83.4	black
9	5,121	1,907	33.5	72.8	black
10	2,500	733	27.3	77.3	black
11	2,277	1,082	23.7	67.7	black
12	4,400	1,021	27.9	81.1	black
13	6,821	3,468	34.7	66.2	black
14	6,877	2,611	34.7	72.4	mixed
15	13,201	3,623	40.8	78.4	black
16	7,138	4,228	32.5	62.8	mixed
17	6,218	5,285	32.5	54.0	mixed
18	2,233	6,776	28.7	62.2	white
19	5,573	3,382	30.0	62.2	black
20	8,665	2,251	33.4	79.3	black
21	7,071	2,864	33.0	71.1	black
22	6,606	1,466	33.0	81.8	black
23	5,607	1,203	32.7	82.3	black
24	2,217	1,106	25.8	66.6	black
25	826	3,914	23.6	82.5	mixed
26	2,749	1,212	32.4	69.4	mixed

Source: Detroit Election Commission

advice of the clergy and voted their morals, a move that was consistent with traditional blue collar ethics. Detroit's economic situation was simply not desperate enough for them to accept legalized gambling as a necessity.

On the whole, Coleman Young has been very successful in his assessment of what issues are important to his constituency. In addition, he knows exactly when to raise an issue and how to link it to a given project or decision in order to obtain the support he deems essential. He is able to convey clear contrasts between himself and the state and federal governments, and

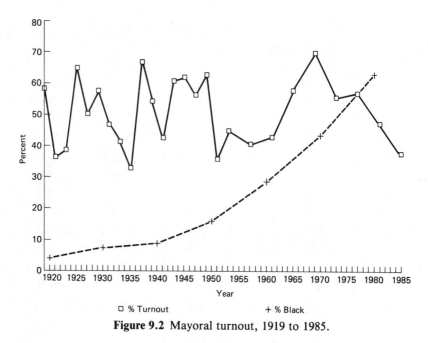

Figure 9.2 Mayoral turnout, 1919 to 1985.

uses these in issue orientation. His success has also been helped by the absence of effective opponents, as well as the impotence of the Republican party in Detroit. Although issues have been debated along partisan lines in the city, Republicans in state government have mainly kept their views in Lansing, and stayed clear of day-to-day city operations and politics.

Conclusions

Raymond Wolfinger began an essay on political machines with the following observation: "Machine politics is always said to be on the point of disappearing, but nevertheless seems to endure."[16] One might turn this sentence around to read: black political machines are always said to be on the point of forming, but never seem to coagulate. The looseness of the Detroit political system can be traced to the city's strong reform tradition of at-large elections. In continuing to allow the city councilperson to run at-large, the city encourages minimachines built around the personality of the councilperson rather than issues or party organizations. Accordingly, name recognition and incumbency are the real prizes in city politics. City councilpersons are not members of a Young machine, neither are they amenable to any type of party discipline. Hence, the reelection strategy is to develop a personal organization and to create one's own resources for the next campaign. This attitude leads to a highly personalized politics built on career survival rather than collective action. As a result, the new black politics in Detroit is constrained by structural reforms that mitigate intraparty conflicts but also obviate party development.

An equally formidable barrier to machine politics is the structure of the welfare system in Michigan. Charles Hamilton has argued that low-income voters need to make linkages between political benefits and voting preferences. Otherwise they are not inclined to regard the political parties or politicians as patrons.[17] If there is no perception of quid pro quo then there is less incentive to support a political leader or party. Indeed, welfare recipients can decide not to vote with impunity. In the past when some welfare services were provided by the parties people voted as clients of the machine. Today, these clients are simply recipients, with obligations only to the bureaucracy. In Detroit there are no data which suggest that welfare recipients view the mayor as their welfare patron. However, black politicians, in general, are expected to lobby for the Department of Social Services budget in the state legislature.

Coleman Young, as state legislator and again as mayor, has established a record as a defender of higher social welfare allowances. Those allowances were frozen in 1979 as a part of the state's solution to its financial problems. There has been no visible protest directed at black politicians in general or the mayor in particular over this. By the same token, no one congratulated the mayor when the freeze was lifted in 1985. Hamilton's observations about linkages would seem to be true, therefore, particularly in light of the recent voter turnout in the mayoral race. The lack of a political reprisal mechanism makes it difficult, if not impossible, for a group or elected official to build a machine based on political benefits.

The ability to manipulate the benefits and services provided by government is also constrained by bureaucratic norms. Bryan Jones found that there was no linkage between political support and service delivery.[18] Municipal bureaucracies are governed by internal procedures and rules, rather than partisan considerations. Accordingly, it is difficult to turn city agencies into political machines. The real problem for Coleman Young has been to convince the bureaucracy that his policies represent those of the general public, as for example his continuing fight with the (mainly white) police bureaucracy over affirmative action and the residency laws. Both the public and the courts support the mayor, but the police continue to press their case.

Another barrier to machine politics is the strong municipal civil service tradition. The job security of city workers is protected by both law and union contracts. The mayor has reacted to the politically insulated bureaucracy by attempting to reform it. Young's efforts with the police and fire departments have not only brought about the inclusion of more minority members and women in these work forces, but have also changed the public images of these departments. Police officers are no longer perceived as particularly antiblack, as they were during the administrations of Cavanaugh and Gribbs. Finally, there is no powerful civil service vote, or for that matter, strong public employee unions that can challenge the mayor electorally.

What then accounts for the mayor's continued electoral success? First, Coleman Young remains extremely popular with his core constituency, the most important of which are municipal blue collar workers. Secondly, he has skillfully nurtured and developed a small group of businessmen/entrepreneurs and middle-class blacks who contribute to his campaign. In each succeeding campaign Young has been able to raise more money. He simply outspends his opponents. This war chest enabled him to mount well-organized and cogent media campaigns.

Lastly, the highly personalized nature of Detroit politics seems to fit the mayor's personality. In many ways Detroit reminds one of the highly personalized politics of the pre-1950 Old South (sans the racism) with its emphasis on personalities and anecdotal references as a guide for voters rather than substantive cues. Coleman Young thrives in this type of social and political environment. Finally, the 1973 Young victory, to use Angus Campbell's terminology, was a realigning election, adjusting to new demographics. The subsequent ones were maintaining elections.[19] They have simply been referendums on Young's mayoral performance, rather than evidence of party stranglehold on the electorate or systematic penetration and mobilization at the precinct level. The image of the Mayor Young as a machine politician may therefore be seen as the media's characterization, reflecting their frustrations in trying to understand the nuances of Detroit politics.

Notes

1.   Paul Friesema, "Black Control of Central Cities: The Hollow Prize," *Journal of American Institute of Planners* (March 1962): 75–79.

2.   See Peter Eisinger, *The Politics of Displacement* (New York: Academic Press, 1980).

3.   All data on city personnel were obtained from city budget reports.

4.   J. David Greenstone, *Labor in American Politics* (New York: Vintage Books, 1969).

5.   Ibid., 125.

6.   Jack Newfield and Paul DuBrul, *The Abuse of Power: The Permanent Government* (New York: Penguin Books, 1977).

7.   See William Kuo, "Mayoral Influence in Urban Policy," *American Journal of Sociology* 79, no. 3 (November 1973): 620–38.

8. See Bryan D. Jones and Lynn Bachelor, "Local Policy Discretion and the Corporate Surplus," in *Urban Economic Development,* eds. Richard D. Bingham and John Blair (Beverly Hills: Sage, 1984).

9. Frederick P. Currier, "Mayor Race Is Too Close to Call," *Detroit News,* November 2, 1969, 1.

10. Edward P. Carrier, "Young Retains Lead Over Nichols," *Detroit News,* November 4, 1973, 1.

11. See Thomas Bray, "Jimmy Carter's Favorite Mayor (Coleman Young)," *Policy Review* (Spring 1984): 37–40.

12. See Wilbur C. Rich, "Bumping, Blocking and Bargaining: The Effects of Layoffs on Employees and Unions," *Review of Public Personnel Administration* 4, no. 1 (Fall 1983): 27–43.

13. Michael Traugott, "Poll Says Young Is Ahead 2-1," *Detroit News,* June 9, 1985, 8A.

14. Angus Campbell et al., *The American Voter* (New York: Wiley, 1960).

15. See Lester W. Milbrath, *Political Participation* (Chicago: Rand McNally, 1971).

16. Raymond Wolfinger, "Why Machines Have Not Withered Away and Other Revisionist Thoughts," *Journal of Politics* 39 (May 1972): 635.

17. Charles V. Hamilton, "The Patron-Recipient Relationship and Minority Politics in New York City," *Political Science Quarterly* 94, no. 2 (Summer 1979): 211-27.

18. Bryan D. Jones, "Party and Bureaucracy: The Influence of Intermediary Groups in Urban Public Service Delivery," *American Political Science Review* 75 (September 1981): 688-700.

19. Angus Campbell, "A Theory of Critical Election," *Journal of Politics* 17 (February 1955).

TEN

Politics and Power in the Sunbelt: Mayor Morial of New Orleans*

Huey L. Perry and Alfred Stokes

This chapter describes and analyzes political participation in New Orleans in connection with the two elections and mayoral administrations of Ernest "Dutch" Morial, the first black mayor of the city. A thorough description and analysis of the major factors operating in contemporary mayoral politics in New Orleans is provided. The chapter also describes and analyzes the role that blacks have played in the city's politics over the last eight years. Additionally, the chapter assesses Morial successes and failures as mayor of New Orleans and the impact that he has had in terms of providing increased social and economic benefits to the city's black population. The extent to which black in New Orleans have benefited as a result of increased participation in the political process is also discussed. We conclude this chapter by discussing and analyzing the election of the second black mayor of New Orleans, Sidney Barthelemy.

Data and Methodology

The primary data collection techniques used to assemble data for this chapter were secondary data analysis, documentary analysis, participant observation, and interviewing. The secondary data analysis component consists primarily of voting data. The primary data analytic methodology used is

*Since this paper was originally written a new black mayor, Sidney Barthelemy, has been elected mayor of New Orleans. The second part of this article discusses his election to office.

longitudinal data analysis. The chapter analyzes the eight years of Morial's mayoral tenure to determine the impact that the mayor has had in terms of providing increased social and economic benefits to blacks in three categories: *municipal employment, executive appointments,* and *municipal contracts.* For municipal employment and executive appointments, the longitudinal analysis also includes a comparative assessment of the benefits received by blacks under Morial as opposed to those received by blacks under Morial's predecessor, Moon Landrieu.

A Demographic and Economic Profile of New Orleans

New Orleans is the largest city in Louisiana, the third largest city in the south,[1] and the twentieth largest city in the U.S.[2] Its location on the Mississippi River is largely responsible for its role as a major commercial center for over 200 years. The city covers a 363.5-square mile area, of which about 200 square miles is land. The boundaries of the city are coterminous with Orleans Parish.[3] New Orleans' population in 1985 was 573,527.[4]

Between 1950 and 1960 New Orleans' population increased by 57,130 or 10 percent. The city's population was 570,445 in 1950 and 627,575 in 1960.[5] Since 1960, however, New Orleans, like most major cities in the U.S., has lost population as residents have moved beyond its municipal boundaries into suburban communities. The population of New Orleans in 1970 was 593,467.[6] This means that between 1960 and 1970 the city's population declined by 34,108 or 5.44 percent. Between 1970 and 1980 the city's population continued to decline; the 1980 population was 557,515.[7] This amounts to a decline of 35,952 or 6.06 percent between 1970 and 1980. Thus between 1960 and 1980, New Orleans' population declined by 70,600 or 11.16 percent. However, between 1980 and 1985 the population increased by 16,012 or 2.87 percent.

Between 1970 and 1980, New Orleans changed from a white majority population to a black majority population. In 1970, New Orleans had a white majority population with blacks comprising 45 percent of the city's population.[8] In 1980, the 308,149 blacks in New Orleans comprised 55.27 percent of the city's population. This amounts to a 15.28 percent increase in the city's black population between 1970 and 1980. By contrast, the 236,987 whites comprised 42.51 percent of the city's 1980 population, which amounts to a 26.72 percent decline in the city's white population since 1970.[9]

As can be ascertained from Table 10.1, New Orleans' primary industries are tourism, oil and gas, wholesale and retail trade, and shipping. In terms of the table's categories, tourism would most likely be included in Services, oil and gas in Transportation and Public Utilities, and shipping also in Transportation and Public Utilities. Manufacturing, once a strong com-

Table 10.1   New Orleans Employment by Major Industry, 1960 to 1981

Industry	1960 Number	1960 Percent	1970 Number	1970 Percent	April 1981 Number	April 1981 Percent
Mining	7,900	2.7	13,900	3.7	18,400	3.6
Contract Construction	17,500	6.1	22,500	6.0	31,000	6.2
Manufacturing	44,700	15.5	53,800	14.4	54,300	10.9
Transportation and Public Utilities	43,000	15.0	44,700	12.0	52,000	10.4
Wholesale and Retail Trade	73,800	25.6	90,500	24.2	124,100	24.8
Finance, Insurance, Real Estate	17,900	6.2	22,900	6.1	30,500	6.1
Services	44,500	15.5	68,200	18.3	110,900	22.2
Government	38,400	13.4	57,300	15.3	78,400	15.7
Total	287,800	100.0	373,800	100.0	499,600	100.0

Source: Adapted from Larry Schroeder, Lee Madere, and Jerome Lomba, *Occasional Paper No. 52: Local Government Revenue and Expenditure Forecasting: New Orleans* (Syracuse: Metropolitan Studies Program, The Maxwell School of Citizenship and Public Affairs, Syracuse University, October 1981), p. 5.

ponent of the city's economy, has declined substantially since 1960. As Table 10.1 shows, in 1960, 44,700 persons were employed in manufacturing, comprising 15.5 percent of the city's total employment. By 1970, the 53,800 persons employed in manufacturing comprised 14.4 percent of the city's total employment; and by April 1981 the 54,300 persons employed in manufacturing comprised 10.9 percent of the city's total employment. This means that manufacturing, as a percentage of the city's total employment, declined 4.6 percentage points, or by 29.68 percent, between 1960 and 1981. By April 1984, the number of persons employed in manufacturing had decreased to 47,500; by March 1985, to 47,100; and by April 1985, to 46,500.[10] This amounts to a 2.11 percent decrease in the number of persons employed in manufacturing between April 1984 and April 1985.

The only other industry which experienced a decline similar in magnitude to manufacturing, between 1960 and 1981, is transportation and public utilities. As Table 10.1 shows, the 43,000 persons employed in transportation and public utilities in 1960 comprised 15 percent of the city's total employment. In 1970 the 44,700 persons employed in transportation and public utilities constituted 12 percent of the city's total employment; and by April 1981, the 52,000 persons employed in transportation and public utilities comprised 10.4 percent of the city's total employment. Thus, manufacturing, as a percentage of the city's total employment, declined 4.6 percentage points, or by 30.67 percent, between 1960 and 1981. The other industries listed in Table 10.1, as a percentage of the city's total employ-ment, either grew or decreased slightly between 1960 and 1981. As the table shows, the three leading sources of employment in New Orleans in 1981 were wholesale and retail trade, services, and government.

Although the various industries listed provide millions of dollars to the city's economy each year, New Orleans continues to have a major poverty problem. A substantial 26.4 percent of the city's residents live below the poverty level, which makes New Orleans the third poorest large city in the United States.[11] The city's economy has experienced only modest growth and almost no diversification since the middle 1960s; and as a result of unemployment, underemployment, and other mal-effects of a longstanding stagnant economy, poverty is pronounced in New Orleans.

According to James R. Bobo the crux of New Orleans economic problem is not growth but inadequate economic development:

> The local economy has experienced economic stagnation tendencies since the mid and late 1950s, with chronic and severe stagnation since 1966, not because there was an absence of economic growth, but because economic development did not provide adequate employment opportunities for an expanding labor force. . . . Employment opportunities have been inadequate since 1966 . . . consequently, unemployment has increased both absolutely and as a percent-age of the labor force since 1966, reaching 9.0 percent in 1975.[12]

Alvin J. Schexnider's list of the economic problems in New Orleans include "low income and poverty, maldistribution of income, unemployment and subemployment, and low educational attainment."[13]

In New Orleans, as is the case in all cities in the U.S., blacks are not doing as well as whites economically. For example, in New Orleans in 1985 the median family income for blacks was $10,516 as compared to $21,544 for whites.[14] This means that the white median family income was more than double that of blacks; or, expressed differently, for every dollar earned by a white family a black family earned 49 cents. The gap between black and white median family income in New Orleans was approximately the same size in 1980 as it was in 1985. In 1980 the median family income for blacks was $7,598 as compared to $14,898 for whites.[15] Thus, white median family income was just slightly less than double black median family in-come. For every dollar a white family earned in 1980, a black family earned 51 cents. The gap in median family income between blacks and whites in New Orleans in 1980 was greater than in any other major city in the United States.[16]

Although blacks in New Orleans fared poorly relative to whites in terms of income in 1980, by 1985 their relative situation had deteriorated even further. Extending the time frame of the comparison to 1970 visibly im-proves black median family income relative to white median family income and at the same time shows how much the economic situation of blacks relative to that of whites deteriorated over the 15-year period between 1970 and 1985. In 1970 the median family income for blacks was $4,745 as compared to $7,445 for whites.[17] This means that white median family income was just over one and one-half times that of black median family income. In other words, for every dollar earned by a white family, a black family earned 64 cents. This compares favorably with 51 cents in 1980 and 49 cents in 1985. In terms of black median family income relative to white median family income, blacks in New Orleans in 1985 were in a slightly less favorable posture than they were in 1980 and a significantly less favorable posture than they were in 1970.

New Orleans Political Culture and Governmental Structure

Most students of politics recognize the importance of understanding the political culture of a locality in order to understand the nuances of how the governmental and political processes work. The political culture of New Orleans is very different from that of most other cities. Thus a knowledge of New Orleans' political culture is especially relevant for understanding the city's governmental and political processes. New Orleans is a cultural mosaic, consisting of a mixture of "French, Spanish, and southern cultures."[18] The cultural mix of New Orleans society gives rise to two important characteristics of the city's political and social culture. One characteristic is that the general pace of life in the city is relaxed. New Orleanians do not appear to be as intense about life, work, and politics as residents of many other large cities. This is especially true of mass citizenry in New Orleans.

Given the easy-going behavioral style of the masses, it seems somewhat incongruous that a second characteristic of New Orleans society is a very rigid social structure. The pinnacle of the city's social sphere is dominated by a small number of wealthy white New Orleanians whose families have been in the city for several generations. The incongruity between the relaxed pace of the masses and the elitism propagated by the leading lights in the social sphere is, ironically, best illustrated during the city's celebrated annual carnival season, otherwise known as Mardi Gras. During the Mardi Gras celebration, while the masses make an art form out of participating in an open, free-wheeling epicurean revelry, the social elites attend elegant balls which "are closed not only to the general public, but also to everyone except those whose families have been . . . (in New Orleans) since the turn of the century."[19]

The rigid social structure in New Orleans resulted in a slow emergence of an expanded and more diversified civic and political leadership in the city. Charles Y. W. Chai provides insight into the negative effects that the social structure has had on the growth of new civic leadership in the city.

> A young executive who moves to New Orleans with his family may soon become frustrated by a system which prevents him from enjoying many of the luxuries he feels he deserves. As a result, he may refuse to participate in community affairs. . . . (Many such executives) see no reason to work with the "locals" on community problems, since the "locals" refuse to socialize with outsiders.[20]

Schexnider provides additional insight into the impact that New Orleans' rigid social structure has had on the emergence of black elected political leadership in the city. Schexnider asserts that the rigid social structure:

> is endemic to the political culture of New Orleans. It is clearly dysfunctional to the political system in general, though its adverse impact on the life fortunes of black citizens is probably more pronounced. It was not until 1967 that the city sent its first black (Ernest Morial . . .) to the Louisiana House of Representatives. Nonetheless, it was easier to send a black to the state legislature than to the New Orleans City Council, which was finally integrated in the mid-1970s.[21]

Additional support for Chai's and Schexnider's observations can be gleaned from the efforts of women to penetrate the elected political leadership domain in New Orleans. Although women were first elected to the state legislature from New Orleans as late as the mid-1970s, the first two women (one black and one white) on the city council were elected as recently as March 1986.

Just as it is well known that a knowledge of the political culture of a locality is relevant for understanding the subtleties of how the governmental and political processes work, the same applies to a knowledge of the governmental structure. The city operates under a home rule charter which became effective in 1954. Under Louisiana's Home Rule authority, "The Louisiana Constitution prohibits the State Legislature from enacting any law affecting the structure, organization or distribution of the power and function of any local political subdivision which operates under a home rule charter."[22]

New Orleans has a mayor-council form of government. The mayor appoints the chief administrative officer and the budget officer. The chief administrative officer, who provides overall executive supervision and coordination of the day-to-day functions of city government, appoints, subject to the mayor's approval, 11 of the 13 executive department heads. The two other executive department heads, the city attorney and the director of the Civil Service Department, are appointed by the mayor and the Civil Service Commission, respectively.[23] The city council is a seven-member body, with five seats elected by districts and two seats elected at large. In terms of the electoral subdivisions of the city, New Orleans consists of 17 wards and 428 precincts.

New Orleans, given its poor economic conditions and its atomistic political culture, clearly constitutes a formidable environment for a black mayor to provide social and economic benefits to the black community. But the austerity of New Orleans as a case study to assess the social and economic impact of the black mayor on the black population is helpful in the sense that it is desirable to know the capacity of black political participation to produce benefits in cities with varying degrees of social and economic resources and characteristics. In terms of theory building in the study of black politics, it is important to know the capacity of black mayors to produce social and economic benefits for blacks in localities where supportive economic resources and characteristics are meager and in localities where supportive economic resources and characteristics are more plentiful. Studies of this nature are needed to produce a general assessment of the capacity of overall black political participation to produce favorable social and economic change for blacks.

The Electoral Support Base of Morial in the 1977 Mayoral Race

Morial was a State Appeals Court Judge when he decided to run for mayor in 1977. Prior to his decision Morial had compiled an impressive list of accomplishments, including several "firsts" for a black person. For example, Morial was the first black graduate of the Louisiana State University Law School in 1954. He became Louisiana's first U.S. Attorney in 1965. Similarly, in 1967 he became the first black since Reconstruction to be elected to the Louisiana Legislature. Morial also subsequently became the first black to serve on the Juvenile Court in New Orleans. In 1974 he also became the first black elected to the Louisiana State Appeals Court.[24]

At the time of Morial's decision to run for mayor, there was not a strong tradition of assertive black political participation in New Orleans, especially with regard to running for public office. Morial had unsuccessfully run for an at-large seat on the city council seat in 1969. Also, Morial decided to run for office only one year after the first black, Reverend A. L. Davis, Jr., had been selected by city council members to fill a vacancy on the council in 1976. Two other factors which seemingly minimized Morial's chances of winning his first mayoral election were that registered white voters outnumbered black voters by 58 percent to 42 percent[25] and "that the major black organizations supported white candidates in the primary."[26] Moreover, Morial "was a long-time foe of those blacks who headed the major political organizations in New Orleans."[27]

In the primary election Morial received the largest number of votes among the 11-candidate field, but not the majority of votes necessary to avoid a runoff. Joseph V. DiRosa, the conservative white city councilman who defeated Morial in the 1969 council race, barely edged out a second place finish over liberal State Senator Nat Kiefer. Toni Morrison, son of former New Orleans Mayor deLesseps Morrison from 1946 to 1961 (before the two-term limit was instituted), finished fourth. None of the other seven candidates was close to the number of votes that Morrison received.[28]

In terms of the racial distribution of the votes cast in the primary, Morial received 58 percent of the black vote and 5 percent of the white vote.[29] DiRosa received 39 percent of the white vote and four percent of the black vote. Thus both Morial and DiRosa received a similarly small proportion of other race support. The two other major candidates, Kiefer and Morrison, received remarkably similar proportions of racially mixed support. Kiefer received 18 percent of the black vote and 28 percent of the white vote; whereas Morrison received 16 percent of the black vote and 25 percent of the white vote. Thus Morial and DiRosa entered into a runoff.

Also in the 1977 primary New Orleans voters elected State Senator Sidney Barthelemy as their first black at-large city councilman.[30] Black turnout for the primary was 66 percent as compared to 74 percent for whites. Thus black turnout in the primary was eight percentage points less than that of whites.

Morial's strategy for the primary election was to appeal to black voters in the hope that he would receive a large enough black vote to put him in the runoff and at the same time take enough black votes away from Kiefer and Morrison to prevent them from entering into the runoff. Kiefer and Morrison were both liberal and would have provided a stronger opposition to Morial in the runoff than the Conservative DiRosa. Morial's strategy, undoubtedly aided by the three white candidates' division of the white vote into three sizable chunks, worked to perfection.[31] Thus Morial finished first in the primary election because he received a majority of the black vote and a small portion of the white vote while his three major white opponents divided the white vote.

Morial's runoff election strategy was different from his primary election strategy. Fully cognizant that he could not be elected by black voters alone, Morial made a strong appeal to white voters in the runoff campaign. This strategy also worked to perfection as Morial won the runoff election by 95 percent of the black vote and 19 percent of the white vote.[32] Morial received 89,823 votes to DiRosa's 84,352,[33] thus defeating him by 5,471 votes. In percentage terms, Morial received 51.57 percent of the votes to DiRosa's 48.43 percent.

Three factors were critical to Morial's victory. Unquestionably one factor was the tremendous support he received from black voters. Morial's impressive performance among black voters is illustrated in Table 10.2. As the table shows, Morial won the two heavily majority black wards and the five racially mixed-majority black wards by overwhelming margins.[34] Although Morial received only nominal support from the major black political organizations,[35] black voters gave him near unanimous support.

A second key ingredient to Morial's victory is the increased interest that blacks manifested in the electoral process following his entry into the runoff. This increased interest was manifested in two ways: one, a greater increase of black voter registration following the primary; and two, a black turnout rate on election day nearly equal to that of whites. With regard to the former, black voter registration increased by 5 percent during the months between the primary election and the runoff election while white voter registration increased by 3.5 percent.

In terms of the nearly equal rates of turnout between blacks and whites, the black turnout rate was 76 percent as compared to the 78 percent turnout rate for whites. It is unusual in American politics for black voter turnout to be nearly equal to that of whites and the fact that it was indicates an increased interest in the electoral process generated by the prospect of a black having a real chance to win the most important office in city government. This mobilization of the black electorate resulted in blacks increasing their voter turnout rate by 10 percentage points or 15 percent between the primary election and the runoff election (66 percent versus 76 percent, respectively), while whites increased their turnout rate by four percentage points or five percent (74 percent versus 78 percent, respectively).

Table 10.2   Registration and Voting Data for the Two Predominantly Black Wards and the Five Racially Mixed-Majority Black Wards Carried by Morial in the 1977 Mayoral Runoff Election

Ward	Voter Registration		Votes Received	
	Black	White	Morial	DiRosa
(Predominantly Black)				
Second Ward	3,289	507	2,304	448
Eleventh Ward	6,028	2,917	4,999	1,803
(Racially Mixed-Majority Black)				
First Ward	1,270	659	903	413
Seventh Ward[a]	16,830	12,764	13,809	8,900
Ninth Ward	29,157	27,405	23,290	19,316
Tenth Ward	3,485	2,091	2,580	1,308
Twelfth Ward	5,645	4,008	5,021	2,297

[a]Data from one precinct are not included in the vote totals for this ward.
Source: Compiled from registration and voting data published in the (New Orleans) Times Picayune, November 14, 1977.

The third and final key to Morial's victory was the fact that he received almost 20 percent of the white vote. Twenty percent is the upper end of the range of support from white voters that most successful black candidates running for public office in biracial political jurisdictions can hope to receive (10 percent is the lower end of the range). Thus Morial's ability to win 19 percent of the white vote was clearly an impressive accomplishment. Table 10.3 provides an indication of how well Morial did among white voters. As the table shows, Morial won all of the five racially mixed-majority wards in the city.

The strength of Morial's showing in the racially mixed-majority white wards is best illustrated in the vote totals from the Sixteenth Ward. Although white registered voters outnumber black registered voters in the Sixteenth Ward by almost a two-to-one ratio, Morial won the ward by almost 700 votes. Since there were 1,830 black registered voters in the ward and Morial received 2,318 votes, this means that Morial received substantial support from the white voters in the ward. The white voters who supported Morial were generally middle and upper income whites.

Morial won 12 of the city's 17 wards, which consisted of the predominantly black wards, the five racially mixed-majority black wards, and the five racially mixed-majority white wards. The remaining five wards won by DiRosa, as Table 10.4 shows, were all predominantly white wards. Although DiRosa won these wards convincingly, he did not win some of them by large enough margins to significantly cut into Morial's lead from the other wards. The Fourteenth Ward well illustrates this point. In the Fourteenth Ward white voter registration exceeds black voter registration by a nine-to-one ratio (13,210 to 1,478, respectively), yet DiRosa won the ward by just under 2,100 votes (6,436 to 4,346, respectively). DiRosa's less than spectacular performance in the predominantly white wards combined with his losing the racially mixed-majority white wards and not doing better in

Table 10.3   Registration and Voting for the Racially Mixed-Majority White Wards Carried by Morial in the 1977 New Orleans Mayoral Runoff Election

Ward	Voter Registration		Votes Received	
	Black	White	Morial	DiRosa
Fifth Ward	3,183	5,528	3,190	3,099
Sixth Ward	1,988	2,229	1,773	1,282
Thirteenth Ward	3,451	4,800	3,864	2,567
Sixteenth Ward	1,830	3,447	2,318	1,619
Seventh Ward	6,846	7,279	6,506	4,642

Source: Compiled from registration and voting data published in the (New Orleans) Times Picayune, November 14, 1977.

Table 10.4   Registration and Voting Data for the Five
Predominantly White Wards Carried by DiRosa in the 1977 New Orleans
Mayoral Runoff Election

	Voter Registration		Votes Received	
Ward	Black	White	Morial	DiRosa
Third Ward	1,232	5,000	1,397	3,389
Fourth Ward	1,525	12,904	2,168	9,099
Eighth Ward[a]	4,093	11,379	3,456	7,469
Fourteenth Ward	1,478	13,210	4,346	6,436
Fifteenth Ward	6,217	14,684	6,646	8,500

[a]*Voting data from three precincts missing.*
Source: Compiled from registration and voting data published in the (New Orleans) *Times Picayune,* November 14, 1977.

the racially mixed-majority black wards are the three principal reasons why DiRosa lost the runoff election.

In sum, Morial won a convincing victory over DiRosa to become the first black mayor in New Orleans' history. Morial's successful electoral support base consisted of a highly mobilized black vote and a sizable minority portion of the white vote, comprised mostly of middle and upper income whites. Morial's strategy to attract a strong black vote in the primary and, in so doing, prevent all but the weakest of his major opponents from entering the runoff worked to perfection. Similarly, his runoff election strategy to attract a significant minority portion of the white vote while holding onto the black vote worked out according to plan. By all accounts Morial's road to the mayor's office was paved by an ingenious strategy that was brilliantly executed.

Morial's 1982 Reelection Support Base

Morial ran for reelection in 1982. In that year, 54 percent of the white voting age population and 46 percent of the black voting age population were registered to vote. Morial's principal opponents were Ronald Faucheaux, a progressive, business-oriented white and State Senator William Jefferson, a liberal black. A runoff election between Morial and Faucheaux was necessary as Morial led the field by receiving 47 percent of the votes cast, followed by Faucheaux who received 45 percent and Jefferson who received 7 percent.[36] Unlike his first mayoral election Morial received a much higher proportion of the black vote—90 percent. Moreover, with a few exceptions, the major black political organizations in the city endorsed his candidacy[37] as compared with no endorsement from those organizations in his 1977 primary election. The overall voter turnout in the primary was 67 percent, with blacks turning out at 64 percent and whites at 69 percent. Thus white voter turnout exceeded black voter turnout by five percentage points.

Faucheaux received practically all his support from whites. His white supporters consisted of some upper income whites, some whites associated with the business community, and the majority of low income whites. While Faucheaux was supported by a few prominent black individuals like then-State Senator Henry Braden, he received virtually no support from the major black political organizations. Faucheaux's showing among black voters in the primary election was very poor, as he received only 1 percent of the black vote. While Jefferson received racially mixed support, he received more support from whites than he received from blacks.[38] A solid portion of Jefferson's white support came from his white constituency in his senatorial district.

The 1982 runoff election provided a greater challenge to Morial's electability than did the 1977 runoff election. This was due to the circumstances regarding the field of candidates and Morial's crafty manipulation of those circumstances, which resulted in Morial facing the weakest of his major opponents in the 1977 runoff. Unlike the Conservative DiRosa, who provided Morial a relatively easy basis for mobilizing black voters and luring a significant minority portion of the white vote, the liberal Faucheaux, who appealed to the same type of white voter most likely to vote for Morial, constituted a much more formidable runoff opponent.

In the runoff election the overall turnout rate was 75 percent, which was eight percentage points higher than the 67 percent turnout in the primary. Of the 189,298 votes cast in the runoff Morial received 100,725 votes, or 53 percent, while Faucheaux received 88,573 votes, or 47 percent. Morial won 10 of the city's 17 wards. Morial received 99 percent of the black vote and 14 percent of the white vote, while Faucheaux received 86 percent of the white vote and 1 percent of the black vote. As Table 10.5 shows, Morial dominated Faucheaux in the three predominantly black wards and won strongly in the five racially mixed-majority black wards. In the predominantly black Second Ward, for example, Morial beat Faucheaux by almost a nine-to-one ratio, receiving 2,763 votes to Faucheaux's 309.

Morial received 5 percentage points less of the white vote than he did in the 1977 runoff (19 percent versus 14 percent). This amounts to a 26.32 reduction in white support, which was in great part attributable to the fact that Faucheaux had some appeal to the upper income white voters who supported Morial in 1977. As a result Morial did not win all the racially mixed-majority white wards in the 1982 runoff as he did in the 1977 runoff (see Table 10.6). In fact Faucheaux won half of the wards in this category. Specifically, he won the Fifth, Sixth, and Eighth Wards. Although Faucheaux barely won the Fifth Ward, he won the Sixth Ward by almost 900

Table 10.5   Registration and Voting Data for the Three Predominantly
Black Wards and the Five Racially Mixed-Majority Black Wards Carried
by Morial in the 1982 Mayoral Runoff Election

Ward	Voter Registration		Votes Received[a]	
	Black	White	Morial	Faucheaux
(Predominantly Black)				
First Ward[b]	1,511	550	1,024	416
Second Ward	3,310	557	2,763	309
Eleventh Ward	6,110	3,891	5,217	1,815
(Racially Mixed-Majority Black)				
Seventh Ward	18,349	12,321	15,948	8,401
Ninth Ward	35,172	27,606	30,004	21,657
Tenth Ward	3,467	2,161	2,909	1,191
Eleventh Ward	6,110	3,891	5,217	1,815
Twelfth Ward	6,140	3,873	5,553	2,191

[a]The double column figures listed do not include absentee votes.
[b]Note that this ward was a racially mixed-majority black ward in 1977.
Source: Compiled from a tally of offical returns recorded by the New Orleans City Council.

votes and the Eighth Ward by almost 3,000 votes. Thus it was crucial to
Morial's victory that he receive a slightly higher percentage of the black
vote than he did in the 1977 runoff (99 percent versus 95 percent) to com-
pensate for the reduced white support.

As expected, Faucheaux, like DiRosa in the 1977 runoff, registered strong
wins in the predominantly white wards (see Table 10.7). Faucheaux's impressive strength in these four wards is best illustrated by the vote totals
for the Fourth Ward. Faucheaux won the Fourth Ward by better than a

Table 10.6   Registration and Voting Data in the Six Racially
Mixed-Majority White Wards for the 1982 Mayoral Runoff Election

Ward	Voter Registration		Votes Received[a]	
	Black	White	Morial	Faucheaux
Fifth Ward	3,502	5,559	3,216	3,271
Sixth Ward	2,083	2,386	1,108	1,988
Eighth Ward[b]	5,358	10,367	4,888	7,687
Thirteenth Ward	3,452	4,982	3,609	2,823
Sixteenth Ward	1,726	3,379	2,075	1,835
Seventeenth Ward	7,117	7,123	6,664	4,841

[a]The double column figures listed do not include absentee votes.
[b]Note that this ward was a predominantly white ward in 1977.
Source: Compiled from a tally of official returns recorded by the New Orleans City Council.

Table 10.7   Registration and Voting Data for the Four Predominantly White Wards for the 1982 Mayoral Runoff Election

Ward	Voter Registration		Votes Received[a]	
	Black	White	Morial	Faucheaux
Third Ward	1,626	5,142	1,650	2,934
Fourth Ward	1,667	12,919	2,384	8,795
Fourteenth Ward	1,387	13,487	3,209	7,717
Fifteenth Ward	6,749	14,750	6,846	9,739

[a]*The double column figures listed do not include absentee votes.*
Source: Compiled from a tally of official returns recorded by the New Orleans City Council.

three and a half-to-one ratio. His 8,795 votes in that ward exceeded Morial's 2,384 by more than 6,400 votes. Thus Faucheaux won 7 wards and Morial won 10 wards. Faucheaux's performance in this regard was 2 wards more than the 5 wards DiRosa won in 1977 and Morial's performance was 2 wards less than the 12 wards he won in 1977.

Seventy-five percent of blacks turned out to vote in the runoff as compared to 64 percent in the primary. This amounts to an increase of 11 percentage points or 17.19 percent. White voter turnout was 74 percent in the runoff as compared to 69 percent in the primary, which amounts to an increase of 5 percentage points or 7.25 percent. Thus there was a 6 percentage point or nearly 10 percent difference in favor of blacks in terms of the increase in turnout between blacks and whites from the primary to the runoff. Most significantly, blacks were so mobilized for this election that their turnout rate exceeded that of whites—by 1 percent, 75 percent to 74 percent, respectively. There was also a 9 percentage point increase in the proportion of the black vote Morial received in the runoff as compared to the primary—99 percent versus 90 percent, respectively.

The 1982 election results reveal Morial's considerable electoral strength. Despite the fact that both Jefferson and Faucheaux were viable candidates, Morial received the highest proportion of the votes in the primary. While Jefferson and Faucheaux were able to attract enough black and upper income white voters to prevent Morial from being reelected in the primary, they were unable to attract enough of those votes to deny Morial a first place finish in the primary. That Morial won the runoff election against Faucheaux, who was a more formidable candidate than DiRosa was in the 1977 runoff, was clearly an important indication of his considerable electoral strength.

Although Morial won reelection convincingly, it is significant that his white support dropped considerably from the 1977 race. Rather than Morial's appeal among white voters increasing over his four years in office, it declined considerably. Although it was basically the same electoral support base responsible for his election in 1977 that reelected Morial in 1982, the difference was that the 1982 support base had a larger black and a smaller white presence than the 1977 support base.

Morial's Election Victories and General Trends in American Politics and Black Political Participation

There are several factors about Morial's electoral victories that are squarely consistent with general trends in American politics and black political participation. One such factor is that Morial was twice elected to the mayor's office on the basis of a large, unified black vote and a significant minority portion of the white vote. This kind of coalition typically elects most blacks to public office in the U.S., with the portion of white voters necessary for victory usually falling in the 10 to 20 percent range. A closely related second factor at work in Morial's victories, which is common to black electoral victories in general, is that the 10 to 20 percent of the white vote that most successful black candidates need to win elections in biracial electorates almost invariably come from middle and upper income whites. Morial's white votes in both the 1977 and 1982 elections decidedly came from the more affluent areas of the city.

A third factor evident in Morial's victories, which is fairly typical of races in which there is a viable black candidate, is an increase in black voter turnout as compared to previous elections. Moreover, it is not unusual in such elections for the black voter turnout to approximately equal white voter turnout. This occurred in both the 1977 and the 1982 New Orleans mayoral runoff elections. In the 1977 election 76 percent of the registered blacks voted as compared to 78 percent of the registered whites. In the 1982 election the comparable figures were 75 percent and 74 percent. These observations are significant because blacks generally turn out less than whites and they show how the presence of a viable black candidate can mobilize blacks to turn out to vote at rates significantly higher than normal, and usually without an equally significant counter mobilization among whites.

A fourth way in which Morial's electoral victories are consistent with general trends in American politics is that the votes were quietly cast along racial lines. In the 1977 runoff election Morial received nearly all of the black vote (95 percent) and DiRosa received the great majority of the white vote (81 percent). The comparable 1982 runoff election figures for Morial and Faucheaux are 99 percent and 86 percent, respectively. Despite this pattern of voting along racial lines, race was not made an issue in the campaign, at least not by the candidates, and there was no manifestation of racial bitterness.[39] This is generally the case in most elections involving ra-

Table 10.8   Registration and Voting Data for the Three Predominantly Black Wards and the Six Racially Mixed-Majority Black Wards for the November 6, 1984 Earnings Tax Referendum

Ward	Voter Registration		Votes Received	
	Black	White	For	Against
(Predominantly Black)				
First Ward	1,613	789	666	525
Second Ward	4,390	619	1,412	638
Eleventh Ward	5,912	3,185	2,929	2,421
(Racially Mixed-Majority Black)				
Sixth Ward	2,379	2,361	1,456	1,369
Seventh Ward	21,223	11,840	10,517	9,537
Ninth Ward	44,185	27,683	22,372	22,516
Tenth Ward	3,668	1,878	1,880	1,220
Twelfth Ward	7,049	4,048	2,485	2,785
Seventeenth Ward	8,640	7,841	4,469	5,156

Source: Compiled from a tally of official returns recorded by the New Orleans City Council.

elections, he could not duplicate that feat for the earnings tax measure. Moreover, the wards in which the measure passed (including the predominantly black wards) did not vote in favor of it by nothing close to the margins that Morial won over his runoff opponents in 1977 and 1982.

The pattern of the vote in the racially mixed-majority white wards and the predominantly white wards was uniformly against the earnings tax, as Table 10.9 shows. In the five racially mixed-majority white wards the measure was overwhelmingly defeated in all but the Thirteenth Ward, where the measure was only narrowly defeated. The Fifteenth Ward best illustrates the strength of the opposition to the earnings tax measure. In the Fifteenth Ward, the measure was defeated by almost a two-to-one ratio, 10,857 against to 5,568 for. In the predominantly white wards the strength of the opposition is best illustrated in the Fourth Ward, where the measure was defeated by better than a two and a half-to-one ratio, 7,318 against to 2,770 for.

Most blacks who voted on the earnings tax referendum overwhelmingly voted in favor of it, whereas most whites who voted on the referendum overwhelmingly voted against it. In 48 black precincts 73.96 percent of the voters voted in favor of the measure as compared with 26.04 percent against. In 72 white precincts 74.25 percent voted against the measure as compared to 25.75 in favor.[41] Thus the proportion of the black population voting for and against the earnings tax was just about inversely equal to the proportion of the white population voting for and against the measure. The reason why the measure lost is explained in terms of the racial differential in the

Table 10.9   Registration and Voting Data for the Five Racially Mixed-Majority White Wards and the Three Predominantly White for the November 6, 1984 Earnings Tax Referendum

Ward	Voter Registration		Votes Received	
	Black	White	For	Against
(Racially Mixed-Majority White)				
Fifth Ward	3,938	5,581	2,431	3,231
Eighth Ward	6,828	9,687	4,265	6,690
Thirteenth Ward	3,808	4,978	2,639	2,946
Fifteenth Ward	9,539	17,814	5,568	10,857
Sixteenth Ward	2,056	4,043	1,628	1,957
(Predominantly White)				
Third Ward	1,886	4,230	1,319	2,299
Fourth Ward	1,965	12,872	2,770	7,318
Fourteenth Ward	1,661	13,748	3,675	6,899

Source: Compiled from a tally of official returns recorded by the New Orleans City Council.

percent of those registered who voted. In the white precincts 71.08 percent of the people registered voted on the measure, as compared to 48.31 percent of the people registered in the black precincts.[42] In other words, black turnout was about one-third less than white turnout; that is the reason why the earnings tax referendum was defeated.

The failure of the earnings tax referendum exacerbated the city's fiscal problem. The one-cent increase in the sales tax's extension ended in 1985. The revenue for the city from the World's Fair did not materialize as the fair was a colossal financial disaster. In addition, the federal government under President Ronald Reagan has reduced federal financial assistance to cities. When Morial began his first term in May 1978, 57 percent of the city's annual operating budget of $214 million came from the federal government and the state government. By 1982, the portion of the city's budget coming from the federal government and the state government had been reduced to 30 percent.[43] Morial has made repeated efforts to solve the city's fiscal problems, but these efforts by and large have not been successful. The city's fiscal situation has continued to deteriorate.

The last major failure of Morial examined in this chapter is one which involved his personal political future. On October 19, 1985 a referendum was held on Morial's proposal to change the city's charter to allow a mayor to run for a third term. Morial actively campaigned for this proposal. It was rejected by the electorate. As Table 10.10 shows the three predominantly black wards voted in favor of the referendum. However, in the six

Table 10.10   Registration[a] and Voting Data for the Three Predominantly
Black Wards and the Six Racially Mixed-Majority Wards for the
October 19, 1985 Third Term Charter Change Referendum

| | Voter Registration | | Votes Received[b] | |
Ward	Black	White	For	Against
(Predominantly Black)				
First Ward	1,686	803	589	468
Second Ward	4,518	613	1,714	465
Eleventh Ward	6,905	3,201	3,037	2,139
(Racially Mixed-Majority Black)				
Sixth Ward	2,400	2,388	1,026	1,346
Seventh Ward	21,456	11,693	8,679	9,144
Ninth Ward	45,173	27,503	18,262	15,094
Tenth Ward	3,709	1,919	7,631	1,204
Twelfth Ward	7,087	4,050	3,095	2,647
Seventeenth Ward	7,869	6,759	3,764	4,950

[a]The voter registration data are for August 1985.
[b]The double column figures listed do not include absentee votes.
Source: Compiled from a tally of official returns recorded by the New Orleans City Council.

racially mixed-majority black wards, the measure was defeated in two of
the wards, the Sixth Ward and the Seventh Ward.

The third term charter change referendum was resoundingly rejected in
the five racially mixed-majority white wards and the three predominantly
white wards, as Table 10.11 shows. In the racially mixed-majority white
wards, the measure was defeated by nearly a two-to-one ratio or higher in
all but the Thirteenth Ward, where it lost by more than 1,200 votes. In the
predominantly white wards, the measure lost by almost three-to-one in the
Third Ward, more than six-to-one in the Fourteenth Ward, and seven-to-
one in the Fourth Ward.

The pattern of the vote on the third term charter change referendum was
remarkably similar to the vote on the earnings tax referendum. While a
majority of blacks voted for both measures, a significant minority of blacks
voted against them. Whites voted against these measures approximately to
the same extent that blacks voted for them. In both referenda the measures
were defeated in two of the six racially mixed-majority black wards, wards
that Morial won easily in his 1977 and 1982 runoff elections. The key to
both defeats was the significant difference in black voter turnout versus
white voter turnout. In both cases black turnout was significantly less than
white turnout. Thus it would be inaccurate to blame the loss of these referenda measures on white opposition, given that the percentage of whites

Table 10.11   Registration[a] and Voting Data for the Five Racially Mixed-Majority White Wards and the Three Predominantly White Wards for the October 19, 1985 Third Term Charter Change Referendum

	Voter Registration		Votes Received[b]	
Ward	*Black*	*White*	*For*	*Against*
(Racially Mixed-Majority White)				
Fifth Ward	3,936	5,551	1,613	3,159
Eighth Ward	6,995	9,525	3,042	6,592
Thirteenth Ward	3,846	4,933	1,808	3,089
Fifteenth Ward	8,574	16,206	3,165	10,094
Sixteenth Ward	1,791	3,171	914	2,088
(Predominantly White)				
Third Ward	1,949	4,114	772	2,269
Fourth Ward	2,055	12,825	1,087	7,642
Fourteenth Ward	1,691	13,583	1,222	7,587

[a]*The voter registration data are for August 1985.*
[b]*The double column figures listed do not include absentee votes.*
Source: Compiled from a tally of official returns recorded by the New Orleans City Council.

voting in favor of them exceeded the percentage of the white vote that Morial received in both the 1977 and 1982 runoff elections. These measures lost, quite simply, because blacks did not turn out to vote in large enough numbers and did not vote for these measures by large enough margins. The electoral coalition of blacks and upper income whites that twice elected Morial could have passed the referenda measures had blacks voted the way they did in the 1977 and 1982 runoff elections.

The Social and Economic Impact of Black Political Participation in New Orleans

One increasingly studied component of black politics involves the extent to which blacks benefit from increased participation in the political process. Previous studies examining this topic assume that since most blacks in the United States are located on the periphery of social and economic advantages, black elected officials are interested in trying to use public authority to confer social and economic benefits upon their fellow black citizens. This assumption is intuitively appealing. In the case of Morial, however, there is first-hand evidence of his expectation that public authority can be used to extract benefits for disadvantaged citizens. Upon his decision to run for the mayor's office while he was a Louisiana State Appeals Court Judge, Morial said: "I enjoy being a judge, but if I can bring a better quality to life to all citizens, and especially to the underclass in our society, then I will be happy."[44] Thus, Morial sought the mayor's office with the hope that he could use the resources of the mayor's office to provide benefits that would enhance the quality of life of the city's disadvantaged citizens.

Morial's position on the use of public authority to help improve the quality of life of disadvantaged citizens provides an additional justification for examining his performance in providing social and economic benefits to blacks. Not only does the fact of increasing scholarly attention to an examination of the social and economic impact of black political participation make this line of scholarly inquiry an important undertaking, but Morial's position on this issue enhances the importance and justification of this line of scholarly inquiry. This section of the paper assesses the impact of Morial's mayoral tenure in terms of the public sector benefits received by blacks in three categories: *municipal employment, executive appointments,* and *municipal contracts.*

Municipal Employment

One increasingly studied component of the research examining the social and economic impact of black political participation is an examination of the extent to which black mayors can increase the representation of blacks on the municipal work force. Peter Eisinger finds that while black mayors exert a slight effect on increasing black municipal employment, a majority black population exerts the single largest influence on increasing black municipal employment.[45] Both variables are present in New Orleans and the evidence suggests that blacks have experienced an increase in municipal employment consistent to Eisinger's findings. When Morial assumed the mayor's office in 1977, blacks comprised a significant 40 percent of the municipal work force. Currently, blacks comprise approximately 53 percent.

A 13 percent increase in the black proportion of the municipal work force over a seven-year period is a significant accomplishment. It is also clearly a significant social and economic benefit that blacks have derived from participation in the political process. The 13 percent increase in the black proportion of the municipal work force is primarily an economic benefit to blacks in New Orleans in that more blacks have been able to obtain employment. Between 1970 and 1985, the percentage of black middle class families increased from 10 to 31 percent. This period overlaps the mayoral administrations of Morial and Moon Landrieu, the most liberal mayors in the city's history. The 13 percent increase is also in part a social benefit in the sense that as blacks participate more in the municipal work force, as whites have always done, and carry out the responsibilities of their job as part of a racially mixed work force tending to the governmental needs of a racially mixed public, they will gain an increased measure of social esteem and well-being.

A point related to the discussion of the 13 percentage point increase in the black proportion of the New Orleans work force is the fact that blacks had obtained a significantly high percentage of the city's work force—40 percent—prior to the election of Morial. The major share of the progress that blacks made in reaching the 40 percent level of the municipal work force was made under the eight-year mayoral tenure of Landrieu. Landrieu, a liberal, had been twice elected with a growing black vote playing a key role in his victories.[46] In return for their support, Landrieu successfully worked to increase the number of blacks on the city's work force.

Executive Appointments

Executive positions in New Orleans include the city's chief administrative officer, department heads, and top mayoral assistants. The importance of blacks penetrating the executive level of city government is at least of three-fold significance. One, executive positions provide additional job opportunities for blacks at a fairly high level of financial compensation and prestige. Two, executive appointees are generally policymakers and thus blacks who are appointed to these positions usually get to influence the formulation and/or administration of public policy. This of course provides the opportunity for black municipal executives to influence the policy process in ways favorable to the interests of blacks if they should so desire. Third, because of the above two factors, blacks who hold executive positions in city government are important sources of symbolic or group pride to the black community. Blacks may feel a sense of racial pride and enhanced social esteem from having members of their race hold high-level positions in government.

Similar to municipal employment, blacks in New Orleans made their greatest initial progress in penetrating the executive level of city government during Landrieu's mayoralty. As part of his push to integrate the city's work force at all levels, Landrieu appointed Terrence Duvernay the city's first black chief administrative officer[47] in addition to appointing blacks to five of the 12 department head positions in city government. This meant that blacks headed 41.7 percent of the departments in city government, which included finance, recreation, welfare, property management, and model cities. It is significant that a black headed the city's finance department, given that municipal finance had been especially resistant to black penetration. In addition to the department head appointments, Landrieu also appointed a significant number of blacks to important administrative positions just below the department head level. These positions included the director of policy planning, manpower director, and the mayor's executive assistant. The most visible of all these appointments was clearly the appointment of Duvernay as the city's first black chief administrative officer.

Under Morial, blacks obtained an even higher proportion of department head appointments as he appointed blacks to seven of the 12 department head positions. This meant that blacks held 58.3 percent of department head positions under Morial as compared to 41.7 percent under Landrieu. In addition to the chief administrative officer and the five departments which were headed by blacks under Landrieu, Morial appointed the city's first black police chief and sanitation department head. The former was clearly Morial's most visible executive appointment, and one which was clearly welcomed by the black community. Morial's appointment of Warren Woodfork as the city's first black police chief, in addition to providing symbolic benefit to blacks, provided the opportunity for substantive benefits to blacks in terms of improved relations with blacks and the police department. The relationship between the black community and the police department in New Orleans has historically been a stormy one with blacks being subjected to a high incidence of police brutality.[48] To the extent that the black police chief succeeds in addressing the problem of police brutality, his appointment provides additional substantive benefits to blacks.

Municipal Contracts

The final area in which this chapter examines the mayoral impact of Morial on the black community is municipal contracts. Until recently municipal contracts have virtually been ignored in studies focusing on the impact of the black political participation. It is surprising that this has been the case because the awarding of municipal contracts to private companies to perform services and provide goods needed by city governments is a very important means of providing economic benefits through the use of public authority. Ethnic public officials made full use of this practice in the early twentieth century by awarding city contracts to businesses run by fellow ethnic group members. While the urban politics literature tends to emphasize the ethnic political machines' use of awarding of municipal contracts to help businesses owned by fellow ethnics, the white Anglo-Saxon Protestants who controlled urban governments prior to ethnic dominance operated on basically the same model, that is, most of the municipal contracts during their governance were awarded to businesses run by fellow white Anglo-Saxon Protestants.

Morial has attempted to use municipal contracting to provide blacks social and economic benefits in two ways: (1) to help them obtain an increased share of the labor force participation on public works and construction projects financed and/or administered by the city and (2) to help black businesses obtain an increased share of contracts awarded by the city. In terms of the former, Morial issued Executive Order No. 83-02 on October 7, 1983, which, among other affirmative action provisions, mandated a 25 percent minority labor force participation rate (based on the total number of work hours on a craft by craft basis) in all city financed and/or administered public works and construction projects.[49] The executive order was later revised to apply to projects in excess of $25,000.[50] The original order was scheduled to go into effect no later than December 22, 1983, but its implementation did not begin until October 1, 1985.

Morial's initial effort to increase the number of black businesses receiving contracts took the form of Executive Order No. 84-01, which was issued on January 24, 1984. This ordinance specified a goal of 20 percent minority subcontracting participation on projects in excess of $100,000.[51] The order applies only to the companies the prime contractors hire, not to the prime contractors themselves. The 20 percent goal of the policy was later dropped and replaced with the goal that the city sought to provide minority businesses "the maximum feasible opportunity to compete for contracts."[52] The original order was scheduled to go into effect no later than April 1, 1984, but its implementation did not begin until October 1, 1985.

Morial's municipal contracting program for minorities suffers from some shortcomings. The shortcoming of Morial's policy for increasing minority participation in municipal contracting can be seen by comparing New Orleans with some other large municipalities. According to Susan Feeney, New Orleans' minority business program lags far behind those in Atlanta, Philadelphia, San Francisco, Chicago, and Washington, both in terms of the size of the commitment and the actual accomplishment.[53] Table 10.12 shows the unfavorable comparison of New Orleans with those cities. Of the seven cities, New Orleans ranks last in terms of minority business participation goals and last in terms of the longevity of the program's implementation. It is not possible to rank the city in terms of proportion of city business actually awarded minority businesses because the city does not have the data necessary for that determination.

A major weakness of the Morial mayoralty is the inability to expeditiously enforce an effective minority labor force participation program and a minority business participation program to ensure that blacks would benefit from municipal contracts, both as individual labor force members and as owners of businesses. Equally as significant as this deficiency is the fact that there is no mechanism in place for monitoring compliance with Morial's order instituting these policies. Thus, there is no basis for evaluating the impact of these policies.

The Post-Morial Era in New Orleans Politics?

Although Morial's mayoralty was not spectacularly successful from a programmatic perspective, there should no doubt that Morial was the dominant political figure in New Orleans for the last eight years. In an uncanny manner, he remains so, despite the fact that he was defeated in his effort

Table 10.12 Minority Business Participation Programs in New Orleans and Other Selected Cities, 1985

City	Minority Business Participation Goal	Rank	Proportion of City Business Actually Awarded to Minority Businesses	Rank	Date of Implementation of Program Began	Rank
Atlanta	35 % of all city business for minorities	1	31%	2	1974 at 25%	1
Chicago	25% of all city business for minorities	3	17%	4	March, 1984	5
New Orleans	20% of subcontracting for construction projects over $100,000	5[a]	Not Available	Unable to rank	October, 1985	7
Philadelphia	15% of all city business	4	17%	4	Mid-1983	4
San Francisco	30% of all city business for minorities	2	20%	3	August, 1984	6
Seattle	15% of all city business	4	15%	5	1980	3
Washington	35% of all city business for minorities	1	38%	1	1976 at 25%	2

[a]An assumption is made in this ranking that, in actual dollars, 20 percent of subcontracting participation for construction projects over $100,000 in New Orleans is less than 15 percent of all city business in Philadelphia and Seattle.
Source: Adopted from Susan Feeny, "City Minority Business Program Sputters," (New Orleans) Times Picayune, June 30, 1985.

to convince the New Orleans' electorate to vote for the charter change referendum that would have allowed him to run for a third term, and despite the fact that he suffered some political embarrassments in the 1986 city elections. One such embarrassment was an unusual outcome to a peculiar city council race in District D.

After the third term charter change referendum was defeated, Morial decided to run for a seat on the city council from District D against an incumbent, Lambert Boissiere, who frequently opposed Morial's policy proposals. Morial's decision was considered by many to be degrading given that Morial was the city's first black mayor, at that time president of the U.S. Conference of Mayors, and considered by many as a strong candidate for Congress one day. Morial's decision was also considered to be petty and vindictive, and was seen as a form of political retribution directed not only toward Boissiere, but principally toward Boissiere's council ally Sidney Barthelemy, who was one of the two at-large members of the city council, the leading candidate to replace Morial as mayor, and Morial's chief opponent on the council during his eight-year mayoral tenure. Morial, surprisingly, finished second to Boissiere among a field of seven candidates. Undoubtedly embarrassed by his showing in a district that had consistently supported him in his mayoral elections, Morial withdrew from the runoff election.

Morial's aborted council race was not the only embarrassment that the 1986 city elections would dish out to Morial. Another major embarrassment was the outcome of the mayoral election. Prior to his decision to run for the council from District D, Morial unexpectedly endorsed State Senator William Jefferson for mayor, who was trailing Barthelemy in the polls by a considerable margin. Morial's endorsement of Jefferson was surprising because he reportedly harbored strong feelings against Jefferson for his decision to run for mayor against Morial in 1982, a decision which may have caused Morial the necessity of waging an expensive runoff campaign against Ronald Faucheaux. Although Morial's endorsement of Jefferson helped him to beat out Barthelemy for a first place finish in the primary among a field of three major candidates (the other major candidate was Sam LeBlanc, "an attorney, former state representative, and a Morial appointee to the city transit authority"[54]), Barthelemy defeated Jefferson in the runoff by an overwhelming margin, 93,049 to 67,698, respectively.[55] Barthelemy won 57.89 percent of the vote to Jefferson's 42.11 percent.

Table 10.13 shows the basis of Barthelemy's victory over Jefferson. Jefferson won the three predominantly black wards. His biggest victory in these wards was in the Second Ward, which he won by better than a two-to-one ratio. Barthelemy and Jefferson split the six racially mixed-majority black wards, with Barthelemy winning the Sixth, Seventh, and Seventeenth Wards and Jefferson winning the Ninth (by less than 500 votes), Tenth, and Twelfth

Table 10.13   Registration and Voting Data for All Wards
for the 1986 New Orleans Mayoral Election

	Voter Registration		Votes Received	
Ward	*Black*	*White*	*Barthelemy*	*Jefferson*
(Predominantly Black)				
First Ward	1,686	803	571	661
Second Ward	4,518	613	795	1,878
Eleventh Ward	6,905	3,201	2,334	3,580
(Racially Mixed- Majority Black)				
Sixth Ward	2,400	2,388	1,605	1,068
Seventh Ward	21,456	11,693	11,989	8,503
Ninth Ward	45,173	27,503	23,062	22,623
Tenth Ward	3,709	1,919	1,368	1,998
Twelfth Ward	7,087	4,050	2,833	3,824
Seventeenth Ward	7,869	6,759	5,407	4,515
(Racially Mixed- Majority White)				
Fifth Ward	3,936	5,551	3,475	1,925
Eighth Ward	6,995	9,525	7,203	3,256
Thirteenth Ward	3,846	4,933	3,047	2,266
Fifteenth Ward	8,574	16,206	9,292	5,561
Sixteenth Ward	1,791	3,171	2,016	1,214
(Predominantly White)				
Third Ward	1,949	4,114	2,407	935
Fourth Ward	2,005	12,825	7,468	1,510
Fourteenth Ward	1,691	13,583	7,277	2,137

Source: "Unofficial Precinct Returns," (New Orleans) *The Times-Picayune/The States-Item,*
March 3, 1986, sec. A, p. 19.

Wards. The remaining wards—the racially mixed-majority white wards and
the predominantly white wards—were all won by Barthelemy by overwhelming margins. In the racially mixed-majority white Eighth Ward, for
example, Barthelemy defeated Jefferson by better than a two-to-one margin. In the predominantly white Fourth Ward Barthelemy defeated Jefferson by almost a five-to-one ratio.

Barthelemy won the election because he won a significant minority of
the black vote and the overwhelming majority of the white vote. The results
of this election suggest that the white vote played the same role that the
black vote used to play in the 1960s and 1970s when it was the minority
component of the electorate. Just as the black vote then used to determine

the winner between two white candidates by voting for the one they thought would be more representative of their interests, whites in the 1986 election cast the pivotal votes in Barthelemy's election. What this portends for the future is that in mayoral runoff contests involving two black candidates whites are going to play a critical role.

The final embarrassment that Morial received in the 1986 city election is that two of the three city council candidates that he endorsed lost to opponents endorsed by Barthelemy. This was a major embarrassment for Morial who just four years earlier successfully engineered the defeat of three opponents on the council by running three candidates against them. The eight-year political rivalry between Morial and Barthelemy had, for the next four years, apparently come to an end with Barthelemy emerging as the clear winner. This development has an important implication both for governance in the city and for the social and economic benefits that blacks may receive from the political process. The New Orleans city council now has a fully elected black majority[56] and the relationship between Barthelemy and the council, unlike the stormy relationship between Morial and the council, should be very positive. With black politics operating from a single center of power in New Orleans, the mayor's office, rather than two centers of power—the mayor's office and the city council, as it did under Morial—municipal governance in New Orleans should be improved and blacks should benefit more than they did previously. Of course the rivalry could resume if Morial runs for the mayor's office in 1990, as many think he will. If he runs and wins, 1986 will not be the beginning of the post-Morial era; rather it will be the beginning of the four-year interlude in the Morial era.

Summary and Conclusions

Black political participation in New Orleans, like black political participation in cities throughout the South, increased substantially over the last 25 years. Black political power is clearly a reality in New Orleans. The increasing black vote in the middle 1960s allowed blacks to play a pivotal role in the election and reelection of Moon Landrieu, the city's most liberal white mayor. Subsequent increases in the black vote and black political development in the city led to the election of Ernest Morial as the first black mayor. Additionally, subsequent developments in black politics in New Orleans has recently led to the beginning of a second generation of black mayoral governance in the city.

Blacks in New Orleans, like blacks elsewhere, have sought to use the political process to achieve some social and economic benefits. By and large, blacks in New Orleans have succeeded in this regard. For example, blacks now constitute a much larger share of the city's work force and the executive level of the municipal bureaucracy than they did in the 1960s. Under Landrieu the black proportion of the municipal work force reached 40 percent and approximately 41.7 percent of all department heads were black. These gains were increased under Morial. Under Morial, the proportion of the municipal work force comprised by blacks reached 53 percent and 58.3 percent of the department heads are black.

Morial's mayoral performance was uneven. From a symbolic perspective, Morial was very successful. From the standpoint of substantive policy accomplishments, Morial was much less successful. In terms of symbolism, the Morial mayoralty has been good for the city and especially for blacks. Morial is very popular among blacks. In the city where poverty is rampant among blacks, it has been a source of pride among blacks to have a black serve in the highest position in city government. Morial is also popular among many upper-income whites. In his two runoff elections he received approximately 20 to 14 percent of the white vote, respectively, which is on the high-end and middle portion of the range, respectively, that a successful black candidate can usually expect to receive from whites. His earnings tax referendum received almost 25 percent from white voters. In all three cases these white voters were middle and upper income whites.

Morial, like many mayors, has had significant difficulties in translating popular appeal into policy successes. He has not done well in getting his policy objectives enacted into public policy. For example, he has experienced repeated failures in his efforts to enhance the city's dismal revenue situation. Several of the fiscal measures that were adopted were not to his liking. Also, the implementation of Morial's minority labor force participation and minority business participation programs was delayed several months. Moreover, the minority business participation program is clearly inferior to that which exists in some other major cities.

Some of the policy successes for blacks in New Orleans came more from blacks on the city council than from Morial. One prominent example in this regard was the one-cent increase in the sales tax which provided the revenue needed to keep the city's bus service from being reduced. The one-cent increase was initially passed for one year, but subsequently extended for two additional years. On both actions blacks on the city council played a vital role, whereas Morial was opposed to the first action and neutral on the second. He rested his argument on the position that these were stop gap measures and the city's dire fiscal problems required more permanent solutions. These measures, Morial objections notwithstanding, were clearly beneficial to the black community since blacks are more dependent on public transportation than whites.

Blacks in New Orleans have considerable political power. It was in huge part that power which elected and reelected Morial as the city's first black mayor. That blacks constitute 51 percent of the city's voters places them in a good position to shape the city's future in a manner favorable to their interests. The 1986 mayoral election results make it clear that blacks will have to share political influence with whites. Whites will now determine the winner of mayoral elections involving two black candidates.

Although blacks in New Orleans have exercised considerable political power over the last eight years, the social and economic impact of that exercise of power on the black community has not been as significant as it could have been. It certainly has not been as significant as the impact of black politics in some other major cities. A principal factor accounting for the less than spectacular success of black politics, in terms of providing increased social and economic benefits for blacks, seems to be that black politics in New Orleans is not consensual, either at the leadership or the mass level. Rather, black politics in New Orleans for the last eight years has had two principal centers of power consisting of Morial in the mayor's office and Barthelemy on the city council. These rival centers of power in the structure of black politics in the city has considerably limited the allocation of public sector resources to the black community.

The challenge that Barthelemy and other black leaders in New Orleans will face is to sustain blacks interests in the political processes at a high level. That will not be easy. As black political participation becomes routinized, emotional and symbolic appeals as a strategy for fueling high levels of black political participation will be less successful. The ability to deliver additional tangible benefits will be more salient for maintaining high levels of black political participation. It will also be much more difficult to realize. The difficulty of the task should be helped by the signs that black politics in New Orleans will operate on a more consensual basis than it has done in the past. It that does not happen, the ironic end result of the enormous political success that blacks have realized in New Orleans over the last 25 years will be that whites will become the institutionalized pivotal center of power in the city's politics. Such an outcome would probably even further limit the capacity of the political process in New Orleans to provide social and economic benefits for blacks.

Notes

1.   Monte Piliawsky, "The Impact of Black Mayors on the Black Community: The Case of New Orleans' Ernest Morial," *The Review of Black Political Economy* (Spring 1985), 6.

2.   Bette Woody, *Managing Crisis Cities: The New Black Leadership and the Politics of Resource Allocation* (Westport, Connecticut: Greenwood Press), 38.

3.   (In Louisiana, parishes are the equivalent of counties.) Larry Schroeder, Lee Madere, and Jerome Lomba, *Occasional Paper No. 52: Local Government*

Revenue and Expenditure Forecasting: New Orleans (Syracuse: Metropolitan Studies Program, The Maxwell School of Citizenship and Public Affairs, Syracuse University, October 1981).

4. Silas Lee et. al., "Ten Years After (Pro Bono Publico?): The Economic Status of Blacks and Whites in New Orleans—1985," (Unpublished report, 1985).

5. Schroeder, Madere, and Lomba, *Local Government Revenue and Expenditure Forecasting,* 2.

6. Ibid.

7. United States Bureau of the Census, *1980 Census of Population and Housing; Supplementary Report: Advance Estimates of Social, Economic, and Housing Characteristics; Part 20, Louisiana Parishes and Selected Places,* PHC80-52-20, (Washington, D.C.: United States Government Printing Office, issued January 1983), 20-4.

8. United States Department of Commerce, Bureau of the Census, *Statistical Abstract of the United States,* 24.

9. Data Analysis Unit, Office of Analysis and Planning, and System and Programming Group, Finance Department, *1980 Census: New Orleans Census Tracts,* City of New Orleans, Ernest N. Morial, Mayor, 1982.

10. (The April 1985 figures are preliminary.) United States Department of Labor, Bureau of Labor Statistics, *Employment and Earnings,* vol. 32, no. 6 (Washington, D.C.: United States Government Printing Office, June 1985) 82–83.

11. Piliawsky, "The Impact of Black Mayors," 6.

12. James R. Bobo, *The New Orleans Economy: Pro Bono Publico?* (New Orleans: College of Business Administration, University of New Orleans, 1975), 1–2.

13. Alvin J. Schexnider, "Political Mobilization in the South: The Election of a Black Mayor in New Orleans," in *The New Black Politics: The Search for Political Power,* ed Michael B. Preston, Lenneal J. Henderson, Jr., and Paul Puryear (New York: Longman, 1982), p. 223.

14. Lee et. al., "The Economic Status of Blacks and Whites," 2.

15. Piliawsky, "The Impact of Black Mayors," 6.

16. Ibid.

17. Lee et. al., "The Economic Status of Blacks and Whites," 2.

18. Schexnider, "Political Mobilization in the South," 222.

19. Charles Y. W. Chai, "Who Rules New Orleans: A Study of Community Power Structure," *Louisiana Business Survey* 2 (October 1971) 10.

20. Ibid.

21. Schexnider, "Political Mobilization in the South," 225.

22. City of New Orleans, *Prospectus, Audubon Park Commission on Improvement Bonds Series 1979,* 1979, 9.

23. Schroeder, Madere, and Lomba, *Local Government Revenue and Expenditure Forecasting,* 4.

24. Piliawsky, "The Impact of Black Mayors," 8; and Jeffrey M. Elliott, *Black Voices in American Politics* (San Diego: Harcourt Brace Jovanovich, Publishers, 1986), 341.

25.   Schexnider, "Political Mobilization in the South," 227.
26.   Ibid., 228.
27.   Ibid.
28.   "Black Judge Enters Runoff for Mayor of New Orleans," *The New York Times.*
29.   All of the electoral data used from this point on in the discussion of the 1977 mayoral election, unless otherwise indicated, were taken from Allen Rosenzweig and John Wildgen, "A Statistical Analysis of the 1977 Mayor's Race in New Orleans," *Louisiana Business Survey* 9 (April 1978), 4–8.
30.   "Black Judge Enters Runoff," *The New York Times.*
31.   For a fuller discussion of Morial's primary strategy, see Rosenzweig and Wildgen, "A Statistical Analysis of the 1977 Mayor's Race," 8.
32.   Ibid., 5.
33.   James H. Gillis, "Black Nearly Solid for Morial," (New Orleans) *Times Picayune,* Nov. 14, 1977, sec. 1; and Walter Isaacson, "DiRosa Contests Election; Ouster of Morial Sought," (New Orleans) *States-Item,* Nov. 14, 1977, final edition.
34.   In this chapter, a predominantly black ward is operationalized as a ward in which black registration exceeds white registration by at least a two-to-one ratio. A predominantly white ward is operationalized as a ward in which white voter registration exceeds black voter registration by at least a two-to-one ratio.
35.   Schexnider, "Political Mobilization in the South," 228.
36.   All of the electoral data used in this section, unless otherwise indicated, were taken or computed from a tally of official returns recorded by the New Orleans City Council.
37.   Garry Boulard, "Power Brokers," *New Orleans,* October 1985, 53.
38.   Piliawsky, "The Impact of Black Mayors," 20. Also, Piliawsky, "The Limits of Power: Dutch Morial Mayor of New Orleans," *Southern Exposure* 12 (February 1984), 75.
39.   Morial reports that while the other candidates did not make race an issue, the media did. For his assessment of this point, see Jeffrey M. Elliot, *Black Voices in American Politics* (1986), 344.
40.   James H. Gillis, "Blacks Voted for Sales Tax," (New Orleans) *Times Picayune,* June 11, 1982, sec. 1, p. 13.
41.   An analysis by the (New Orleans) *Times Picayune* operationalizes black and white precincts as precincts in which fewer than 10 voters are members of the opposite race. See James H. Gillis, "The Black and White Voting Split," (New Orleans) *Times Picayune,* Nov. 7, 1984.
42.   Ibid.
43.   (New Orleans) *Times Picayune,* Oct. 16, 1982, 15, cited in Piliawsky, "The Impact of Black Mayors," 9–10.
44.   Alex Poinsett, "Mayor Ernest N. Morial Finds: Running New Orleans Is No Mardi Gras," *Ebony,* December 1978, 34.
45.   Peter K. Eisinger, "Black Employment in Municipal Jobs: The Impact of Black Political Power," *American Political Science Review* 76 (June 1982), 391.

46.   Schexnider, "Political Mobilization in the South," 226.

47.   Poinsett, "Running New Orleans," 38.

48.   For a brief discussion of the issue of police brutality in New Orleans, see Piliawsky, "The Impact of Black Mayors," 16–17.

49.   Executive Order No. 83-02, Mayor's Office New Orleans, Louisiana, Oct. 7, 1983.

50.   Policy Memorandum No. 209, Chief Administrative Office, New Orleans, Louisiana, July 11, 1985.

51.   Executive Order No. 84-01, Mayor's Office, New Orleans, Louisiana, Jan. 24, 1984.

52.   Policy Memorandum No. 183 (Revised), Chief Administrative Office, New Orleans, Louisiana, April 10, 1984.

53.   Susan Feeney, "City Minority Business Program Sputters," (New Orleans) *Times Picayune,* June 30, 1985.

54.   Ibid.

55.   "Unofficial Precinct Return," (New Orleans) *The Times Picayune/The State-Item,* March 3, 1986, sec. A, p. 19.

56.   The city council became majority black in 1985 when Ulysses Williams was selected by council members to fill a seat on the council vacated by the resignation of Wayne Bobvovich.

ELEVEN

Black Independent Electoral Politics in Philadelphia and The Election of Mayor W. Wilson Goode

Bruce Ransom

On January 2, 1984, W. Wilson Goode was sworn in as the 126th mayor of Philadelphia, the nation's fourth largest city. Mayor Goode's ascendancy to the office was achieved by turning back two-term Mayor Frank Rizzo in the Democratic party's primary and then becoming mayor with a majority of the votes in a three-candidate general election.

The 1983 mayoral elections in Philadelphia, unlike those months earlier in Chicago, were not shaped by overt racial acrimony and conflict. Yet race was one of the most significant elements in the elections. Former Mayor Frank Rizzo's tenure was marked by stormy race relations, and the city's black community mobilized to oppose him through his administration. The 1983 mayoral elections were momentous, but to understand fully their importance, the analysis must be placed in the context of previous research, the black independent political movement in Philadelphia, and Wilson Goode's tenure as Philadelphia's managing director. This approach connects voting patterns in Philadelphia with those in other cities that had successful black mayoral candidates, and the unique circumstances surrounding the election of Wilson Goode.

Strategies for Electing Black Mayors

Several models for explaining alliances between black and white, for instance, voters in elections with aspiring black mayoral candidates, may be found in the literature. These models may be useful for explaining the Goode election. Although the percentage of blacks in the city's population, especially if it is considerably above 50 percent, is the most important contributing factor to black mayoral success,[1] coalition strategies are well represented in the literature on cities without a working black majority.[2]

First, a conservative coalition of blacks and a city's white business and financial community is possible. While such coalition does not elect a black mayor, it does support white "progressive" candidates. Prior to Maynard Jackson's 1973 mayoral victory in Atlanta, such an alliance existed in Atlanta. A variant of this strategy is found in municipalities where city council members select the mayor from among themselves. Richmond's current mayor, Roy West, was apparently selected by this arrangement. Second, blacks may form an alliance with lower-income whites and create a biracial and class-based coalition.[3] However, an analysis of municipal elections in several southern cities revealed that such a coalition was difficult to form for a black candidate.[4] The evidence in ethnically diverse northern cities is similar.[5] Third, a liberal coalition of blacks and Hispanics, labor unions, and liberal whites is a fairly common winning coalition in contemporary municipal elections. Fourth, the independent black political strategy is common; it has two variants. First, if blacks are not in the majority, but represent a large independent bloc of votes, those votes may be delivered to a liberal-progressive white candidate in exchange for political accommodations. Increasingly evident, however, is the near majority and black majority city in which black candidates have sufficient black electoral base to focus their campaigns almost exclusively on the black community: Washington, Detroit, Gary, Newark, are just a few examples.

Crossover voting by at least a fifth of the white voters is one of the keys to successful black mayoral candidacies in cities with black populations that are nonetheless below 50 percent. A viable black candidate with only one white challenger, a fairly high level of black voter registration and turnout, along with about 20 percent crossover voting among whites may win. Indeed, the conclusion in an analysis of winning alliances for black mayoral candidates of nearly a decade ago supports this observation:

> The victory of black candidates could be attributed to the large percentage of the black population . . . to intensive black voter registration drives; to high turnout in the black community; and to the cohesion of black voters, who cast from 88–97 percent of their ballots for black candidates. . . . In fact, in most cases, black candidates have been unable to capture more than 25 percent of the white vote.[6]

A more recent study comes to a similar conclusion:

> To win a citywide race, a black candidate usually must have resources that reach beyond the black community. If a city is dominated by whites, numerically or otherwise, then at least some support must come from the white

community, ordinarily from its more "liberal" elements. . . . The election of a black mayor can be thought of as the joint product of the conditions that cause blacks to be nominated (or to choose to run) and those that affect their chance of election once they are candidates.[7]

The focus of this chapter is one city—Philadelphia. The findings in the literature about black and white voting alliances are applicable to Philadelphia, but the election of Wilson Goode is also the outgrowth of a *viable* black independent electoral movement which began over a decade before the 1983 elections. In fact, since 1971 a number of blacks had run for mayor; none succeeded. And the success in 1983 was in no small part due to crossover voting by whites.[8] In addition, the campaign avoided racial acrimony while maintaining a solidified black electoral base. The black independent electoral movement, the candidate's neighborhood reform orientation and managerial experience provide the context for understanding the election of Mayor Wilson Goode.

Data Base

The data for this study are derived from two primary sources: election returns and personal interviews. Beginning with the 1971 mayoral elections, returns for Democratic mayoral primary elections and general elections were examined. In each mayoral election between 1971 and 1983, a viable black mayoral candidate entered the Democratic primary or the general election, though usually not both. The 1978 city charter-change referendum, a benchmark election, is also a part of the election data base. Voter registration data, election returns, and demographic data are analyzed citywide, and by neighborhoods. Finally, in addition to extensive personal interviews conducted with key Goode campaign officials and supporters, position papers and campaign research documents and materials were inspected for relevant information.

Black Independent Electoral Politics

In 1968 a movement for black independence in electoral politics was initiated by Hardy Williams, Dave Richardson, and W. Wilson Goode.[9] Although Goode was not one of the more active members of the movement, he was an integral component in the drive to run and elect blacks to offices at all levels of government.[10] The aggressive leadership of Cecil Moore of the Philadelphia chapter of the National Association for the Advancement of Colored People in the 1960s, and the movement for black participation and control in the city's antipoverty programs produced some strains in the relationship between blacks and the city Democratic party.[11] Blacks seeking local and state offices independent of the support of the Democratic City Committee marked the transition from the politics of confrontation to participation in electoral politics.

The 1971 mayoral election marked the beginning of a sustained effort for full and independent black participation in mayoral elections. Although Frank Rizzo, a street cop and the police commissioner in the James Tate administration (1962 to 1970), obtained the Democratic party's mayoral nomination, Rizzo's handling of black protest demonstrations in the 1960s and his "law-and-order" tactics produced police brutality charges and cries of racism from many of the city's black leaders. Further, many blacks viewed Rizzo as the candidate for white working class and ethnic residents. Hardy Williams, a black state legislator and organizer of the black independent movement also ran for the Democratic party's nomination. In a three-candidate race Williams carried only three wards (in West and North Philadelphia) and collected 45,026 votes (13 percent). Rizzo won the nomination with 51 percent of the votes and went on to win the general election with 53 percent of the votes.

Mayor Rizzo's tough law and order position was too strident for many liberal and white reformers, and blacks in particular. There was also dissatisfaction in other corners. Rizzo was rejected by the Democratic City Committee in the 1975 primary election. The ward leaders supported Louis G. Hill, a state senator, in a losing effort.[12] Charles Bowser, a lawyer and former director of the Philadelphia Antipoverty Action Committee (PAAC) and a deputy mayor in the Tate administration, bypassed the Democratic party primary and ran for mayor in the general election on an independent slate, the Philadelphia party. Although Rizzo was reelected with 57 percent of the votes, Bowser received 138,783 votes (25 percent), an improvement over William's total in the 1971 Democratic primary.

Mayor Rizzo's relations with the black community became more strained in his second term. Several weeks after Rizzo's second inauguration, his administration disclosed that the city was running a massive deficit and that the debt would be resolved by huge increases in the real estate and wage taxes. Mayor Rizzo was widely criticized for backing away from his no-tax-increase promise during the campaign. He was also, and more fundamentally, criticized for his inability to demonstrate solid management skills. In the spring of 1976 a coalition of liberal and reformist whites and blacks (Citizens' Committee to Recall Rizzo) formed to recall the mayor under provisions of the city charter. An impressive number of signatures (over 200,000) were collected, but the Pennsylvania Supreme Court voided the signatures and declared the city charter's recall provision unconstitutional.[13] In 1978 Mayor Rizzo and his supporters initiated a drive to revise the city charter and remove the prohibition on two successive mayoral terms.

The "charter-change election," or referendum, became a Rizzo/Anti-Rizzo referendum. Philadelphia's black leadership was united and determined; dissatisfaction with Mayor Rizzo was shared by many whites as well.

A major voter registration drive was launched to increase the number of black registered voters. It was a huge success. Between 1971 and the time of the charter change election in 1978, total registration in Philadelphia rose by 8 percent, from 966,084 to 1,041,799. Black voter registration, by comparison, rose by 46 percent, from 268,707 to 391,461.[14] The number of white registered voters declined from 631,626 to 603,991, a decrease of 4 percent. Further, in the year preceding the November 1978 balloting, five blacks registered to vote for every one white.

The 1978 charter-change election was a major defeat for Mayor Rizzo and a victory for a coalition of liberal and reformist whites and blacks (Committee to Protect the Charter). In the balloting, 67 percent of the votes were against changing the charter provision. Moreover, the 710,307 votes cast in the election were 26 percent above the turnout for the 1975 mayoral general election. In the black neighborhoods of North Philadelphia, West Philadelphia, Chestnut Hill-Mt. Airy, and Germantown-West Oak Lane, the opposition to charter revision ranged from 89 percent to 93 percent of the votes cast (see Table 11.1). The heavily white-liberal and in-town Central Philadelphia area was also overwhelmingly opposed to charter change—80 percent of the votes were against Mayor Rizzo's proposal. Significantly, in two predominantly white neighborhoods that had been key elements in Rizzo's electoral base, the voters rejected the charter revision: in the sprawling Northeast, 54 percent of the voters were against changing the city charter, and in Roxborough-Manayunk the opposition vote was 53 percent. Only three working class ethnic neighborhoods—Kensington-Bridesburg (62 percent), South Philadelphia (62 percent), and Southeast Philadelphia (57 percent)—voted to revise the city charter. In light of Mayor Rizzo's command to "vote white," the coalition of liberal and reformist whites and blacks recorded a victory of unexpected magnitude. For the black community, the drive to increase voter registration and turnout (estimates suggest that 71 percent of the black voters turned out, and 96 percent of them voted "No") was a portent of things to come.

The momentum of the black independent movement in mayoral elections continued into the 1979 Democratic primary. Although the election commission "cleaned-up" (purged) the voter registration rolls, the black proportion of the registered voters remained stable at about 37 percent of all registered voters between November of 1978 and the 1979 elections. Black activist Charles Bowser, the Philadelphia party nominee in 1975, ran in the Democratic party primary. Bowser faced former congressman William Green, a favorite among white liberal-reform Democrats and some black leaders. After some maneuvering, most black leaders supported Bowser.

Table 11.1   Neighborhood Returns Against the 1978 Charter Change and Support for Bowser and Goode

		Voting Outcomes (in Percent)	
Neighborhoods[a]	Voting "No" in 1978 Charter-Change	Voting for Bowser in 1979 Democratic Primary	Voting for Goode in 1983 Democratic Primary
The Northeast	54.1	7.0	19.1
West Philadelphia	89.9	81.4	82.8
Kensington-Bridesburg	38.3	4.4	13.0
South Philadelphia	37.3	29.6	31.4
Central Philadelphia	79.6	36.1	69.0
North Philadelphia	92.5	85.8	89.6
Chestnut Hill-Mt. Airy	88.6	71.6	86.7
Roxborough-Manayunk	53.0	11.4	22.5
Germantown-West Oak Lane	89.4	78.9	87.0
Olney-Oak Lane	51.0	8.5	20.3
Southwest Philadelphia	42.8	28.6	31.8

[a]Note: Wards were assigned to neighborhoods in accordance with the delineation developed by Lou Antosh, The (Philadelphia) Evening Bulletin, May 21, 1975, p. 6, and The Philadelphia City Planning Commission, "1980 Census Special Population Summary for Philadelphia Census Tracts," especially maps on pp. 7–8. Bruce Caswell, research director for the Institute for the Study of Civic Values, compiled the black and Hispanic data composition for each of the city's wards.
Source: City of Philadelphia, Office of City Commissioners, Voter Registration Division.

Although he lost, Bowser garnered 178,376 votes (43 percent), 37,366 less than Green and received landslide majorities in the black neighborhoods of North Philadelphia, West Philadelphia, Germantown-West Oak Lane, and Chestnut Hill-Mt. Airy; all of these nighborhoods had voted against the charter revision in 1978 (see Table 11.1). In the other neighborhoods that had voted against the charter change in 1978, Bowser ran poorly. Although he received 36 percent of the votes in racially mixed and liberal Central Philadelphia, he obtained only 11 percent of the votes in Roxborough, 9 percent in Olney-Oak Lane, and 7 percent in the Northeast. However, the black voting precincts in Southwest Philadelphia and South Philadelphia gave him 29 percent and 30 percent of the votes, respectively.

Bowser did not readily accept defeat. He charged that voting irregularities and fraud prevented him from securing the nomination. After a recount and investigation, the May primary results were certified in late June. Common Pleas Court Judge Harvey Schmidt ruled that no improprieties had been found. Bowser subsequently supported Green in the general election, even though another black, Lucien Blackwell, a city councilman, ran on the Consumer party line. Green received 53 percent of the votes cast in the general election, and Republican David Marston received 29 percent. Blackwell received 17 percent of the votes. In exchange for Bowser's support and that of other black leaders', newly elected Mayor Green honored a campaign promise and appointed a black, W. Wilson Goode, to the city managing director's position, Philadelphia's first black chief administrative officer.

Managing Director Goode and Neighborhood Issues

Wilson Goode, a participant in the black independent movement, became Philadelphia's number two city official. The managing director is appointed by the mayor and approved by the city council. The primary responsibilities of the position include the management of service delivery in the areas of police, fire, health, streets, recreation, welfare, water, public property, licenses and inspections, and records. The managing director appoints 10 commissioners, subject to the mayor's approval, to administer each service area. The commissioners report directly to the managing director.

Wilson Goode brought a number of skills and experiences to the position. He is a graduate of Morgan State University in Baltimore and recipient of a master's in public administration from the Wharton School of the University of Pennsylvania. In addition, he had nearly two decades of experience with neighborhood and housing issues, including the leadership of the Paschall Betterment League in his neighborhood, and for 12 years he served as the executive director of the non-profit Philadelphia Council for

Community Advancement (PCCA). In 1978 he was named chairman of the Pennsylvania Public Utility Commission. Goode was thus well-qualified to manage the day-to-day operations of Philadelphia's city hall, the more than 30,000 city employees, and a budget in excess of $1 billion. Goode's tenure with the PCCA and the Pennsylvania Public Utility Commission, especially during the Three Mile Island crisis, established his reputation as a tireless worker with a business-like no-nonense approach to public management.

Sound and prudent management skills would be crucial for meeting the challenges of the 1980s. The Green administration began after a period of population decreases and economic decline experienced by many north-eastern cities. The U.S. Census Bureau reported within weeks of Mayor Green's inauguration that Philadelphia had lost a sizable number of residents during the 1970s. The city's population dropped from 1,948,609 in 1970 to 1,688,210 in 1980—a 13 percent decline. (In the Philadelphia Metropolitan Area, the population declined by only 2 percent.) Significantly, the number of both blacks and whites declined, although the rate of decline for whites was considerably higher than the rate for blacks. Whites comprised 58 percent of the city's population, blacks 38 percent (up from 34 percent in 1970), and Hispanics 4 percent. More importantly, a nationwide study of urban decline by the Brookings Institution identified Philadelphia as a declining and distressed city,[15] located in a declining metropolitan area.[16] The tax increases of 1976, the lowering of the city's bond rating, and the loss of over 100,000 jobs motivated the Green administration to pursue an economic recovery strategy which focused on revitalizing the central business distict (CBD).

Managing Director Goode established priorities for delivering services to the CBD and the residential neighborhoods. The equitable distribution of police, fire, street, sewerage, sanitation, and housing services and the priority given to services for neighborhoods in the city budget helped establish a working relationship between Managing Director Goode and neighborhood leaders.

Neighborhood and housing issues were not new for the managing director; he had tackled similar problems during his leadership of the Paschall Betterment League and the PCCA. Again, Goode showed that he was sensitive to the problems of neighborhoods and receptive to a search for solutions. In the summer of 1981 he began to meet regularly with representatives of neighborhood groups in order to familiarize them with the budgetary process and to permit them to examine the city's service distribution system. These initial sessions led the managing director to conduct citywide town meetings, between October 1981 and March 1982, in each of Philadelphia's 23 police districts. These were given high marks by Edward Schwartz, the director of the Institute for the Study of Civic Values, a research and service organization for neighborhood and reform groups, and successful at-large city council candidate (and major Wilson Goode supporter) in the 1983 elections:

> Over 5,000 citizens, collectively, attended the meetings, which emerged as the most ambitious attempt to acquaint citizens with local government in recent Philadelphia. . . . While a wide range of complaints surfaced in the various gatherings, it was not hard to identify the common concerns—deteriorating physical conditions ranging from streets and sewer systems in the Northeast and Northwest to thousands of abandoned houses in North Philadelphia and Kensington; serious deficiencies in the City's educational and recreation programs for young people, contributing to juvenile drug use and street crime and economic hardships growing out of unemployment, abandoned commercial strips, and Reaganomics. Above all, neighborhood residents wanted to be taken seriously as active partners in City-run improvement programs, instead of merely being the "clients" of agencies that rarely seemed to respond adequately to community concerns. Indeed, as the meetings unfolded, it was clear that governmental accountability was the overriding concern, underlying complaints in virtually every area.[17]

On April 29, 1982 the leaders of 45 neighborhood organizations from across the city testified at a city council budget hearing and presented their six-point Neighborhood Agenda: replace lost jobs, acquire and dispose of abandoned houses, develop an energy conservation program for city residents, reduce crime, design a comprehensive program to improve the quality of the public school system, and design a comprehensive system of citizen planning for neighborhoods in service delivery.[18]

Following the budget hearings and the budget's approval, neighborhood organization leaders met regularly with the managing director to implement their proposals. Neighborhood leaders were successful in working with Managing Director Goode in developing a new housing plan, organizing regular meetings with Town Watch organizers and city officials to improve neighborhood crime prevention, developing a new strategy to combat juvenile unemployment, and designing a comprehensive energy conservation and fuel assistance program. Not surprisingly, a $500,000 proposal from the managing director to establish citywide Neighborhood Planning Councils was rejected by the city council. These councils would have been organized in each of the 23 police districts, but city council viewed them as unnecessary and a threat to individual council members. Consequently, the neighborhood leaders, with Managing Director Goode's support, independently organized Neighborhood Coordinating Teams in every police district. The neighborhood teams engaged in monitoring and coordinating neighborhood service delivery by working closely with Managing Director Goode. The city administration's process for neighborhood participation received high praise from Edward Schwartz for the "many months of meetings and discussions between neighborhood representatives and the City's

Managing Director over the best way that community groups and city government could work together to combat major problems facing the City."[19]

Not surprisingly, when Mayor Green disclosed that he would not seek a second mayoral term, Wilson Goode resigned as managing director and announced his candidacy for the Democratic party's mayoral nomination. Goode's tenure as managing director was largely an outgrowth of the black independent political movement, but once in office he incorporated neighborhood and reform issues into the city's administrative process. At the same time he expanded his own visibility. More importantly, Wilson Goode reinforced his reputation for effectiveness and efficiency in government. Indeed, he demonstrated that good management and social responsibility are compatible.

Goode's Election Strategy

W. Wilson Goode's campaign strategy is intimately intertwined with the black independent movement. In a conversation with the authors, William Leggett, Goode's campaign field coordinator in the general election and Philadelphia's current deputy mayor, explained how the campaign built upon and carried further a long-standing effort in the black community:

> Wilson Goode is the benefactor of several incremental stages taken by the black community over the last 13–14 years, starting with the independent campaign of Hardy Williams and Charles Bowser. Further, the Rizzo administration, especially as personified by the recall drive and attempted Rizzo-backed charter revision, created enthusiasm and spurred mobilization of the black community. The black community's overwhelming rejection of the move to remove the two-term limitation on mayoral terms, especially in light of the failed attempt to recall Rizzo, crystalized into a movement to elect a black mayor. Blacks led the move to stop the charter revision and they supported Bill Green. Yet the candidacy of Lucien Blackwell, an independent candidate in the 1979 general election, following Charles Bowser's close defeat in the Democratic primary, symbolized the desire of the black community to elect one of its own to the mayor's office. Indeed, the election of a black mayor was transferred to Wilson Goode and became the *cause celebre* in the black community.[20]

William Miller, the campaign field coordinator in the primary and political consultant for the primary and general elections, emphasized that despite all the good work that had gone on before, it was clear that the campaign would not be easy:

> The Goode campaign was not to be your typical "black campaign." Goode's entry to the political community was made in the primary—he distilled the notion of aloofness, demonstrated a sense of politics, and the like. Rizzo had

the Democratic political structure and experience. Goode had to organize and unify black constituents and integrate the liberal community into the campaign. He had no political party organization. He also had to raise money and raise issues. Goode: man of the future who can bring the city together; Rizzo: man of the past, divisive, living image of what we are not proud of, a politics of corruption and political demagoguery. Goode represented competency; a vision of bringing all Philadelphians together; hard work; and a new Philadelphia. Yet he needed a big black vote. There had to be a massive and effective voter registration campaign.[21]

Events of the 1970s, especially the 1978 charter-change election, convinced Goode's campaign officials that the black community wanted a change and could be mobilized. They also believed the white community was ready for change. Rizzo was not only viewed as a racist in the black community, he had also alienated a large segment of the white community, especially the liberals. Therefore, the key element in the campaign strategy was tapping the enthusiasm in the black community and demonstrating that W. Wilson Goode, as mayor, would make all Philadelphians proud.

Campaign Issues

Goode's major campaign theme was Philadelphia's decline during the 1970s and the link between that decline and Mayor Rizzo. At the same time Goode was projected as the leader who recognized the city's problems and had the skill and vision to solve them. Goode's advisors constantly reminded the media and the public of the failures of the Rizzo administration. These failures included the loss of nearly 100,000 jobs in the city during the 1970s; the lowering of the city's bond rating; the historic tax increase of 1976; the low level of performance in many city schools; the deterioration of family life in the city, especially the high incidence of female-headed households; and the high rate of joblessness and poverty. Philadelphia, like many cities in the Northeast, had become poorer, dirtier, and less safe during the 1970s, the years of Frank Rizzo's leadership.

The U.S. Bureau of Labor Statistics reports that between 1972 and 1983 the number of unemployed individuals in Philadelphia rose by 23 percent. Furthermore, the number of manufacturing jobs in the city declined from over 207,000 to around 109,000, a drop of 47 percent. Services by comparison rose by 20 percent, with much of this growth in the area of health services and hospitals. Interestingly, in the Philadelphia Metropolitan Area, employment in manufacturing declined by 23 percent between 1972 and 1983, but the service area rose by 49 percent. The employment decline in manufacturing and growth in services occurred in the city and the region, but in the city of Philadelphia the rate of decline in manufacturing jobs was much higher than in the region, and in the service area the growth in the region was considerably higher than the city rate.

Wilson Goode was projected as the leader with the vision, skills, confidence, and determination to see that once again "Philadelphia's on the Move." (Not be confused with the group MOVE.) The cornerstone of Goode's issues strategy was contained in a position paper entitled "Philadelphia and Jobs: The Second Renaissance" (Goode for Mayor Campaign Committee, 1983). The document was billed as "an economic blueprint for the new Philadelphia of the 1980s." Wilson Goode's objective was to return Philadelphia to prosperity; as he said during the campaign:

> The most important question to face this city in the 1980s: Which mayoral candidate will best be able to strengthen the city's economy and promise the jobs and income which are indispensable to the city's well-being?. . . . The generation and maintenance of jobs, income, and economic growth for all of the people of Philadelphia will be the number one priority of my administration. Our people need jobs for a decent life, and this city needs the solid low-rate tax base which full employment provides. . . . I intend to be both an innovator and an advocate for the people of Philadelphia, tirelessly pursuing programs to attract and maintain the jobs and economic growth which are the very life-blood of the city.

Goode linked economic growth with neighborhood revitalization and emphasized his support of neighborhoods during his tenure as managing director:

> Neighborhoods are the strength of our city. The preservation and improvement of neighborhoods will be a central concern of my administration as Mayor, just as it was one of my central concerns when I was City Managing Director. Philadelphia's neighborhoods are important because it is in the neighborhoods that all the problems of the city become most acutely focused. Each of the 20,000 abandoned houses citywide translate into a problem on somebody's block. Growing unemployment throughout the region translates into a neighbor who recently lost his job. . . . As Managing Director, I made myself available to neighborhood groups and neighborhood residents throughout the city on a continuing basis, attending over 500 neighborhood meetings in three years. As Mayor, I will renew that commitment to bring government closer to the people to listen to what people in the neighborhoods have to say, and to work directly with them to solve problems that confront them.

The position paper on neighborhoods contained specific proposals for dealing with the problems of jobs and economic recovery, education and employment for youth, housing, crime prevention and reduction, energy conservation, education in the public schools, clean neighborhoods, community gardening. The creation of an Office of Neighborhoods would also be a priority of a Goode administration.

Goode addressed Philadelphia's housing crisis by reminding residents of his experience and accomplishments. In particular, he stressed his record with the nonprofit PCCA; his more favorable record in the number of rental housing units rehabilitated during his three years as managing director when juxtaposed to the record from 1975 through 1979, the first five years of the federal Community Development Block Grant program and the last five years of Frank Rizzo's administration; and his nearly 17 years of experience in the housing area. He also presented a program for housing which included assisting the homeless, reorganizing the Philadelphia Housing Authority, utilizing vacant properties, assisting the private rental housing market, providing emergency mortgage assistance to homeowners, constructing new housing, creating a Mayor's Advisory Committee on Housing, and appointing a Director of Housing with cabinet status. The housing position paper, and others, emphasized Goode's experience in problem-solving, management, and especially his record as Philadelphia's managing director and his demonstrated ability to effectively and efficiently lead Philadelphia forward.

While the issues raised and debated during the campaign were important, campaign strategists did not regard them as the key to victory. As a high ranking Goode strategist explained:

> Issues in the campaign were part of the media strategy—satisfy people and treat certain interests. Issues legitimated Wilson in the eyes of whites. Economic development, housing, crime, service delivery, Philadelphia on the Move, and the like, were issues that appealed to everyone. We took issues and positions that everyone could find appealing. We searched for a consensus, for a coalition. Blacks and whites, for different reasons, are concerned about public housing. Issues legitimated the candidate; Wilson would have gotten his base (95 percent of it) without issues. Position papers were documents that served as a model for campaigning.

Another campaign strategist was even more emphatic:

> This was not an "issues" campaign. We had people who were interested in housing, education, crime, etc., but the real issue was a new future for Philadelphia and whether people had confidence in Wilson Goode or would they resort to the past or remain stationary.
>
> The campaign went through two issues directors. After the second director, we did not fill the position. A lot of time was spent firing off issues papers. Special interest groups wrote the papers and the campaign organization coopted them. There were a series of task forces—housing, aging, minority set-asides, reorganizing city government, etc. The pollsters, Paul Masland and Pat Caddell, found out what concerns people had. But issues were not important from the standpoint of developing a winning strategy. Issues were media hits, the press secretary had the most to do with them. He made policy statements about how to get it done.

Campaign issues may have been media hits to "legitimate" Wilson Goode with white voters, but black voter registration and turnout were the major elements in the campaign strategy. A Goode primary election campaign document discloses that: "Both campaigns (Rizzo and Goode) intended to shift the registration balance through intense registration efforts, the race would be predicated on turnout in the Black and White communities and success would come to the candidate who was best able to cross over to the other's base while retaining their core of support."[22] For this reason both major candidates in the primary developed strategies to maximize voter registration and turnout among their constituencies. But, largely due to the 1978 charter-change election, neither side made appeals on explicitly racial grounds, for fear of mobilizing the other's voters in opposition. They did not want a repeat of the "vote white" appeals of the earlier campaign; that strategy had failed. Moreover, no one wanted a repeat of what had recently occurred in Chicago. All were aware that the same thing could happen in Philadelphia.

The Primary Election

The campaign strategy in the primary largely consisted of increasing black voter registration by organizing voter registration drives and increasing black turnout by developing an efficient election day operation.[23] The objective was to "build a political apparatus to annihilate the old (Rizzo) political army and build an army for Wilson and get him elected."[24] The Goode campaign assumed that the Rizzo forces would seek to expand their base primarily by Republican party crossovers. That is, enrolled Republicans would change their registration to the Democratic party. The Democratic City Committee was neutral. The Goode forces were determined to mobilize and turn out black voters at almost the same rate as white voters. Goode, so the strategy assumed, could win with only 20 percent of the white vote, but an aggressive black voter registration and turnout was paramount.

The strategy had two components: (1) expand the universe of registered voters and (2) train a corps of field operators who would do nothing but make plans for getting out the vote. These duties were handled by the deputy field director for registration and the deputy field director for operations, respectively. Eleven field offices were opened in black and Hispanic neighborhoods and one predominantly white neighborhood in the Northeast. Excluding the office in the Northeast, the field operations essentially bypassed the white community. With over $2 million available for the campaign, the media effort (especially television) was directed at the white community.

Black organizations were solicited to work for the Goode campaign in their neighborhoods. Black churches were the organizational base for the campaign, and the ministerial alliances were solidly behind Goode, who was a deacon in his church. Goode visited several churches each Sunday during the campaign. Black organizations—churches, neighborhood groups, fraternities and sororities, operation PUSH, NAACP, Urban League, radio stations, and the like not only spearheaded voter registration drives, but purchased advertisements in *The Philadelphia Tribune,* the black newspaper. The black media, especially radio, played a significant role. Goode periodically appeared on the city's two most popular radio talk and call-in shows—Mary Mason on WHAT and Georgie Woods on WDAS. The field operation also engaged in fund raising: "The black community had an opportunity to vote for itself. Wilson symbolized the best of what could come out of the campaign, not only could people vote, but they could give the campaign 50 cents."[25]

The result of all these efforts was most impressive. Table 11.2 shows the changes in the number of enrolled Democratic party voters between the November elections of 1982 and the mayoral primary in May 1983. The number of registered Democrats in Philadelphia rose by 29 percent. Black Democrats are one half of the growth in enrolled Democrats; whites are 45 percent; and others make up the balance. Stated differently, blacks and other minorities represent over half of the growth in Democratic party registration. Significantly, the proportion of white Democrats declined from 56 percent of all registered Democrats in November 1982 to 53 percent of Democrats in May 1983. During this six-month period, the proportion of black registered Democrats increased from 42 percent to 44 percent. Moreover, approximately 90 percent of Philadelphia's voting age residents were registered for the primary elections. Further, 83 percent of voting age whites and over 90 percent of blacks were registered. In addition, enrolled black Democrats were over 90 percent of the city's black voting age population; white Democrats were only 62 percent of voting age whites.

Both camps apparently picked up some formerly registered Republicans. Between the two elections, the Republican party lost 11 percent of its registered voters. Whites continued to represent slightly more than four-fifths of registered Republicans; however, the number of white Republicans declined by 10 percent. Interestingly, the number of black Republicans declined by 22 percent, and their proportion of Republican voters dropped from 17 percent to 15 percent.

As Table 11.3 shows, Goode easily won the Democratic nomination, receiving 53 percent of the votes;[26] former Mayor Frank Rizzo pulled 43 percent. Citywide turnout among registered Democrats was 70 percent. Bruce Caswell, research director of the Institute for the Study of Civic Values and a Goode supporter and campaign researcher, estimates that 70.1 percent of the enrolled white Democrats turned out and 69.3 percent of the black Democrats went to the polls.[27] The virtual closing of the city's traditional 5 percent gap between black and white turnout was one of the keys to Goode's victory.

Table 11.2 Major Party Registration for November 1982 and May 1983

Registrants by Party and Race	Number of Registered Voters				Change in Registration, November 1982-May 1983	
	November 1982	%	May 1983	%	Number	% Change
Democrats	695,228		899,882		+204,654	+29.4
White	387,357	55.7	479,419	53.3	+ 92,062	+23.8
Black	291,977	42.0	395,071	43.9	+103,094	+35.3
Other	15,894	2.3	25,392	2.8	+ 9,498	+59.8
Republicans	198,031		176,930		− 21,101	−10.7
White	163,822	82.7	147,463	83.3	− 16,359	−10.0
Black	34,208	17.3	26,727	15.1	− 7,481	−21.9
Other	1	0.0	2,740	1.6	+ 2,739[a]	

aThis represents a large percentage increase in other groups.
Source: City of Philadelphia, Office of City Commissioners, Voter Registration Division.

Table 11.3 Neighborhood Returns for the 1983 Democratic Primary (Top Three Candidates) and General Election for Mayor

Neighborhoods and Citywide	% Black	% Hispanic	Democratic Primary				Voting Outcomes	General Election		
			% Turnout of Registered Democratic voters	% Voting for:			% Turnout of All Registered voters	Democrat Goode	Republican Eagan	Leonard for Mayor Leonard
				Goode	Rizzo	Lomento				
	1980									
The Northeast	5.1	1.1	69.5	19.1	80.3	0.5	64.6	19.9	64.9	15.2
West Philadelphia	72.8	1.1	70.6	82.8	11.2	6.0	64.5	87.9	9.5	2.5
Kensington–Bridesburg	1.6	7.4	68.7	13.0	85.7	1.3	60.9	20.3	69.7	10.0
South Philadelphia	30.5	1.8	74.5	31.4	66.0	2.6	62.3	42.9	51.3	5.7
Central Philadelphia	32.2	6.5	65.5	69.0	28.8	2.2	58.4	59.0	26.9	14.1
North Philadelphia	66.1	9.9	63.5	89.6	6.1	4.3	60.2	93.2	4.8	2.0
Chesnut Hill–Mt. Airy	61.6	1.0	75.8	86.7	10.2	3.1	69.6	81.4	13.5	5.1
Roxborough–Manuyunk Germantown–West	3.6	0.8	70.8	22.5	77.0	0.5	62.8	24.1	61.6	14.2
Oak Lane	71.5	6.2	69.7	87.0	7.8	5.2	65.0	91.1	6.6	2.2
Olney–Oak Lane	3.7	4.6	67.2	20.3	79.1	0.6	60.0	24.3	60.6	15.1
Southwest Philadelphia	25.3	0.8	75.5	31.8	66.5	1.7	64.5	38.8	52.5	8.7
Citywide	37.8	3.8	69.5	52.7	43.2	3.0	62.3	55.3	36.8	8.0

Source: City of Philadelphia, Office of City Commissioners, Voter Registration Division.

A second reason was that Goode not only won the predominantly black neighborhoods (Charles Bowser won only these neighborhoods in the 1979 Democratic primary), but carried Central Philadelphia, which includes many upper-income Jewish residents in Central City and Society Hill, with 69 percent of the votes (Table 11.1 and 11.3). In the remaining neighborhoods, Goode's proportion of the vote was generally significantly higher than the black percentage of the neighborhood's population. For example, blacks are only 4 percent of the population in Roxborough-Manuyunk, but Goode received 23 percent of the neighborhood's votes.

Third, Table 11.1 shows clearly that Goode and Bowser were not able to capture the "No" votes for the 1978 charter-change election in the predominantly white neighborhoods, but Goode ran considerably better than Bowser in those neighborhoods. For example, in Roxborough-Manuyunk 53 percent of the voters voted against removing the two-term ban on successive mayoral terms; only 11 percent of the neighborhood's electorate voted for Bowser in 1979; yet Goode collected 23 percent of the neighborhood's votes. Fourth, the NBC Exit Poll reveals that 98 percent of the black voters cast their ballots for Goode, as did 24 percent of white voters.[28] (Bruce Caswell of the Institute for the Study of Civic Values discloses that his regression analysis of the city's 1,794 voting districts reveals that Goode captured 19 to 20 percent of the white vote.) The NBC poll also indicates that the whites voting for Goode were largely Jewish; had at least a college degree; were liberal to moderate in political ideology; were under 50 years of age; and were employed primarily in professional/managerial and other white collar professions.

Wilson Goode's victory in the Democratic primary reflects a large amount of voting along racial lines. Neighborhood voting patterns for Bowser in 1979 and Goode in 1983 show that both candidates ran very well in black neighborhoods. Goode, unlike Bowser in 1979, was able to benefit from some decisive crossover voting among whites. The poll data and the comparison of the Bowser and Goode votes from predominantly white neighborhoods, especially Central Philadelphia, show that Goode ran much better than Bowser in the predominantly white neighborhoods. Nonetheless, Goode carried only one of the four predominantly white neighborhoods that voted against the charter change (see Table 11.1 and 11.3). In short, Goode was able to make a strong appeal to black voters, but in addition and, unlike Bowser, he was also able to appeal to a sufficient number of white voters, especially Jewish and other liberal whites.

The General Election

With a decisive victory in the Democratic primary, the Goode campaign added an additionally appropriate element to its general election strategy. William Miller explains:

In the general election we moved somewhat differently than we had in the primary. We had increased the pool of voters in the primary. In the primary our aim was to render the Democratic party organization to impotency. We took the Democratic structure apart. The primary was a crusade and attack army; now in the general election, we started building or molding the party for Goode. All patronage and perks would continue to be done by and for Democrats. White ward leaders and all ward leaders had more to lose if there was a Republican victory. The real issue was: What would the party loyalist do to save their behinds by getting their constituencies to vote for Goode? Goode became the "consumate Democrat." He sought endorsements from ward leaders in white areas—Northeast, South Philly, River Wards. He got those ward leaders to endorse him. A Unity Dinner was held and we got the Democratic City Committee to endorse Goode. Rizzo endorsed Goode. Goode now had an organization in every ward. White ward leaders had to deliver their constituencies, and help Wilson and themselves. Many of the ward leaders worked hard, but what could they do![29]

Bruce Caswell concurs with Miller by stressing: "Goode just wanted to be the party standard-bearer; he emphasized his party loyalty by making pro-Democratic and anti-Republican statements. He realized that he needed the party to run or govern the city."[30] Consequently, the Goode strategy for the general election contained essentially two elements: "(1) reassuring party leaders of Goode's loyalty and (2) telling the black community, one more time!"[31]

A major thread running through the Goode strategy was the importance placed on experienced and effective leadership. Goode accentuated his proven administrative and managerial skills, and his ability to construct a new policy agenda for the city and all Philadelphians. In short, he argued that he would lead the entire city and he demonstrated his leadership capacity by reaching out to all the major leadership elements of the Democratic party establishment (80 percent of registered voters are Democrats and the party has won every mayoral election since 1951). For example, he informed ward leaders: "I believe in patronage. I believe there are jobs to be given out by the mayor on a discretionary basis. And, those jobs will go to those people who have been loyal . . . and *productive* party members."[32] In addition, Goode met with the members of city council, the city's delegation to the Pennsylvania State Legislature, the State Legislature's Black Caucus, the state Democratic Committee; he also addressed the State Legislature. Miller feels that these meetings were extremely important:

> He stressed a new era—Philadelphia would now be a full partner in state party politics; not just a taker. Goode had to reinforce the message in Philadelphia by using party pundits. He said good things about Philadelphia and the possibilities under a Goode administration. The black community was still the base, but we had a Democratic structure and apparatus to deal with. Goode

now moved to solidify his support with the party and show his loyalty by running as a Democrat.[33]

In terms of patronage, policy, and leadership for the new Philadelphia, the strategy was to present Wilson Goode as a good and loyal Democrat who recognized the imperative of a symbiotic relationship with the party establishment for purposes of effectively governing the city.

By embracing the largely white Democratic party establishment, there were some who had the fear that Goode would lose some support in the black community. This did not occur:

> Goode was able to hold on to his base though a white appeal was presented in the press. Blacks did not scrutinize Goode. It was Goode's time because blacks wanted their own mayor; they had elected other mayors. The white-oriented media campaign did not soften Wilson's base. Nonetheless, many blacks did not like the ads . . . But blacks had an agenda—the election of one of their own to the office of mayor. Wilson Goode was the recipient of the black community's agenda.[34]

In short, the Goode campaign strategy in the black community was similar to the plan in the primary. With the decisive primary victory in hand, the Goode campaign tactic was to direct the field operation so that the black base could be cultivated and maintained. Just as important, the plan entailed demonstrating that Wilson Goode would forge those alliances needed for governing Philadelphia.

This campaign strategy in fact produced a huge victory margin. W. Wilson Goode captured 55 percent of the votes (Table 11.3). The Republican nominee received 37 percent of the votes and the third candidate, a liberal independent, collected the remaining 8 percent. Although Democrat Goode won in only those neighborhoods that had been in his column in the Democratic primary, generally he improved his percentage of the primary votes in predominantly white neighborhoods. For example, in South Philadelphia, Rizzo's base, Goode's share of the vote rose from 31 percent to 43 percent. Goode was victorious in Central Philadelphia, the home of many "Limousine Liberals," but votes garnered by the liberal independent candidate cut into Goode's victory margin (see Table 11.3).

Citywide the turnout was 62 percent, around 7 percent points below the Democratic primary turnout rate. The turnout rate in those wards with at least 90 percent white registered voters was 64 percent; the ward with predominantly black registration had a turnout rate of 66 percent. Furthermore, in the predominantly white wards only 21 percent of the votes went to Goode. White liberals in Center City, Society Hill, and Chestnut Hill were Goode's base in the white community. For example, in Ward 8 in Central Philadelphia, a predominantly white area, Goode collected 51 percent of the votes, and the liberal independent candidate received 15 percent. Not surprisingly, in the predominantly black wards, Goode garnered 97 percent of the votes. The voting pattern for Goode in the general election was similar to the model in the primary—a rate of turnout in the black community that is similar to the rate among whites (perhaps higher), a virtual monopoly of the black vote, and at least 20 percent of the white vote. According to Leggett, the Goode campaign field coordinator for the general election:

> The election of Wilson Goode was the product of timing, incremental steps, black enthusiasm (locally and nationally), hype, black voter registration and turnout, and support from white liberals. Wilson was legitimated by not being in the mold of Harold Washington of Chicago, this had more importance in the white community. Yet the returns and exit polls reveal that Goode's support among whites was not markedly higher, though higher, than the white support received by Washington.[35]

Caswell of the Institute for the Study of Civic Values agrees.

> There was enthusiasm among blacks and liberals for Goode. Nineteen percent of whites voted for Goode. Lots of whites voted against the charter change; but they gave Wilson Goode only 19–20 percent of their votes. The election was significant for the city. A good feeling about Wilson Goode has developed among whites since the election.[36]

While the voting patterns reveal that the road to victory for Wilson Goode was not very different from those for Harold Washington in Chicago, it is significant that race-baiting and intense racial conflict were not a part of the campaign strategy, though race was omnipresent. In part this was due to the desire of leaders in black and white communities to overcome the rancor of the Rizzo administration and the 1978 charter-change election. A "Chicago Style Campaign" would have been a return to 1978 and before. More importantly, Goode did not portray himself as a "black" candidate for mayor; instead, he campaigned as the former city managing director—he was familiar with city services; he knew the budget; he had demonstrated his managerial skills; and he had a vision of Philadelphia on the move. Goode's low-key managerial style enabled him to project himself by explaining that economic growth and equitable service distribution was the way to build the new Philadelphia. He stressed his background and experience, plus he voiced the necessity of a working public-private partnership.

> I intend to make Philadelphia's government the best-run company in this town. . . . We will invest our scarce capital resources widely; we will manage departmental budgets prudently and productively; and we will work in close partnership with business, labor, political, neighborhood and institutional leaders to bring about our common goal—economic revitalization. . . . I intend to create a climate where diverse groups such as government, management and labor can sit together to develop and offer solutions to the city's

economic problems. . . . I intend to work hand-in-hand with the city council and the Philadelphia delegations in Harrisburg and Washington to bring about economic recovery. . . . The economic revitalization of Philadelphia requires the marshalling of all of our talents to take this city into a new and strong future.

Wilson Goode presented himself as the candidate with the strongest leadership characteristics—confidence and determination—for constructing the new Philadelphia. Goode conveyed a vision of a better Philadelphia and challenged all Philadelphians to pull together under his direction. Nonetheless, an overwhelming black vote and support from white liberals are his electoral base. Not surprisingly, an exit poll for *The Philadelphia Inquirer* and Channel 10, a local television station, disclosed that most of Goode's voters perceived him to be the most experienced mayoral candidate; the candidate with specific plans for Philadelphia; and the person to unify the city.[37]

The election of Wilson Goode was the culmination of a series of attempts by the black community to select a black mayor. Significantly, he had been an initial organizer of the city's black independent political movement. Moreover, Goode's educational background in public administration and public policy, along with his experience and record with PCCA and the Pennsylvania Public Utilities Commission, and the management of Philadelphia's service delivery system, established his credentials as a first-rate public manager. Furthermore, these experiences created visibility for Goode and shaped his reputation. In short, Goode's public expertise, leadership ability, and vision of a new Philadelphia became natural elements in his campaign's efforts to present him as a proficient public manager and competent executive leader.

Goode succeeded in increasing black voter registration and turning out blacks at the same rate as whites, thereby providing a large enough base to include white liberals in a winning alliance. Previous mayoral elections, in particular the 1979 Democratic primary, had demonstrated that a black candidate could come close, but still fall short of victory. Without question, Wilson Goode's experience and competence in the city's black political movement helped mobilize the black community and to achieve finally the goal of electing a black mayor begun back in 1971. Although Goode collected more white support than the black mayoral candidates before him, the highly activated black electorate is responsible for his victory. The enthusiasm in the black community and Wilson Goode's public record combined to make him the ideal candidate.

While the Goode campaign developed a winning alliance for the 1983 elections, the process of governing requires making choices and setting priorities. Moderation and innovation are tests of the stability of Goode's electoral alliance. Mayor Wilson Goode is an historic figure. Yet the measure of Goode's political skills is his ability to govern in a way that his electoral base is maintained and expanded. The success of the Goode administration is predicated on economic revitalization (for Center City and the neighborhoods) and the widespread distribution of public services and programs across Philadelphia's neighborhoods.[38]

The Future of W. Wilson Goode in Philadelphia Politics After MOVE

Wilson Goode was elected mayor of Philadelphia by overwhelming support from black voters, but his winning coalition consisted of support from other quarters as well, especially liberal whites and some of the city's labor unions. In addition, candidate Goode promised to work with loyal Democratic party ward leaders. Indeed, challenging patronage and the problem-plagued city police were not prominant during the campaign.

Rather, Goode articulated positions on economic development and disclosed that development would be a top priority in his administration. His vision for economic revitalization won him support, especially campaign contributions, from Philadelphia's top business leaders. The Greater Philadelphia First Corporation, an organization representing the Philadelphia area's top corporations, was the core of Goode's support in the business community. Clearly, Wilson Goode convinced a cross-section of Philadelphia's stakeholders that he was capable of leading the city, solving her problems, and creating better times for city residents. For a little more than 16 months, the Goode administration enjoyed a blissful honeymoon.

The Honeymoon

By fulfilling his campaign pledges, Mayor Goode sought to demonstrate that his administration had indeed "hit the ground running." Prior to his inauguration on January 2, 1984, Goode instructed his Transition Team to develop an action plan for this administration's first 100 days. After 15 weeks in office Mayor Goode issued a document outlining his young administration's accomplishments.[39]

He claimed credit for progress on programs and projects that had become "entangled and enmeshed in discussion and disagreements." He argued that his administration was overcoming the political impasse which stymied issues such as cable television, abondoned car removal, constructing a new convention center, providing more shelter for the homeless, creating bold new initiatives with summer jobs for youth, literacy advancement, volunteerism, and anti-graffiti programs. Furthermore, Mayor Goode reported that his administration had begun its economic revitalization strategy by surveying the city's 37,000 businesses to determine their public service needs; he also convened a panel of business and corporate leaders to advise his administration on economic revitalization; and he also developed a framework for development.

General optimism about Mayor Goode permitted his administration to enjoy an abundant honeymoon. For example, in the summer of 1984 he was interviewed by Democratic party presidential nominee-to-be Walter Mondale, between the last primaries and the convention, for his vice-presidential running mate, becoming the first black to be considered for this office by one of the major political parties.

Further, a Cambridge Survey Research poll[40] in July of registered voters in the 13th congressional district (most of suburban Montogomery County and two wards in Philadelphia), the congressional district with the highest median income in the Philadelphia metropolitan area, disclosed an 86 percent favorable rating for Mayor Goode, topping Republicans such as President Ronald Reagan (65 percent), Pennsylvania Governor Richard Thornburgh (60 percent), and local Congressman Lawrence Coughlin (51 percent). Indeed, as Mayor Goode approached the end of his first year in office, a Teichner Associates poll of Philadelphians conducted in November revealed that 76 percent of city residents gave Mayor Goode a excellent or good general approval rating.[41]

On January 2, 1985 Mayor Goode's completed his first year in office and reported on his administration's first year accomplishments. In his "State of the City" address, mayor Goode pointed to the success of his aggressive 100 days plan and summarized his administration's first year by arguing: "We have made considerable success toward our goals. We have had some disappointments. And, we have resolved some unexpected crises."[42]

In the speech and a more detailed "Mayor's Annual Report," Mayor Goode itemized as accomplishments for 1984 several progressive steps in revitalizing Philadelphia's economy and creating jobs, improving the city's infrastructure, revitalizing neighborhoods, meeting human needs, and improving public management.[43]

He also listed five critical continuing and unresolved issues requiring "immediate and consistent attention." The challenges for 1985 outlined by Mayor Goode included: resolving long-term solid waste disposal and management requirements; adopting an equitable reform of the differential in the city wage tax rate for city residents and commuters; improving effectiveness in coordinating the delivery of human, physical, and basic services to neighborhoods; continuing to build a strong fiscal base and balancing the municipal budget; and taking aggressive and systematic steps to rid neighborhoods of illegal drug activity.

Fault-Finding Murmurs

Although Mayor Goode continued to enjoy a high approval rating on job performance, grumbling surfaced in some quarters of the political landscape in interviews, especially those conducted in the late winter of 1985, with leaders in politics and business. The plethora of reports and planning documents led to some criticisms, particularly from those outside city government. For example, some questioned his commitment to neighborhood economic development after the original draft of the mayor's economic development strategy overlooked the topic. The inclusion of a section on neighborhood economic development in the final draft generated questions about whether Mayor Goode had produced a nice-looking and inclusive document on economic development, but omitted priorities. Some wondered if Mayor Goode could make the needed hard choices.

Further, while Mayor Goode was widely praised for keeping the Eagles, the National Football League franchise, from moving to Phoenix, a few critics wondered how the financial package, including the building of sky-boxes at Veterans' Stadium, to keep the Eagles in Philadelphia could be consistent with the mayor's economic development strategy document! Some wondered if Mayor Goode would develop specific strategies for encouraging black entrepreneurship. Others questioned Mayor Goode's management and problem solving skills; the perceived over-attention to ceremony and public relations; and the competence of some high-level city appointees.

Unquestionably, these criticisms did not penetrate Mayor Goode's high overall approval rating among the general population. Indeed, the mayor's critics admitted that Goode's historic status, including his climb from the rural South, as Philadelphia's first black mayor, and his accessibility and visibility created credibility and goodwill among city residents that appeared almost impossible to uproot.

Broken Fortunes

Events in the Cobb Creek area of West Philadelphia, a predominantly working class and middle-income black area, tragically exposed the Goode administration's vulnerability. In August 1978, during the Rizzo administration, there was a police assault on a house in Powelton Village occupied by MOVE—a radical back-to-nature black cult that favored dreadlocks, uncooked food, stray animals, a build-up of trash and human waste, and the surname "Africa." The confrontation ended in the death of a white policeman and the wounding of five firemen, but all MOVE members survived. Nine MOVE members were sent to prison.

The situation on Osage Avenue, the primary MOVE house after Powelton Village, had reached the top of the Goode administration's agenda by late May 1984. The efforts of current MOVE members to force the release of their members from prison led to a squalid fortified house at 6221 Osage Avenue. From this house MOVE members directed foul-mouthed harangues from the rooftop to neighbors at all hours of the night. After months of complaining from neighbors and grumbling because of the lack of corrective action from the Goode administration, on May 13, 1985 the Philadelphia Police Department responded by attempting to serve arrest warrants on MOVE members accused of disturbing their neighbors with loudspeakers and unsanitary living conditions.

Tragedy occurred as a gun battle (police fired 10,000 rounds) and an unchecked fire ignited by an explosive device dropped by city police from a state police helicopter destroyed life and property. The MOVE house was engulfed in flames that city officials initially decided not to extinguish, destroying 61 rowhouses (Mayor Goode promised to build new houses and have them ready for occupancy by Christmas of 1985; the date for occupancy had to be moved to March 31, 1986) and damaging several others in the 6200 blocks of Osage Avenue and Pine Street. Eleven persons, including five children, inside the MOVE house perished. (One child and an adult are known to have escaped from the burning MOVE house.) Other area residents were evacuated on May 12, but over 250 persons lost homes and contents valued at more than $5 million.

Reaction to the dropping of a bomb in a highly dense area and killing 11 persons, especially 5 children, was one of general outrage among blacks across the country, but some Philadelphia residents appeared to be more understanding. U.S. Representative John Conyers represented the general opinion of black leadership when he said, "We are totally outraged" and added that Philadelphia's bombing of a residential area is "the most violent eviction notice ever given."[44] However, some residents left homeless by the fire, admitted a mistake was made, but there was a reluctance to criticize Mayor Goode, and some praised him.[45] Much of the support for the action, however, came from law enforcement officials. Indeed, Police Chief Darryl Gates of Los Angeles appeared on CBS TV's "Face The Nation"[46] and called Mayor Goode a hero and urged him to run for national office. On the day following the bombing and its live coverage on Philadelphia television stations, 69 percent of the city respondents in a Teichner Associates poll rated Mayor Goode's handling of the MOVE confrontation excellent to good.[47]

Mayor Goode accepted responsibility for the events of May 13, but he also appointed a commission to investigate what went wrong and who is to be blamed. Although the Philadelphia Special Investigation Commission began its work during the summer, the events of May 13 did not begin to emerge in detail until the 11-member commission heard testimony from 90 witnesses, including the city's top four decision makers in the MOVE confrontation, in 18 days (100 hours) of televised testimony in the fall.

Philadelphia's top decision makers—Mayor Goode, Managing Director Leo A. Brooks, Mayor Goode's representative on the scene (Brooks resigned shortly after the seige), Police Commissioner Gregore J. Sambor (who resigned shortly after the hearings ended), and Fire Commissioner William C. Richmond—appeared before the commission separately, but the gaps, inconsistencies, and contradictions on key aspects of the events of May 13 in their testimonies led the commission to recall them to appear together in the closing days of the hearings. Further, Mayor Goode charged his subordinates with failing to inform him fully and ignoring his orders. The mayor's testimony was contradicted by his subordinates and they disagreed with each other on several other important aspects of the planning and implementation of the police assault.

With testimony shattering Mayor Goode's image as a hard working, hands-on problem solver and manager, *The Philadelphia Inquirer* concluded:

> After 90 witnesses, after the final, stone-faced four, the MOVE hearings have recessed now, leaving a painful record, an image of police "professionalism" in shreds, an image of mayoral leadership battered, a city groping for ways to repair a government that has warred against its own people.[48]

Claude Lewis, a black member of *The Philadelphia Inquirer's* editorial board, summed up the commission's hearings:

> The panel's chief value was that it documented what nearly everyone had suspected: The confrontation with MOVE was crowded with incompetence, seared by insensitivity, crippled by a corrupt plan and made obscene by an arsenal of weaponry that might have been more properly used to topple a small army rather than to evict six children and seven armed and barricaded adults.[49]

The Fall Out

What is the impact of MOVE and the commission's hearing on the political future of Mayor Goode? One source for developing an answer is *The Philadelphia Inquirer*/WCAU-TV survey of Philadelphians conducted by Teichner Associates, a polling organization. (The Teichner surveys of 400 Philadelphians have a margin of error of plus or minus 5 percent.) Table 11.4 shows that between May and November of 1985, the proportion of Philadelphians giving Mayor Goode an excellent and poor rating for his handling of the MOVE confrontation moved inversely, reversing their per-

Table 11.4   Approval Rating of Mayor Goode's Handling
of the MOVE Confrontation

	Excellent	Good	Not Very Good	Poor	Undecided
May 14, 1985 (Day After MOVE)	30%	39%	12%	12%	7%
October 5, 1985 (Just Before MOVE Hearings Began)	12	47	12	21	8
October 17, 1985 (After Mayor Goode Testified at MOVE Hearings)	9	39	18	28	6
November 9, 1985 (After Conclusion of MOVE Hearings)	8	39	21	29	3

Source: Teichner Associates as Reported in *The Philadelphia Inquirer,* November 11, 1985, p. 16-A.

centages. The day after the confrontation 30 percent of city residents gave Mayor Goode an excellent rating, but just before the beginning of the commission's public hearings in October, only 12 percent rated the mayor that way. After the conclusion of the hearings, only 8 percent of the city's residents gave the mayor an excellent rating.

Conversely, the proportion of Philadelphians rating the mayor's handling of the confrontation poor, rose from 12 percent in May to 21 percent just before the beginning of the hearings. At the conclusion of the hearings, 29 percent of the city's residents gave Mayor Goode a poor rating. Interestingly, with the exception of the 47 percent giving Mayor Goode a rating of good just before the hearings began in October, the proportion of city residents selecting a good rating was stable. Nonetheless, the proportion of city residents rating Mayor Goode excellent to good declined from 69 percent in May to 47 percent after the hearings concluded. Clearly as Philadelphians obtained more information about the events of May 13, including Mayor Goode's testimony, the proportion of city residents rating his handling of the situation excellent and poor reversed itself.

Another piece of information is Mayor Goode's general approval rating. Mayor Goode continues to receive a high general rating on his job performance. Table 11.5 illustrates the point. Indeed, the apparent slippage, given the 5 percent margin of error, may not be significant. For example, in November 1984 during Mayor Goode's most popular period, he received an

Table 11.5   Mayor Goode's General Approval Rating

	Excellent	Good	Not Very Good	Poor	Undecided
November 6, 1984	25%	51%	16%	5%	3%
October 5, 1984 (Just Before the MOVE Hearings Began)	16	63	13	5	3
November 9, 1985 (After Conclusion of MOVE Hearings)	19	51	21	8	1

Source: Teichner Associates as Reported in *The Philadelphia Inquirer,* November 11, 1985, p. 16-A.

excellent rating from 25 percent of Philadelphians. By the October 1985 public hearings, his excellent rating dropped to 16 percent but the proportion rating his general performance as excellent stood at 19 percent as the hearings ended in November. Although the proportion of city residents rating Mayor Good's job performance as being good rose from 51 percent in November 1984 to 63 percent just before the beginning of the October 1985 hearings, the proportion feeling this way did decline after the conclusion of the hearings, but it stood where it had been back in 1984, at 51 percent. Slightly more city residents gave Mayor Goode a negative rating between the fall of 1984 and the conclusion of the hearings in the fall of 1985, yet 70 percent of Philadelphians gave Mayor Goode an excellent to good general approval rating in the fall of 1985, down from 76 percent in 1984 and 79 percent just before the hearings began.

The evidence reveals that Philadelphians do not give Mayor Goode high ratings for his handling of the MOVE controversy. Their approval rating of his handling of the conflict dropped from 69 percent the day after the bombing and fire to 47 percent after the conclusion of the Philadelphia Special Investigation Commission's hearings. Yet city residents continue to give Mayor Goode a high rating for his general job performance or non-MOVE activities.

Even so, Table 11.6 discloses that if Philadelphians were voting on the reelection of their mayor at the time the hearings ended, Mayor Goode would not be reelected.

According to *The Philadelphia Inquirer*/WCAU-TV survey, only 38 percent of Philadelphia voters would vote for Mayor Goode in an election on November 9, 1985. A third of the voters would not vote for Mayor Goode and the remaining 29 percent are undecided. A quick glance at Table 12.3

Table 11.6   Support for Mayor Goode if Reelection Was Held
on November 9, 1985

	All	Black	White
Voted for Goode in 1983 And:			
Would Vote for Him Today	29%	49%	20%
Wouldn't Vote for Him Today	13	14	14
Don't Know If Would Today	17	20	15
Didn't Vote For Goode in 1983 But:			
Would Vote For Him Today	9	5	11
Wouldn't Vote For Him Today	20	7	25
Don't Know If Would Today	12	5	15

Source: Teichner Associates as Reported in *The Philadelphia Inquirer,* November 11, 1985,
p. 16-A.

shows that only 29 percent of those who voted for Mayor Goode in 1983
would do so now. Significantly, only 49 percent of blacks would vote for
him now, but the proportion of whites is only 20 percent. Although about
one-seventh of the voters, blacks and whites, who voted for Goode in 1983
indicate they would not do so now, a sizeable proportion of those who voted
for Goode in 1983 are undecided about voting for him now—20 percent
among blacks and 15 percent for whites.

Turning to those who did not vote for Mayor Goode in 1983, Table 11.6
shows, not unexpectedly, that most of those who did not vote for Mayor
Goode in 1983 and would not vote for him now are whites. Even so, 12
percent of those who did not vote for Goode in 1983 are uncertain about
voting for Mayor Goode now—15 percent among whites and 5 percent for
blacks.

From the evidence at hand, it is clear that if Mayor Goode sought reelection on November 9, 1985, a few days following the end of the commission hearings, he would not be reelected, but the evidence also reveals
that his erosion of support must be coupled with the sizable proportion of
voters who are undecided, especially among blacks who voted for him in
1983. In addition, among whites who voted for Mayor Goode in 1983 and
those who did not, many of them are undecided about voting for the Mayor
Goode now.

Healing the Breach?

The evidence suggests that Mayor Goode is vulnerable. Many voters, however, are undecided. At midterm, the Goode administration was in trouble.
The MOVE confrontation transformed Mayor Goode from a shoe-in for a
second term to a mayor who must battle back. Can he do it? He clearly

has problems. Black voters are dissatisfied. In large measure, Mayor Goode's electoral future depends on his ability to get back-on-track by making progress on those issues he pledged to resolve in 1985. That is, by taking the recommendations of Philadelphia Special Investigation Commission (which were not expected before early spring of 1986) and implementing needed changes, reforming the police department, and combining with them already identified critical and unresolved issues such as building a new convention center, getting the city's fiscal house in order, maintaining high quality public services, solving the city's trash disposal problem, and avoiding disruptions among municipal workers whose labor contracts expire this year are the kind of issues and problems that Mayor Goode must derive some succcsscs from in 1986.

Mayor Goode must also show that he can be the type of mayor voters elected in 1983. In the words of Claude Lewis:

> If Goode is to survive the politics of May 13, several administrative changes must immediately be made. He must demonstrate his capacity for toughness when it is needed. He must gain control of the police, fire and medical examiner's office, as well as other city departments. He must never again allow an order from the mayor to be ignored. . . . Goode must dispel the image of weakness his recent leadership has engendered. He must become the "hands-on" mayor of his early reputation.[50]

Yet some believe such acts will not be enough. One local leader has been quoted saying:

> . . . the myth of Goode the manager is gone—gone, its gone. If nothing else, what you have is a graphic, visual demonstration that there was and is no capacity to manage anything. MOVE is a methaphor. It is a vortex in which all of the things Wilson has done and will do will get caught up in.[51]

Clearly, those who began to critize Mayor Goode prior to the MOVE incident will try to seize on the mayor's political troubles and attempt to dissuade him from seeking reelection or deny him a successful reelection bid.

Others may challenge the mayor because of his handling of the MOVE incident and the perceived harm it has imposed on Philadelphia's image. Rumors have already surfaced that former Mayor Frank Rizzo will switch to the Republican party and run for mayor in 1987; former Mayor William Green is also rumored to be interested in seeking the 1987 Democratic party nomination. There is also interest in the influence Democratic Congressman William Gray will have in the next mayoral election. As the Goode administration reaches the midway point, there are reports that Mayor Goode has already raised nearly $500,000 for 1987. Nonetheless, in addition to Rizzo, several other Republican contenders for 1987 include John Egan (the 1983 GOP nominee), Chamber of Commerce president G. Fred DiBona, and city councilwomen Joan Specter.

Politics is the art of the possible; 1986 is a crucial year for Mayor Goode. If Mayor Goode can repair his political base and demonstrate leadership on his agenda, it is possible for him to rebuild his electoral base, especially among those who are uncertain—especially blacks. His task is not an easy one, but polls are only a snapshot of one point in time.

MOVE, however, will not fade away. For example, in early February of 1986, Romana Johnson Africa, the lone known adult survivor from the burning MOVE house, was acquitted of 10 serious charges, including assaulting and endangering police officers in the May 13 confrontation. Yet she was convicted of two lesser charges—criminal conspiracy and riot charges.[52] Philadelphia's political landscape will be largely colored by the continuing after-effects of the incident, such as the Romana Africa trial, as attempts are made to determine blame: MOVE or the city administration, Mayor Goode or the police, or should blame be apportioned more broadly. In addition, the reports and findings of the Philadelphia Special Investigation Commission's and other investigations, plus the outcome of other anticipated criminal proceedings, will unfold during 1986 and beyond, receiving front page coverage in local newspapers and lead-story status on radio and television news programs.

All of these events will color and shape Philadelphia politics as Mayor Goode tries to recover. The additional damage to be inflicted from on-going developments surrounding the May 13 confrontation is a major variable in Mayor Goode's political future. Just as important are the successes he can score in 1986 and the political baggage of those who challenge him in 1987, assuming Mayor Goode will seek reelection. Unquestionably, the matrix of local circumstances and matters in 1987, not the outrage of those who do not vote in Philadelphia, will determine Mayor Goode's political future.

Notes

1. Albert K. Karnig and Susan Welch, *Black Representation and Urban Policy* (Chicago: University of Chicago Press, 1980), 54.

2. Harry Holloway, "Negro Political Stretegy: Coalition or Independent Power Politics?" *Social Science Quarterly* 49 (December 1968):534–547; and Holloway, *The Politics of the Southern Negro: From Exclusion to Big City Organization* (New York: Random House, 1969).

3. Chandler Davidson, *Biracial Politics: Conflict and Coalition in the Metropolitan South* (Baton Rouge: Louisiana State University Press, 1972), 181–219.

4. Richard Murray and Authur Vedlitz, "Racial Voting Patterns in the South: An Analysis of Mayoral Elections Form 1960 to 1977 in Five Cities," *The Annals of the American Academy of Political and Social Science* 439 (September 1978): 29–39.

5.   Ira Katznelson, *City Trenches: Urban Politics and the Patterning of Class in the United States* (New York: Pantheon Books, 1981).

6.   Halan Hahn, David Klingman, and Harry Pachon, "Cleavages, Coalitions and the Black Candidate: The Los Angeles Mayoralty Elections of 1969 and 1973," *Western Political Quarterly* 29 (December 1976): 508.

7.   Karnig and Welch, *Black Representation and Urban Policy,* 46.

8.   Charles S. Bullock III, "Racial Crossover Voting and the Election of Black Officials," *Journal of Politics* 46 (February 1984): 239–251.

9.   Unless otherwise indicated, specific information about black politics in Philadelphia and more general information about the city's politics and mayoral elections was obtained from personal interviews.

10.   Wilson Goode was active in a number of organizations; among them the Philadelphia Council for Community Advancement (PCCA), The West Philadelphia Independent Democrats, and the Americans for Democratic Action.

11.   Miriam Ershkowitz and Joseph Zikmund II, eds., *Black Politics in Philadelphia* (New York: Basic Goods, 1973); and Peter C. Buffum and Rita Sagi, "Philadelphia: Politics of Reform and Retreat," in *Crime in City Politics,* eds. Anne Heinz, Herbert Jacob, and Robert L. Lineberry (New York: Longman, 1983), 97–149.

12.   Adam Tuitt, ed., *Bulletin Almanac—1976* (Philadelphia: Bulletin Co., 1976), 18.

13.   Buffum and Sagi, "Philadelphia," 134–35.

14.   Voter registration in Philadelphia is by political party, major and miscellaneous ones. Registering votes may also enroll in a nonpartisan capacity. Voter registration data are also compiled by race and whether or not an enrollee is foreign born. The Office of City Commissioners, Voter Registration Division, issues formal reports annually. Less formal reports on the number of registered voters by race and party are released periodically, especially during campaign periods.

15.   Katherine L. Bradbury, Anthony Downs, and Kenneth A. Small, *Urban Decline and the Future of the American City* (Washington, D.C.: The Brookings Insitution, 1982), 54.

16.   Ibid., 60.

17.   Edward Schwartz, *The Neighborhood Agenda* (Philadelphia: Institute for Civic Values, 1982), i.

18.   Schwartz, *The Neighborhood Agenda.*

19.   Ibid., i.

20.   Interviews with William Leggett, April 5, 1984 and September 6, 1984.

21.   Interviews with William Miller, June 12, 1984 and September 10, 1984.

22.   "Goode Campaign Report of the Democratic Primary Election" (Goode for Mayor Campaign Committee: 1983), 3.

23.   Ibid.

24.   Interview with William Miller, op. cit.

25.   Ibid.

26.   Knowledgeable persons suggest that the closeness of the Wilson Goode and Frank Lomento levers on the voting machines confused some Goode sup-

porters. Perhaps, they suggest, some Goode voters unintentionally pulled Lomento's lever.

27. Persons familiar with voter registration administration—among them Bruce Caswell—speculate that the turnout rate for blacks was actually higher than the rate for whites. The Voter Registration Division was flooded with new enrollees and already registered voters who wanted to change addresses or party affiliation. Blacks are believed to be a high proportion of the changes in address, and thereby are more likely to be listed twice on the rolls. Indeed, the registration totals reveal that 83 percent of the white voting age population is registered and over 100 percent of voting age blacks are registered.
28. NBC Election Voter Poll Results (1983), Philadelphia Mayoral Primary.
29. Interview with William Miller, op. cit.
30. Interviews with Bruce Caswell, August 14, 1984 and September 12, 1984.
31. Interview with William Miller, op. cit.
32. *The Philadelphia Inquirer,* October 9, 1983, 1.
33. Interview with William Miller, op. cit.
34. Interview with William Leggett, op. cit.
35. Ibid.
36. Interview with Bruce Caswell, op. cit.
37. *The Philadelphia Inquirer,* November 9, 1983, 64.
38. The author is presently examining mayoral leadership, economic development and neighborhood revitalization in Atlanta, Newark, Philadelphia, and Richmond.
39. Office of the Mayor, "Report of Actions on the 100 Day Agenda," Philadelphia, 1984.
40. Cambridge Survey Research Poll, "13th District Results Memorandum," August 3, 1984, A-4. Unpublished.
41. *The Philadelphia Inquirer,* November 12, 1985, 16-A. Philadelphia, 1985.
42. Wilson Goode, "State of the City Speech," January 2, 1985, 2. Philadelphia, 1985.
43. Wilson Goode, "Mayor's Annual Report," Philadelphia, 1984.
44. *The Wall Street Journal,* May 21, 1985, 64.
45. Ibid.
46. CBS-TV, "Face the Nation," 1985.
47. *The Philadelphia Inquirer,* November 12, 1985, 1-A, 16-A.
48. Claude Lewis, Editorial, *The Philadelphia Inquirer,* November 8, 1985, 20-A.
49. Claude Lewis, Editorial, *The Philadelphia Inquirer,* November 9, 1985, 9-A.
50. Ibid.
51. *The Philadelphia Inquirer,* November 8, 1985, 19-A.
52. *The Philadelphia Inquirer,* February 10, 1986, 1 & 9A; *The New York Times,* February 10, 1986, A-12.

About The Authors

Lucius J. Barker, Ph.D., Illinois, is Edna Fischel Gellhorn Professor of Political Science and former chairperson, Department of Political Science, Washington University. He is the author of *Black Americans and the Political System* (with Jesse J. McCorry, Jr.), and coauthor of several books in the judicial politics area, including *Civil Liberties and the Constitution* (with Twiley Barker).

Twiley W. Barker, Jr., Ph.D., Illinois, is a professor in the Department of Political Science, University of Illinois, Chicago Circle. He is the author of *Civil Liberties and the Constitution* (with Lucius Barker), and numerous other articles on judicial politics.

Mary Delorse Coleman, Ph.D., candidate at University of Wisconsin–Madison, is currently an assistant professor of political science, Jackson State University. Her major teaching areas are public law, senior research and law-related courses, and women and politics. She has written "Teaching Black Politics in Political Science" (with Leslie Burl McLemore) and is currently writing a book on Mississippi politics (with Professor McLemore).

Lenneal J. Henderson, Jr., Ph.D., Berkeley, is currently a professor in the School of Business and Public Administration at Howard University. He formerly served as associate director of research at the Joint Center for Political Studies, director of Ethnic Studies at the University of San Francisco, NASPAA fellow in the U.S. Department of Energy, and a fellow of the Moton Center for Independent Studies. He has edited *Black Political Life in the U.S.* (1972); coedited *Public Administration and Public Policy: A Minority Perspective* (1977), and authored *Administrative Advocacy: Black Administrators in Urban Bureaucracies*

(1979). His articles have appeared in the *Public Administration Review,* the *Black Scholar,* the *Annals, the Review of Black Political Economy,* and other publications.

Charles P. Henry, Ph.D., Chicago, is an associate professor in the Afro-American Studies Department, University of California–Berkeley. He is the author of *The Chit'lin Controversy: Race of Public Policy in America* (with Lorenzo Morris), "Money, Law, and Black Congressional Candidates," "The Role of Race in the Bradley-Deukmejian Campaign," and "Ebony Elite: American's Most Influential Blacks," plus numerous other articles on a variety of subjects.

Leslie Burl McLemore, Ph.D., University of Massachusetts–Amherst; Post Doctorate, Johns Hopkins. He is former chairperson, Department of Political Science, Jackson State University. Currently he is the Dean of the Graduate College and is a top advisor to the Rev. Jesse Jackson.

William E. Nelson, Jr., Ph.D., Illinois, is currently a Distinguished Professor of Research, Department of Black Studies, The Ohio State University. He was the former head of the Department of Black Studies for over 15 years and is also a professor of Political Science. He is the author of *Electing Black Mayors* (with Phillip J. Meranto), "Black Elected Administrators" in *Public Administration Review* (with Winston Van Horne), and numerous other articles on black and urban politics.

Huey L. Perry, Ph.D., Chicago, is associate professor at Southern University in Baton Rouge. He is the author of *Democracy and Public Policy: Minority Inputs into National Energy Policy of Carter Administration.* He is also the author of numerous other articles on black and urban politics.

Michael B. Preston, Ph.D., University of California–Berkeley is currently a professor of political science at the University of Southern California. He was formerly a professor at the University of Illinois–Urbana. He is the author of *The Politics of Bureaucratic Reform, Race, Sex, and Policy Problems* (with Marian Lief Palley), "Black Politics in Chicago: 1971–1983," "The Election of Harold Washington, 1983," "The Limitation of Black Urban Power: The Case of Black Mayors," and "Who Voted for Jesse Jackson and Why?," plus many other articles on urban and black politics.

Paul L. Puryear, Ph.D., Chicago, is Dean, Afro-American Affairs, University of Virginia. He is the author of numerous articles on black and American politics (especially southern politics).

Bruce Ransom, Ph.D., Virginia, is currently Executive Director of Urban Affairs Center at Stockton State College in New Jersey. He is currently working on a book about Mayor Wilson Goode of Philadelphia.

Wilbur C. Rich, Ph.D., Illinois, is director, MAPA Program and an associate professor at Wayne State University, Detroit. He is the author of *The History of the New York Civil Service System,* "Political Power and the Role of Housing Authority," "Civil Servants, Unionism, and the State of Cities," and "Municipal Civil Service Under Fire," *Public Administration Review.*

Alfred Stokes is an associate professor at Xavier University in New Orleans. He is currently on leave and is serving as the executive assistant to the Mayor of New Orleans for Intergovernmental Relations.

Linda Williams, Ph.D., Chicago, is an associate professor of political science at Howard University and is currently on leave to serve as Research Director for the Joint Center for Political Studies. She is the author of *Race, Class and Urban Politics* (with Dianne M. Pinderhughes) and numerous other articles on black and urban politics.